Biting the Moon

Writing American Women

Carol A. Kolmerten, *Series Editor*

Other titles in Writing American Women

Biting
the
Moon

A Memoir of
Feminism and Motherhood

Joanne S. Frye

SYRACUSE UNIVERSITY PRESS

Some names have been changed in the interest of privacy.

Syracuse University Press
Syracuse, New York 13244-5290

First Edition 2012
12 13 14 15 16 17   6 5 4 3 2 1

∞ The paper used in this publication meets the minimum requirements of the American National Standard for Information Sciences—Permanence of Paper for Printed Library Materials, ANSI Z39.48-1992.

For a listing of books published and distributed by Syracuse University Press, visit our Web site at SyracuseUniversityPress.syr.edu.

ISBN: 978-0-8156-0969-8

Library of Congress Cataloging-in-Publication Data
Frye, Joanne S., 1944–
    Biting the moon : a memoir of feminism and motherhood / Joanne S. Frye.
        p. cm. — (Writing American women)
    ISBN 978-0-8156-0969-8 (cloth : alk. paper) 1. Working mothers.   2. Motherhood.
3. Feminism.   I. Title.
    HQ759.48.F79 2012
    306.874'3—dc23   2012000991

Manufactured in the United States of America

05 12

For Kara and Adriane

Contents

Prologue

Icy Bridges

I noted the warning, though it was commonplace: BRIDGE MAY BE ICY. I usually find such signs amusing, heedless of seasonal change, incongruent in eighty-degree weather. But I know their purpose is serious: to remind of danger that can arise unexpectedly.

On this January day in 1998, the danger was very real, and I was not laughing. I had come to a halt on the freeway, with ice glazing the road and snow blurring the air. There was just one car ahead of me, but in front of it two highway patrol cars blocked the road, preventing further progress. At a dead stop on I-80 in the middle of Pennsylvania, I watched the snow fall into the ravines around me and onto my windshield, gathering on all sides. I peered through the glass, trying to see the highway ahead. Across the icy bridge, I could barely discern numerous lights flashing, red and blue: emergency vehicles drawn to a catastrophe on the other side of the chasm.

I had debated whether or not to make my departure from Ohio that morning. The weather forecast had been iffy, and the five-hundred-mile drive would be exhausting. But I had already picked up the rental car the night before, loaded the trunk with my computer and books and clothes, old journals and photos and letters, and arranged to get the key to the New York apartment in which I would be staying for the next four months. I was ready to be on the road and had decided to take this risk. Behind me were my husband, my teaching job at a liberal arts college, my small-town home. Ahead of me were my grown daughters, a city apartment of my own, and the opportunity to take on a writing project that had been haunting me for years.

I was glad to have with me a book on tape: *The Good Mother*. As long as my gas supply held out, I could keep the engine running and sit in a warm car, listening to the Sue Miller novel in relative comfort. I had chosen this tape deliberately as a way to focus my thoughts toward the writing that lay ahead of me. The project was to write my experience as a mother—primarily a single mother. My questions had emerged out of years of thinking about narrative and self and motherhood and feminist change. What does it mean to be a mother and a self at the same time? How does my experience as a single mother shed light on the notion of a mother–self? More painfully: What kind of mother was I? What kind of life have I made, and what are the costs of that life—for my daughters, for their father, for me? Most immediately: Can I use this gift of time to *write*, as I had always meant to do?

Toward the end of *The Good Mother*, Anna, also a single mother, assumes the blame for losing custody of her daughter: "There was no one I blamed so much as myself. . . . It was a chain of events set in motion by me, by my euphoric forgetfulness of all the rules." As I sat in the car, frozen in space and time, I heard these words and grew angry at Anna for entirely different reasons. I was not angry at her for being a "bad mother" or for breaking the rules—I would certainly not judge her for wanting to have a sexual life and a self-definition beyond "mother." I was angry at her for failing to anticipate consequences that she could have prevented and for so easily relinquishing all of her desires to the demands of "the rules." I was angry at her for succumbing to the cultural definition of a good mother: selfless, without a self.

When the accident on the other side of the bridge finally cleared, the highway patrol officers left their cars blocking the road and walked past my car to the vehicles behind me. In my side-view mirror, I watched them talk to a truck driver in the next vehicle back and then walk farther down the line. That truck driver and then another eventually pulled out and moved to the front of the now very long line of vehicles. With patrol cars leading, lights flashing, the two trucks followed side by side, setting our speed for us as we moved across the treacherous bridge and on down the highway: forty miles an hour, passing Clearfield at a steady pace defined by the dangers of ice and the highway patrol's cautionary strategies.

I looked seriously at the Clearfield exit and then the next exit, too. The traffic gradually resumed highway speed, but icy conditions persisted.

Adrenaline pumped through me as I drove on, wondering whether I should continue this hazardous journey or pull off the highway and stop for the night. I thought: Kara and Adriane and Ron will be furious at me if I die on the highway this way. But I also thought: I need to proceed with the plan, to drive on through the snow and ice into the city this evening in order to meet up with my daughters and begin my writing sabbatical.

I arrived safely in New York, despite hazardous roads. Kara and Adriane had picked up the key to my apartment and were ready to help me unload the car and turn it in at the rental station. They were there, together, to welcome me into New York, *their* city. For the next four months, my daughters would be my primary social world. The apartment in the Village—Twelfth Street near Seventh Avenue—would provide a writer's retreat, a room of my own.

Kara, twenty-six, had moved to New York directly after her college graduation with a degree in international studies; she had worked in international business and then in publishing before entering an interdisciplinary master's program in literary cultures at New York University. Now settled in a studio in the East Village, she had earned her identity as resident New Yorker. Adriane, twenty-two, had arrived in the city the previous summer, a recent college graduate with a double major in English and French; she shared an apartment on the Upper West Side, not far from the small private school where she and her roommate taught two- and three-year-old children.

Ron, my husband of nearly nine years, would tend the home fires, maintaining his own work life in Wooster, Ohio, and periodically flying to New York for weekends with me and for shared time with Kara and Adriane. Though the four of us were deeply connected, I planned in these months to reembrace the sense of *myself*, alone.

EVEN AFTER EIGHT AND A HALF YEARS, I did not exactly feel married. Too much of who I knew myself to be was still defined as *single mother*. And yet I knew Ron to be my life partner, had even seemed to recognize him the first time I had seen him.

That was December 1987, when I was en route to San Francisco for the annual meeting of the Modern Language Association. When the plane touched down in Detroit to pick up additional passengers, I had turned farther toward the window, work papers spread in front of me. But when a late passenger walked down the aisle, I looked up and into eyes that felt *known* to me, even from the first. When he took the aisle seat, I could hardly believe my good fortune. When the woman who sat between us began to question him, I listened covertly to all his answers.

Who was this man so full of the joy of a recent family holiday in Detroit, now returning to his home in Oakland? Who was this man who spoke so respectfully of his sisters, his nieces, even his former wife—this man who cared deeply about politics, who talked of writing stories and thought about the workings of language? Who was this man who—when I looked up from my work to eat lunch—turned his attention to me and listened to my own answers thoughtfully? Who was this man with brown eyes the color of all colors, deep enough to fall into and wide enough to encompass untold vistas?

Upon my return from San Francisco, I picked up my daughters from their holiday visit in Bloomington, Indiana, with Lawrence, their father. In the car, they told me of their Christmas—fraught as always with the tensions of their father's prickliness, his demands on them, his thorny love for them. And then I told them of my new encounter: I had met someone on the airplane, had walked on windswept hills with him above Ocean Beach and on wet sand along the ocean shore, talking of literature and politics, Wobblies and Bakhtin, Longshoremen and general strikes, Jack London and James Joyce and Virginia Woolf and Tillie Olsen. I told them that I had accepted from him a ride to Sacramento, where my brother, their uncle Don, lived. I told them that he was someone special, who spoke a language of social change that I recognized, someone who listened to me, alert to what I was actually saying. And I told them that he was a proud truck driver and union activist who wrote short stories and had a visible respect for women, for his sisters—one of whom was a single mother—and for me. I did not yet tell them of our first kiss, there on the hills above the ocean where the trees are perpetually blown back, like hair brushed away from the sea. Nor did I yet tell them of his eyes, the color of all colors.

My daughters, ages twelve and sixteen, listened attentively, hearing hidden messages and something new in my voice. And then they responded: "That's like a novel, Mom. That's like a movie!"

I, always ready to criticize easy romantic feelings—and an anxious mother—said to them, "Yes. But don't you consider meeting someone that way until you are at least forty."

A YEAR AND A HALF LATER, when Ron and I married in August 1989, we wrote our own vows and incorporated lines from an Adrienne Rich poem, "Origins and History of Consciousness." Though the poem speaks specifically of lesbian love, we affirmed our own love in Rich's words, hoping this was not a transgression:

> It was simple to meet you, simple to take your eyes
> into mine, saying these are eyes I have known
> from the first . . .

> What is not simple: to wake from drowning
> from where the ocean beat inside us like an afterbirth
> into this common, acute particularity
> these two selves who walked half a lifetime untouching—

Also in the ceremony, which we held in our home—Kara's and Adriane's and mine—with only immediate family present, Ron thanked Kara and Adriane for accepting him into their family.

I knew that Ron was sacrificing a great deal to move to the midwestern home I had made with Kara and Adriane, to give up his urban life and his California home, to be with us. None of it could be easy for him—even if we would spend our first year of marriage in Berkeley, California, rather than in Wooster, Ohio, because I had a research leave to work on my book on Tillie Olsen. Nor could it be easy for Kara and Adriane to forge a new family bond with someone they were only beginning to know. When I had asked them what they thought of the possibility of this marriage, which would follow upon our thirteen years as a single-parent family, they had told me that they wanted me to do what felt right to me. And then they had added: "But we like Ron. And it *would* be easier if we knew what to call him"—a stepfather, not their mother's "friend." It helped that Ron listened carefully to Kara and Adriane and that he had no wish to take control of our family—only wanted to join us. Early on he had said: "The three of you are the most functional family I know." Even so, for all of us, the adjustments would be many. For me, the hardest part would be letting go of my identity as a single mother.

I struggled to hold on to the lost identity, though I could not have imagined a smoother transition from one kind of family to another. Since my divorce from Lawrence, I had been a critic of marriage as of the hazards of romance. Indeed, Ron and I had already made this critique a subject of our initial conversation on that singular airplane trip. I had long claimed this idea of single mother as my *self*: independent, self-sustaining, responsible to children and to work, making a family from shared lives, not from assumed roles. I wanted to blend my life with Ron's, but my daughters would have to remain central, as would the idea of myself that I had worked so hard to earn. As token of this commitment, I kept the name that tied me to my daughters: Joanne Frye.

From the beginning, Ron had acknowledged that Kara and Adriane did not need a father, for they already had one. And their father was a continuing part of their lives as they spent regular holidays and summer vacations together, sharing in ongoing conversations over the years. Though Lawrence and I had been divorced for thirteen years by the time Ron joined our family, he had never ceased being my daughters' father: Lawrence Frye.

We tried to remember that even Lawrence had a place in our changing family as Ron settled in Wooster, Kara went off to college, followed four years later by Adriane, and all of us kept trying to figure out just what our web of relations really was.

BUT THEN A SHOCK tore into that web and left threads hanging loose in tattered disarray. Without preparation, I answered the phone on July 5, 1994, and took the shock into my body. A voice told me: "Lawrence took his own life yesterday. I'm sorry to call you with this news. Yours was the only number we had for contacting Kara and Adriane. We thought you should be the one to tell them—as their mother."

Their mother. This was the role that held me steady, even as I had resisted letting it become my whole identity. And in the face of their father's death— his suicide—we would once again have to hold each other steady. But suicide forces other questions upon survivors, and I will not be able to ignore those even as I try to hold steady. Questions, old and new, push to the surface and threaten prior complacencies: What could we have done to prevent this loss? What will this do to Kara and Adriane? What will follow in the trail of this grief? And crowding in again are my own questions: What kind of mother have I been and can I now be to them? What kind of life have I made, and what are the costs of that life—for my daughters, for their now dead father, for me?

NOW, JANUARY 1998, nearly four years later, I have arrived in New York, haunted by all the questions, trying to find a way to the immediate one: Can I write this story? My daughters are close by, my books and letters and journals and photos are here for the grappling. My space is arranged for writing. I am prepared to try to make sense of it all: the dead father, yes, but more crucially the beautifully grown daughters, the living and loving husband—and me. This is the story I need to tell.

I pace the floor, peering into the past. I shake the kaleidoscope of memory, discerning something new each time I shake it. Sometimes nothing takes shape at all, though I keep trying to arrange the broken pieces into coherent stories. I make a story of pain and guilt, but also of joy, small pleasures, felt accomplishments, survival, and love. But mine is not what people expect from a mother's story. In it, I am first a mother in a rifted family and then a single mother, unprotected by traditional family structure, freed from that structure. Throughout, I am a mother, of course, but also a woman struggling to understand who I am.

Though I am safely here in New York, I am newly dizzy with circling back over the years—with the chasms I must cross, the choices I will revisit, the dangers of slippery highways and exits taken or bypassed. I prepare to face additional perils, knowing that old certainties and prior identities are sure to rupture.

PART I

Family with Fissures
1968–1976

1

Nascent Self

When I was twenty-two and a first-year graduate student, a man who wanted to sleep with me said, "You're just like a twenty-eight year old librarian." He meant to insult me: to him, librarians were uptight, and twenty-eight was ancient. He spoke in clichés; I resisted the insult. He had already told me that his goal was to find a little woman to tend his garden within a white picket fence: no picket fence for me; no easy bedding either.

I was no longer a virgin, but I intended to protect my borders, and though I admired librarians, I had no wish to become one. I had long since rejected my engineer father's suggestion that library work would be an appropriate life plan, just because I loved books: he thought I should do something practical. But I loved books as a private pleasure, not as a career plan, even as I enrolled in a PhD program in English literature. I did not consider myself ambitious: I was only nurturing my own desires. I meant to tend my love of words and books in my unkempt way, not to cultivate someone else's garden.

And yet a mere one year later, I recommitted to graduate school and married Lawrence. I bound my life to his, even ended up tending his garden. Why would I do such a thing?

LAST SUMMER, still in Wooster, I raised this question with Ron as he and I sat on our porch, sharing a glass of wine, the evening before us. I thought of *Martha Quest* and chafed at my similarity to Doris Lessing's protagonist, who marries at age nineteen, thinking underneath, that she won't *stay* married. That same Martha Quest, five days after her wedding in *A Proper Marriage*, thinks of herself as "formless, graceless, and unpredictable, a mere lump of clay." Worried at my youthful similarity to her, I wondered aloud: Why did I marry Lawrence? How can I know if I ever even loved him?

11

Generously, Ron led me to remember all the reasons I would have been drawn to this man, this marriage. And now, here in New York, I revisit that decision in solitude, going back thirty years to January 1968.

AFTER A YEAR AND A HALF of intense graduate study and haphazard social life, I had my first date with Lawrence, dinner at his apartment—veal chops in cream sauce, completely unlike the food I had known as breaded veal in the college dining room or at home when Mom had cooked a Sunday dinner especially to please Dad. I didn't even know that you could get veal in the form of thick succulent chops and then eat it with a delicate sauce and asparagus on the side. Nor did I know that, after dinner, sitting on the couch, you might put Beethoven on the stereo and pull glossy fine-art books off the shelves, paging through modernist painters and then slowing down to examine Picasso's move from early realism to cubism, puzzling out the meanings of art.

A basic college course in art appreciation had given me phrases and names, but not this passion for discovery. When Lawrence paused to point out *Guernica*'s rendering of wartime carnage, I silenced my pacifist horror at war, as well as my ignorance about the Spanish Civil War, and concentrated instead on aesthetic appreciation, a budding awe at form. But my stomach clenched against the images of destruction.

My stomach continued to clench as we moved from couch to floor, to stretch out on the oriental rug, after Lawrence changed the music from Beethoven to Alban Berg's opera, *Wozzeck*. This, too, was new to me. As a student at Bluffton College, I had made an outing with a professor to hear the Metropolitan Opera perform in Cleveland, but I had never experienced music like this. The dissonance grated harshly on my ears as Lawrence explained the brutal lives plotted out in this lurid tale. I tried to take in the vehemence of the music along with Lawrence's nuanced explanations of the German play on which it was based and the complicated reception of the opera itself.

I was listening carefully, even analytically, but was also being swept into new currents as I lay on the floor beside the man who had recently been my German professor, taking pleasure in the words he spoke, having eaten the food he prepared. Beneath us was a finely woven antique rug in geometric patterns from a nomadic culture in Asia. On the table where we had eaten was a Persian tray with decanter and tiny goblets, delicately etched silver, and an equally delicate pillar of white jade, Chinese, intricately carved, no more than two inches tall. Everything seemed so sophisticated, so worldly, so utterly new to me.

When Lawrence turned to kiss me, I moved into these currents with a surprising readiness. As the night deepened toward morning, I was in thrall.

Yes, I said, I will spend the night. I will move to the bed to lie there with you—just keep enticing me with words. But I will keep my skirt and sweater on, maintaining physical boundaries carefully, even as I begin to yield.

I don't remember Lawrence's response to my insistence on remaining clothed. But I do know that we lay together on his bed through the rest of that night, fully clothed, girdle and all.

WHEN WE BEGAN DATING THAT JANUARY, I was a twenty-three-year-old graduate student at Indiana University, studying British and American modernism, recent graduate of Bluffton, a small Mennonite college at which my grandfather had been dean; Lawrence was a thirty-three-year-old assistant professor of German, soon to be tenured. I had met him the previous semester as a student in his course in German-language study for graduate students—a workaday course among his seminars for advanced undergraduate or graduate students in German romantic or modernist literature. He was tall and handsome and unapproachable, his comments terse, hinting at brilliance. He smoked in class, dropping ashes casually into the wastebasket, posing derisive questions to the ill prepared, and gazing out over our heads as if searching for the brilliance we lacked. From fellow students, I had heard rumors of his mysterious exploits, his silk bathrobe, his volatile personality, and his challenging intellect.

When the course ended, Lawrence lent me a book and invited me for coffee. When we moved on to conversation and then dinners together, I delighted not only in his cultured aesthetics, but also in his willingness to cook for me. He introduced me to exotic new foods that I had never even thought to taste, some I had never even heard of: steak tartare, sweetbreads in cream sauce, kohlrabi, whole artichokes, capers. Savoring these new foods, escaping his disdain for the ignorant and the uninquisitive, I was captivated—by his words, his enigmatic presence, his sophistication, but most of all by the sense that I was exceptional in his discriminating judgment.

This encounter gradually began to feel fated: my college friends had predicted that I would meet a future lover through a common interest in Franz Kafka, *my* alienated Jewish writer from Prague. And now here was Lawrence—former Fulbright scholar to Germany, nearly associate professor at a prestigious university—working on an article on Kafka's wordplay. When he told me this, I shyly mentioned that I had written my senior thesis on Kafka's sense of alienation, his novels and stories as an expression of a search for meaning. I was not so bold as to tell him that our coming together had been foretold.

THE RELATIONSHIP PREVAILED, though I had already applied for the Peace Corps—distressed by what felt like sterility in my student life and confused by the social protest that rose in great waves around me: student activists, draft resisters, demonstrations against the Vietnam War—and had been assigned to Morocco and scheduled for training in Colorado. I had sat in tense opposition among shouting students when Dean Rusk had visited the Indiana University campus, and I had felt the urgency of antiwar activity and political activism. But I had been unable to throw myself into group protests, unable to join in what so often seemed like ill-considered action for the sake of action, and so I had hesitantly chosen the Peace Corps. Now I backed off; I was not quite ready to give up on graduate school or to leave behind this new relationship. Might this odd kinship with Lawrence yield a new sense of purpose and still allow me to persist in my love of books?

It was a strange way to seek continuity, this bonding in a shared passion for Kafka, this opening onto a world of intellectual sophistication. Despite growing up in South Bend, Indiana, which had no Mennonite church, I had always thought of myself as Mennonite. I was a Schultz, which also meant I was a Bargen and a Detweiler and a Zook, with threads of kinship extending back to rural Minnesota, to Russia, to Germany, to the Europe in which the followers of Menno Simons had been persecuted. Even as I moved toward a union with Lawrence, I felt that I belonged in this family to which I was born.

I belonged to my father, Harold Bargen Schultz, ingenious inventor, reliable engineer, responsible parent—sometimes severe, often nurturing,

always rational. As a child, I spent hours in the garage with him, holding riv-
ets while he built a collapsible trailer of his own design. I wrote a junior high
report on patents so that I could display a copy of the patent he had earned
for this unique aluminum trailer with solid walls and a kitchen and enough
beds for our family of five. I felt sustained in my own shyness by the story of
his youthful shyness, pretending to knock on doors to sell newspapers during the Depression—hesitant to intrude on neighbors with an actual knock.
I took great pleasure in learning calculus in part because this confirmed a
talent I shared with my father.

Much admired by his younger brother and sister, Harold was the oldest
son of a dedicated professor at Bluffton College and his energetic wife, who
volunteered for the Mennonite Central Committee and performed gustatory
feats of magic in the kitchen. Growing up in that small town, dominated by
the college, my father had absorbed from his parents a sense of rectitude and
duty, a commitment to justice, as well as the necessity of church on Sunday.
From them he also took the smell of sawdust from construction in the basement and of yeast and flour in the kitchen, the presence of books in several
parts of the house, and words handled with care. Most of these values he
handed on to me.

And I belonged to my mother, Emma Detweiler Schultz, preacher's kid,
attentive listener, homemaker, public-school teacher, and Planned Parenthood educator, active and curious and gregarious, drawing other people to
her like filings to a magnet. She was the youngest child of three and only
daughter of parents whose youthful voyage to India as Mennonite mission-
aries had been cut short by my grandmother's ill health, a thyroid condition that weakened her then and would eventually cause her death years
later; perhaps it was the same condition that would prompt my own thyroid
removal when I was twelve years old—a surgery that had been unavailable to
my grandmother.

Before my mother was born, her parents had settled in Goshen, Indiana,
where they made their home into a haven for international travelers. There
my grandfather suffered new travails as a liberal-minded minister among
judgmental conservatives. When his church rejected him, they moved on
to Ohio. My grandmother was—my mother told me—an early follower of
Maria Montessori and a rigorous enforcer of good behavior: no dancing,

no card playing, no short hair. But her death came early, in her daughter's arms. My mother, not quite eighteen years old, helped her mother to dress, clasped her mother's dying body, and then became her father's mainstay as she herself prepared for college, her head still crowned by a coiled braid of uncut hair. I am told that twelve years later, when I was a toddler, not yet two, I roamed my grandfather's house the day after his death, asking, "Ba-pa? Where's Ba-pa?" By then, my mother's hair had been trimmed to the more practical length that my father preferred. I'm not certain if my mother had yet decided just what she herself preferred.

As a child, I climbed trees and played neighborhood hide-and-seek. I read books and tried to figure out the relationship between truth and story. Like my father, I treasured the precision of math, but unlike him I preferred the play of words and the spell of stories. Like my mother, I loved to read and had a keen interest in understanding other people's lives. I wanted to know the truth but sometimes mistrusted facts. From my great-uncle Bill, I learned the word *hyperbole,* but from his sister, my grandmother, I learned to be careful not to exaggerate. She and my grandfather played *Scrabble* and anagrams, toying with words, though they otherwise used them carefully and tended scrupulously to truth.

Like my father, I had severe myopia and like my mother an overbite— needing glasses and braces from a young age. Still, I thought myself lucky, smart, much nurtured, willing to be outshone by my older sister, Eileen, and my younger brother, Don—both of whom were more gregarious and athletic than I. A middle child, I shadowed my older sister in craven admiration and beseeched my younger brother to play with me. Otherwise, I liked being alone with my books, nestled in a loving family. Always I looked for meanings.

I WAS STILL A CHILD when I confirmed nonviolence as an article of faith at an extended family reunion in Mountain Lake, Minnesota. We arrived at the family homestead with a sense of festivity, crossing the expansive lawn toward the old farmhouse, being greeted by relatives I barely knew as well as by my much loved grandparents. We ate zwiebach and watermelon and potato salad and corn on the cob from large tables set up outside. But what I most remember is meeting my father's cousin, who had spent five months in prison for his refusal to participate in the Korean War. Jail! I joined the other children gathered around him—cousins and second cousins and siblings—mesmerized by his stories and his lively eyes. Steeped in that family atmosphere, I aligned myself with his belief in pacifism, his resolute integrity.

In sixth grade, I was invited to my first boy–girl party by a friend who knew of my Mennonite background. She took me aside and advised me to find someone to teach me how to dance—I alone among the party-goers did not have the benefit of dancing lessons. Once I was at the party, though, I still suffered, not only from my clumsy attempts to dance but also from my fumbling ignorance in a game of charades: I simply knew none of the current cultural references—to movies or songs or television shows. Our family did finally get a television that year, and my sister was beginning to bring home a few rock-and-roll records. But I couldn't seem to catch up with peers who saw me as overly serious, unfamiliar with popular culture, and lacking a bodily ease that might have come with the liberty to dance freely.

Born into this history, I seemed destined to attend a Mennonite college, following my parents and my sister to Bluffton, a college at which daily chapel was required and dancing and drinking and smoking were explicitly forbidden. Lawrence hardly fit comfortably into this value system, with his cigarettes and his accumulation of expensive objects, his sarcastic judgments, and his secular worldview.

But I needed to wrench against my family identity without losing it: my Mennonite heritage, full of teachers and war resisters and even an occasional missionary; my parents, who supported my academic pursuits but suggested I study something more practical and worried that I seemed drawn to alienated writers. Work hard and speak the truth—those imperatives were deep inside me, as were other values I had culled from my heritage: live simply, love others, seek justice for all people, refrain from violence, develop the mind. Equally deep was my attraction to alienated writers.

WHEN I MET LAWRENCE, not only Kafka but also Camus and Sartre and Kierkegaard—those existentialists—were my touchstones, as they were for many others at the time. As a college student, I took from *The Myth of Sisyphus* the notion of the absurd hero and the defining question of whether to commit suicide, coupled with the threat of an amorphous self: "nothing but water slipping through my fingers." I committed to authenticity and choice and constructing one's own meanings, and I tried to blend them into what I saw as my family legacy. But I still felt formless.

During the college years, I sought out new ways to think about religion. For the course "Philosophy of Religion," I wrote a paper comparing mysticism across cultures—Meister Eckhart and Ramakrishna—a pursuit that hit a dead end when the professor suggested that since I wrote so well, I should make it my goal to write Sunday school literature. I kept reading and reading, turning more and more toward literary texts, especially those of the twentieth century, at that time called, after Auden, the "age of anxiety."

One afternoon, alone in my parents' home on break from college during my sophomore year, I faced my own crisis of anxiety. No longer sharing in the family faith, I succumbed to my reading of Camus's *Caligula* with its themes of despair, violence, transience, mortality. I still hated violence, but I was otherwise unmoored from previous convictions; I could find no sense of purpose and had even lost the ease of mind and body that I had felt in early childhood. In an empty house, I paced and cried out against a nameless pain.

Back at college, I lingered for a while with Paul Tillich and Martin Buber, religious existentialists who might bridge my conflicting value systems, but then turned toward more immediate concerns. During my senior year, I did student teaching and earned certification, even as my senior project kept me steeped in Kafka, in words and books and the search for meaning. Finally, I chose to go to graduate school, resisting the advice given by one of my professors: to teach high school so that I could be home for the children I didn't yet imagine having. In this choice, I equivocated, following my urge to keep reading and thinking about meanings, choosing a markedly secular path, but not yet embracing a decisive purpose. I did not say, "I want to be a professor."

Now drawn to Lawrence, as if he were an unfamiliar wine I was just learning to taste—though I really had no knowledge of wines at all—I kept my one thread of continuity: I read and I read and I read, out of a deep hunger for other people's stories, for understanding how they make sense of their lives. And in this new stage of life, I thought that books shared with a life partner might well be a way toward who I could be and even a heady escape from loneliness.

I PHONED MY PARENTS that April to tell them of our decision to marry in June. I had prepared them a bit for this possibility in an earlier letter so that the actual news would not come as such a shock—they had barely heard of this man whom I now told them I would marry within a few short months. I followed the phone call with another letter, trying to explain why everything was moving so quickly.

My parents' response—typed and rather formal, from both of them at once—cautiously agreed that Lawrence and I might make a "meaningful marriage," though it also expressed concern that I had left behind my religious heritage. They tried to ease these differences by referring to their own "searching and evaluating" beyond church membership, and they included a lengthy quotation from a book called *Love and Marriage,* which describes religion as a "way of hungering and thirsting after righteousness" rather than attendance at a specific church. Two and a half of the remaining three typed pages were devoted to specifics of time and place and people for the simple wedding that they were willing to help me plan on such short notice.

My parents, of marked Mennonite history and deeply rooted values of pacifism, simple living, independent thinking, were working hard to understand this highly secular marriage plan, this apparent turn away from my heritage, and the abrupt retreat from the Peace Corps. But as their letter attests, they found a way to base their response on a deep appreciation of learning and to honor my independence as well as my lifelong love of reading, my attempt to understand life through books. Their letter ended in my mother's voice: "Frankly I'm very thankful and grateful to know that you'll have a fine strong man to love and to cherish you, and that he in turn will have you."

AS WE MADE OUR PLANS, the world around us continued to roil and rupture. On April 4, just as Lawrence and I were reaching our decision to marry, we heard the news that Martin Luther King Jr. had been assassinated—an event so horrific as to be nearly inassimilable. The night of King's death, Robert Kennedy—campaigning for the presidency a few miles north of us in Indianapolis—replaced his scheduled speech with some brief remarks that have since become famous. As he told the gathered political crowd, largely African American, of the news they had not yet heard, he remembered his own anger at the assassination of John F. Kennedy five years earlier. He conceded that anger and desire for vengeance were potent reactions, but he urged the crowd to recommit to King's own nonviolence.

I was unaware of that speech at the time; I do not even recall exactly where I was when King was shot, though I have vivid memories of the television images of the motel balcony, the chaotic events in Memphis, and the tumultuous aftermath throughout the country. And I know that I, too, felt anger as well as grief at the senseless death, the ongoing racial and economic injustices—and I felt the absolute futility of revenge.

In a further convergence of events, Robert Kennedy was then also assassinated that June just a few days before Lawrence and I were to be married. Of this assassination, I have only what I have since reconstructed; I have no real memory even of the anguished loss I must have felt while carrying on with wedding plans. I cannot merge such enormous events with my own personal history. How can they possibly be brought together into one frame of reference?

In that same year marked by assassinations and demonstrations and political ferment, though it seems much later, I again sat in tense emotion, watching as others shouted. But this time violence broke out on the television screen in front of me: the 1968 Democratic National Convention in Chicago. By then I was already married and on a delayed honeymoon to San Francisco, where Lawrence and I stewed in our own early marital tensions in my aunt and uncle's living room, watching their television in overwrought silence. I'm not sure what I had done with my urge to make change or my yearning for purpose, though I resisted viscerally all of the violence I saw around me: the war and the police brutality, of course, but also the rock throwing and bomb threats and guns of a few antiwar and antiracist activists.

PAUSING NOW at the rifts in my story, I pace along the wall-length desk on which I have spread out the books and documents that I brought with me to New York. I pull out my box of photos, sifting for visual clues to who I was when I married Lawrence: how young I look! Indeed, I *am* young—twenty-three, twenty-four—though I look not just young, but blurry. When I look at pictures of the young Sylvia Plath—wife, poet, not yet mother—I can see a little of this same quality of blurriness, though she was in those roles half a generation before I was in mine, and despite the roles she always had a sharply defined sense of her poetic gifts, her ambition. But Plath already had within her the seeds of deep despair. Photos hide so much, even photos of me: that inner pacing, that undertow of alienation.

In those same photos of our early married life, Lawrence, too, looks very young, though he was ten years my senior and had already been married once. His apparent youthfulness is also tempered by his stance toward the camera, as toward the world: at six feet two inches, he carries himself with authority. Where I seem vague, he seems sharply defined: dark hair, professorial glasses, head held high, long legs planted firmly. Or maybe that is simply my later insight. He was, in fact, "Larry" then, not "Lawrence" at all, but even in memory I cannot undo his renaming of himself—a considered act of self-reconstruction that he enforced on friends and family several years later.

In the snapshots of our wedding in June 1968—a small affair at my parents' house—he, at thirty-three, was still young; his hopeful smile is nearly as soft as mine, his eyes frank rather than assertive. We look almost the way newlyweds are supposed to look: pleased with ourselves and our celebration, glowing with happiness. But what, then, of the hostilities that were already brewing—his anger at my parents for not wanting to serve alcohol in their home or his disdain for my bond with my sister? What of my apprehension that even in his caring gestures he seemed self-absorbed, performative rather than considerate? What of the question I had put to my sister: How can I know if I should marry him when he sometimes seems so selfish? What of the heady rush through a mere six months of getting acquainted?

In the photos at least, I cannot see his capacity for rage or his distrust of family ties. Nor can I see my own uncertainty, obscured by my bright smile and sleeveless street dress, sky blue. In our wedding vows—made in the living room in front of our parents, his brother, and my brother, sister, and brother-in-law—we quoted Rilke and pledged to be "two solitudes [that] protect and border and salute each other." In the photos, we stand together.

In photos taken slightly later—in 1970 while we were on a six-month sabbatical in Europe—we look even happier. With a time-delay camera, Lawrence had taken pictures of both of us on the Acropolis, at Delphi, Sparta, Crete. On the beach on the island of Mykonos, we grin at the camera, sunburned faces surrounded by sharp blue sky and white sand. In many of the European photos, I wear clothes that he had helped me to select on shopping trips in London: clothes with designer names previously unknown to me, inconceivable for someone like me, simple, straightforward, plain living. He is often wearing a camel's hair sport coat or a perfectly fitted dark suit, both of which he had had tailor made during those same weeks in London.

Not evident in the photos: the night in Venice when we argued and I wandered alone along the canals and through Saint Mark's Square until I finally bought myself a cheese sandwich out of a desperate hunger. Or the lonely days looking up at the castle in Tübingen where his near-native German and my bare expressions kept me in a kind of forced isolation, a silent wifely shadow, alone in the hotel, reading and rereading Virginia Woolf for my stalled dissertation work. The photos instead show almost perpetual smiles, seeming to affirm a happiness that I cannot recall. Did I, in fact, experience "the moon, or happiness" that Caligula purports to be pursuing? Or did I merely wear a mask for the camera, for some public charade?

Also not evident in the photos: the terrible shock at the invasion of Cambodia and further shock at photos and reports of student protesters killed at Kent State and then at Jackson State. Out of the country during this period of cultural anguish, we remained two people given to complex analyses rather than concrete actions—and committed to protecting our solitude.

WHEN I BECAME PREGNANT, we were back in Bloomington in our second apartment: a three-bedroom unit, spacious compared to our first one bedroom. Chosen to accommodate our writing lives, it had a bedroom we would share, a study for him, a study for me. The latter was a delicious luxury, a room of my own—not then the cliché that it has since become. A room of my own in which to prepare the classes I taught as an associate instructor in graduate school. A room of my own in which to continue work on my dissertation examining the novels of Virginia Woolf. Still resisting explicitly feminist approaches to Woolf—this dissertation was begun in 1969, and I cannot claim to have been boldly ahead of the time, when Woolf was not to be read in feminist or political terms—I did at least know the value of a room set aside to do my own work. But I also knew the obvious: Lawrence, ten years my senior, a newly tenured associate professor, was the family "provider." His claim upon the larger study was indisputable. So, too, was his claim on the *only* study when we needed to convert one study into a nursery.

So here I was: married, "all but dissertation"—ABD, in the vernacular—and pregnant. Pretty much on track for 1971. But still vague, unformed. I think of young mothers now who speak in outrage and shock about losing their identity when they have children. But I was of a different generation, taught not to be defined too early on, expected to remain open to the possible changes that would come from mating with a more sharply defined partner and subsequent responsibilities for children. Older by then than Rachel Vinrace in Woolf's first novel, I nevertheless had that same quality that so irritated her aunt Helen—lack of color and outline, nothing hard or permanent or satisfactory. And my few journal entries of this period show me yearning for a love I cannot feel from behind "a wall of ice" at the core of our marriage.

Now that we were resettled in Indiana, the country still simmering around us, I simply continued the academic life as my way to be both traditional and resistant, teaching my own courses through 1970–71. On my syllabus for composition courses, I included Eldridge Cleaver's *Soul on Ice*, essays about the civil rights movement and the My Lai massacre, and Stanley Milgram's sobering study of obedience. But I did not see a clear way to work more actively to make change. The women's movement was growing, especially in major urban centers, but I was in Indiana, in this life that I had both chosen and drifted into. I finished the semester in maternity clothes, still blurred around the edges.

JULY 1, 1971. Inside me, the tensions roiled up. I felt the movement of limbs other than my own, pressing against my physical borders, the movement of unknown changes pressing against the walls of identity.

As my due date approached—July 4, Independence Day, with its multiple meanings—I saw only glimmers of what might come next. I could not, then, have known all the ruptures I had yet to face. Nor could I have had any idea of the somber meaning this particular date would acquire twenty-three years later when it became the date of Lawrence's death.

But of the meanings available to me in 1971, I did know this much: I yearned to be freed from this pregnancy. I did not like being led by my abdomen and breasts, feeling grotesquely swollen and perpetually nauseated. I did not know how to move through space, could not bend over properly, sit comfortably on a desk to talk with my students, or find my way through narrow passages. I wanted my own body back—even if it had never been a limber dancing body—and I wanted "the kid" to be in the world.

We were blithely ignorant of this child's sex—no sonogram photo albums or scientific verifications as most parents seem to have these days—but we enjoyed the play of providing an affectionate, gender-neutral label for our baby: "the kid." And we anticipated a "natural" or "prepared" childbirth in a conventional hospital setting. Not given to group activities, we had foregone the childbirth classes, relying instead on our own preparation with books and exercises. I knew how to time my contractions, pace my breathing, stay active for as long as possible. I was ready.

When my water broke in the postmidnight hours of July 2, everything seemed according to plan. Here was a considerate advance notice: no contractions yet, but all indications were that the baby would arrive within twenty-four hours, as the books suggested. Momentarily pleased by anticipation and wet sheets, I lay quiescent—a fleeting luxury—before moving into action, changing the bedding, checking my packed suitcase. I phoned the doctor, who told me to get some rest: labor should start soon; he'd like to see me in the office in the morning. In recollection, I see that I did all of this alone; I do not know what Lawrence was doing or thinking, but I imagine him working late, as was his pattern—still in his study when my water broke.

Sleep, of course, was slow to come. Labor, too, was slow to start. The night was endless, and the clock immobile. But like the good student that I had always been, I had done my homework; I knew not to be worried. "Dry labor" was merely a myth, and my breathing exercises were as clearly assembled as the objects in my overnight bag. All I needed to do was wait, lying there alone in my marital bed, my husband at his books.

But what I wanted was to be done waiting. I felt that I had always just been a solitary observer: even in marriage and pregnancy—choices I had made in private retreat from public turmoil. During my pregnancy, I had read about the many changes my body and my baby were going through, but I did not feel like an active participant.

Now here was this long night and more waiting. I watched the clock as I had watched the calendar for the past nine months. Minute by minute, hour by hour, such a slow accretion and no perceptible change. I must have dozed; Lawrence must, eventually, have come to bed. But in the morning

I still had no contractions. When I saw the doctor as directed, he sent me home, still to wait. Lawrence went into his study to work; I tried to read, seeking distraction.

By late afternoon, I insisted that we go to the hospital. But I had made only a few centimeters progress. Though I had pledged to try for a medicine-free birth, I finally succumbed to the doctor's medicine-ready worldview and agreed to a little Pitocin inside my lip. This yielded a slight tightening, nothing more. My body and my baby were not yet ready. Together they conspired against my wish to participate: I stood aside and waited.

As the evening progressed, I could not foresee any independence day of the kind I yearned for—to be free of this pregnancy, to return to a self I thought I knew—but at least I could finally become part of this birthing. Finally, I not only timed mild abdominal spasms but also joined effort with increasingly strong contractions. Labor. At last, work I could do.

Even Lawrence finally had a role as he drew on the book knowledge we had developed together. With more caring and tenderness than I had ever felt from him, he stood behind me and pressed firmly on my back. The pains tightened against my lower spine, fanned out around my pelvis, gripped my abdomen. When I was told to lie flat—no more pacing in the halls—I bucked against the pains, feeling like a beetle flipped arbitrarily onto my back and waving my limbs in empty space, though in truth my feet were firmly anchored in stirrups.

At last I was liberated to an active role, the very hard work of giving birth. This was the moment that so many women say that nature conspires to make us forget, that religious stories have told us is our punishment for sexual knowledge. This *was* the moment, but, for me, not of punishment and pain but finally a chance to participate. No longer a watcher—not even interested in observing what was happening—I immersed in the physical, sensing every muscle and nerve ending. With one clear goal, I felt *present* in a way that I had felt *absent* throughout most of my pregnancy, much of my marriage, even much of my relationship to the culture around me. With the authorization to *push*, I finally came alive to a clear sense of bodily purpose.

I could scarcely see her, but I knew she was there, in the world at last: covered with blotches of white cream, tiny and splotchy red beneath the vernix coating, but breathing real air, clearing her lungs assertively, waving her arms and legs at the edges of my vision as I lay flat on my back. No longer "the kid," she was now a healthy, whole baby girl who nestled briefly on my chest before they took her away to be cleaned up.

Now we could name her, begin to place her in the world: Kara Antonia Frye. It was July 3, 1971, 12:49 AM, not yet Independence Day, but a new era for me. I still did not know how to participate in the culture around me. Nor did I know how to be Lawrence's wife. But I was, at least, this body, this self, and now Kara's mother.

EACH DAY, as I try to wrench this story free from its constraints, I pace my study, a New York room of my own, catching new refractions of light from my cherished crystal, a gift from Ron. It is both beautiful and simple: egg size, egg shaped, multifaceted.

Sometimes I lie on the bed naked, alone, and settle the crystal in my physical center, resting it against the concave of my navel. It seems to fit there—as it fits in more public moments in the palm of my hand—its heft in either case holding me to myself. In my navel, it marks the first scar of self, the knot tied at birth.

Like the crystal, a self is multiple, responsive, always changing yet somehow the same. Unlike the crystal, a self is an agent of its own multiplicity.

With the crystal nestled against my navel, I muse upon my birth and my birthings, my work and my loving and my losing, my daughters' growing and my own.

This much is clear: beginning with Kara's birth, my thinking had new fissures in it as it opened onto an altogether different sense of self than what I thought I had been struggling with. I had thought I needed either to stand aside or to join a group, though no group quite fit my needs. Then I had thought I had to choose between assertion and accommodation—between a selfishness I thought I saw in Lawrence and a selflessness I thought I aspired to. And I kept thinking I had to find a way to protect my solitude though I chafed at loneliness. But now I was experiencing something else altogether: a nascent self, perhaps, but cracked open, ready to rethink my very assumptions.

2

On the Farm

Among the documents I brought with me to New York, I find a small blue box of ivory note cards, some blank, a few of them written on, left-over announcements of Kara's birth. I remember hand lettering them with a fountain pen and black ink, keeping them modest and to the point: her name, date of birth, length, weight—her bodily presence in the world. The only other message was the phrase "sharing the news of our happiness," followed by our names: Lawrence and Joanne. On the front of the folded note card, I had printed a quotation from Hölderlin that Lawrence had selected and translated from the German and that we both agreed on: "A child is wholly what it is, and thus it is so beautiful."

The claim is too simple, but I must admit: Kara was amazingly, from the beginning, *integral*. I cannot think of another word for it. Perhaps it is true of all young children, but I think not. In Kara, we and others very early on recognized that she was a presence unto herself, whole and magnetic. Later, as a toddler, she would stand in the middle of our living room, surrounded by guests attending a baby shower for an expectant mother. Others noticed her. Some anticipated that she would be the proverbial "heartbreaker," but that was not the question at all. Really, it was a simple sense that she knew who she was, and whether Hölderlin had it right or not, her wholeness was beautiful.

WHEN KARA WAS BORN, my mother wrote to me that now I would be able to understand the love that she and my father felt for me. I remember being startled by this observation. It had not occurred to me that anyone could ever have loved me as I loved this new person: her perfectly shaped head and clear brow, the whorls of her ear, the glint in her eye, her tiny clenched fists and reaching fingers, and her long and lean body barely couched in tender flesh.

It was not that I doubted my parents' love for me. I had always felt well nurtured. My attentive mother had nourished in me her own love of words and stories and thoughtful choices; she had even made me feel special for having inherited her marked overbite. So too with my responsible father, who had given me his myopia but had cherished me with quiet affection, seeing in me his own talent for mathematics and reasoned thought. Nestled in this family—between my sister, Eileen, three years my elder, and my brother, Don, a year and a half younger—I had always thought myself much cared for.

But the intensity of my feeling for this baby, of me and beyond me, was completely new.

WHEN I WAS ELEVEN YEARS OLD, in the car with my mother on an errand—we were crossing a bridge—I asked her, "But who am I, really? What makes me *me* if I inherit this part from you and Dad and the rest comes from everything else around me?"

I remember the moment with stark clarity: the car, the bridge, my mother's attentive ears, the riddle I could not solve. What part of me is *mine*?

Now a parent myself, I returned to that question with a new ferocity. Who is this new person—Kara—so immediately whole? And who am I, hers and yet my own?

BEFORE KARA'S BIRTH, I had thought of myself as more mind than body: a reader who searched for meanings. As a child, I had joined in neighborhood games of hide-and-seek or kick-the-can, but clumsily, without the pleasure of muscle and sinew. I had climbed trees joyfully but had usually taken books to read and a pillow to cushion my flesh as I lost myself in other worlds. With my Mennonite heritage, I had missed the ease of body that might come from dancing. In my life with Lawrence, I had fully embraced a secular life of the mind.

Now I struggled with my earlier belief in mind over body, reason over matter. While pregnant, when my body would not yield to any simple assertion of will, I knew that I was of the flesh. Even more, after Kara's birth, mind and body seemed newly entangled by my love for this small creature, who needed me to understand her, who required my full attention—even required the nourishment that my body provided—but who had altogether a distinct being, a mind of her own. I knew that she was separate from me and I from her, but I was still bound to her by silken threads that seemed to issue from my body or, more complexly, from my whole being.

THIS NEW WEAVE of mind and body, self and child, tightened when we moved from our apartment near the university in Bloomington to a farm twenty miles out through the limestone quarries and rolling hills of southern Indiana. I had not anticipated or yearned for the rural life, though I did want a place larger than our small apartment—a place with a yard and a freer access to the outdoors to match a child's need for space and motion. Instead, late that summer, Lawrence—never one for half-measures—found the farm. Neither of us had any experience with farming, but he wanted to try this experiment in living differently, and both of us were ready to forge a new life in a new place with our new daughter. No doubt we were in part influenced by the counterculture movement, then swelling in many parts of the United States, the urge to live simply and "naturally," eschewing a consumer culture. But we felt this experiment as something we were doing ourselves in all our singularity, framed by the distinctive stresses of our own lives.

To my surprise, I succumbed to the farm, a response that was both visual and visceral. Awash in the sensory life of early motherhood, I could not differentiate my falling in love with the farm from my physical and emotional love for my new baby. Was it temporary or permanent, this new intertwining of the physical with the intellectual and the emotional?

The intensity of these new maternal feelings deepened the colors and sharpened my senses on the day that we first visited the farm: Kara and Lawrence and I in our newly acquired Datsun station wagon, the family car that had incongruently replaced Lawrence's sleek Porsche, remnant of his bachelor days sold to help finance the farm. Now we had this modest station wagon, forest green, to serve our new needs as a family. With Kara's arrival, most of our values were in flux.

Gazing out the windows of the purely functional car that was part of our life transformations, I was stunned by the beauty of the farm as we drove up the curved driveway to the one-story white house, small and set well back from the road. Spikes of red cannas stood tall by the fence surrounding the house. Red salvia clustered in front of the porch. One hundred and ten acres in all: behind the house lay the back fields, ready to till and plant; behind them were gloriously useless woods and gullies, brambled and untamed, and a scrawny creek way out back. We knew from the realtor that the farm included places that were locally named "Becky's Bluff" and "Rattlesnake Holler," and rumor had it that we could count on finding Indian artifacts if we looked very carefully. Even without looking hard, we would quickly spot an old Indian grinding stone on the pathway to the backwoods.

As we walked toward the house on that first visit, we could look off to our left, down the hill, where we barely saw the roof of the barn and a glimpse of the pond. To the left as well, but not far from the house, stood the gleaming two-car garage, newly built, and behind that, the decrepit chicken coop. Against the tree in the chicken yard leaned an old wagon wheel—remnant of past lives and token of rustic beauty. The wagon wheel sealed my response: this would be our new home.

ON OUR MOVING DAY a month and a half later, the beauty of the landscape was infused with change: recently harvested fields and the raw colors of autumn leaves spattered against plangent blue sky. This October encompassed the seasonal cycle, harvest and hints of spring air to come, all at once. It seemed the perfectly fitting month for us to move our belongings from town to farm. We were full of hope and sensory pleasure.

Perhaps our new place was, after all, only an ordinary, small midwestern farm. But to me it was the place of my newfound love of the senses, my new love affair with my daughter, my new awareness of my own body. Perhaps here we could be a family—Lawrence and Kara and I—premising our lives on a much more physical existence, even a luxuriant growth, while keeping our intellectual commitments.

We knew that we were taking on much that was new to us, even though the real work of the fields and the farm would be hired out. We had not only our new baby, but also a new puppy, two new kittens, a few white Plymouth Rock hens and two roosters, gardens we would dig once spring arrived, and the plan to develop a small herd of beef cattle in the future. And I feared that the new demands on both of us would only increase our emotional isolation from each other. Kara's gleeful smiles and grasping fingers had drawn an unfamiliar warmth from Lawrence when he held her or gazed fondly on her, but he and I seemed as distant from each other as if that wall of ice still stood between us. In his emotional absence, I came very close to making of Kara my whole emotional world.

Still, I tried to hope that here, with all this newness, we would be better able to twine our three lives together.

IN THE EARLY AUTUMN of our first months on the farm, the urgency of the earth and the seasons paused. But the days were still filled with life and color; the leaden sky had not yet settled over the barren ground. In that season of the farmer's respite, Kara and I—when Lawrence was away—would sometimes claim an afternoon just to sit on the porch swing and inhale the newness of this life. We had no rocking chair, so the porch swing served as occasional substitute during her feeding times. I could sit quietly with that easy movement between free associative thought and pervasive bodily sensation. Sometimes I would read a book; sometimes I would just sit, stroking her foot or head or cheek, nuzzling the fine strands of her baby hair, speaking aloud my random thoughts, nestling her tiny body against my own curves and protrusions.

I've heard these sensations described as erotic. And surely for me they were intensely sensuous in a way that my body can still recall: nerve endings fully activated not just by the gentle tugging at the breast or the more vigorous sucking that pulled milk palpably through the ducts that looked like white rivulets winding across my breasts, converging in the nipple. I felt both lethargic and alert, both self-absorbed and given over to Kara's comforts. Here was no separation between mind and body: fully engaged, I felt intellectually alive as well as bodily present. Though the skeptical voice now taunts me—*Well, which was it: intellectually alive or bodily present, lethargic or alert?*—I must insist that in those moments I really felt *both*: that was the wonder of it.

Even the work with the body that so many new parents find distressing—the endless diapers, the messes of food and excrement, the cleaning and caring—in the beginning, even these did not much disturb me. For one thing—others mock me when I say this—I did not find new baby shit offensive. As long as Kara's only nourishment was breast milk, her diapers always seemed to smell sweet and the cleanup to be simple. It is true that the laundry—the rinsing and washing and hanging to dry and folding of all of those diapers and baby stretch suits—seemed endless. And I admit to some repressed irritation that all of this physical work fell to me, never to her father. But there was, at least, a rhythm to it even in its repetitions. And I yearned to be physical—not just a sterile vessel for other people's ideas, as I had again begun to feel in my studies.

IN A SPIRIT OF PARTIAL COOPERATION, Lawrence and I even managed to work out the details of our university commitments, trying together to make a life that felt whole. Lawrence carried on with his teaching and research, inviting the occasional dissertation student or graduate seminar for a country outing and adopting the veneer of a crusty farmer to supplement his professorial presence. Although I was making little visible progress on my dissertation, I told myself to think of this as a time that my dissertation director called "fallow"—a time when I could read and reread, a time when my thinking could deepen without my scrambling to put further words to paper, a season of respite. And I continued with a class I was teaching at the university.

Since we had only the one car and the twenty-mile commute, I would twice a week spend the day on campus, attending to Kara's infant needs as well as to my own work. As a graduate student, I had no real office space of my own, so I would camp out in Lawrence's office while he taught his classes or attended meetings and would leave Kara there with him during the one hour when I went off to teach my class. By the end of the semester, she had been dubbed the "German department baby." We were assured that she would be much missed during the second semester when we were able to make other accommodations. I would miss the social interactions but not the added stress.

IN OUR FIRST SEASONS on the farm, both Lawrence and I made valiant efforts to throw ourselves into the new life around us. We dug up not just one garden, but two; we put in perennials, fragile asparagus, hardy rhubarb; we special-ordered apple trees, peach trees, apricot trees, even English walnut trees and almond trees; we tapped our long-standing maple trees in late winter, boiled large vats of sap, and sealed jars of the amber syrup. We picked blackberries for jam and pies; we tried out elderberry recipes; we sought the edible wild mushrooms; we spent endless hours, into the early morning, boiling and processing pea pods and dandelions, attempting to make new exotic wines. All of this was at Lawrence's insistence, for he was driven, though I developed my own passion for it, too.

From the plowing and tilling, the planting and cultivating, the harvesting, our two large gardens yielded glistening jars in the fruit cellar and a freezer full of carefully labeled packages: applesauce and tomatoes and corn and beans and so many other vegetables, both familiar and strange. I treasured the fruit of our labors in such luxuriant abundance. But I fought with the sense that Lawrence saw me as his assistant in these labors, under his direction—the subordinate custodian of the harvesting and freezing and canning.

As Kara grew, we enmeshed her in the profusion of life around us. Unmindful of the tension between her parents—both of whom so clearly loved her—she learned to laugh at the surrounding natural world. She learned to roll, to sit up, to crawl, and then to walk—reaching out gleefully toward Tofa, our Norwegian elkhound, her arms thrown out, her bare feet grasping the earth beneath the blades of grass. She kept me company—first in her baby carriage, then in her playpen, eventually free in the fenced-in yard—as I worked the soil, tended the emergent life, while her father went farther out into the fields. When he was closer by, in the garden, she also worked with him, helping to place the cut potatoes in the troughs he had prepared. She explored the milkweed pods, blew the dandelion fuzz, poked her fingers in the dirt. She threw her head back with abandon as Lawrence lifted her high to see the newly blooming lilac bushes; she climbed proudly on the recently gathered bales of hay. She trailed confidently behind either of her parents or the dog or the cat with the clear sense that the land and its abundance belonged to her.

Sitting on her bedroom floor, looking out the low bedroom window—past the old wagon wheel against the tree and toward the chicken coop—she watched the chickens pecking in the dirt, the birds arriving in flocks for seasonal migration, the passing of sunshine and midwestern thunderstorms. She learned her first words, *chi* for chicken, *ca* for cow, "Tata" for our dog, as well as the more typical *hi* and *shoes* and *da* for daddy. Did she say "mama"? I think that was later, for I did not name myself as she and I named the world together.

As Kara persisted in learning her environment, she also took up "cooking," getting all the pans and mixing bowls out of the cupboard and stirring together nuts and blocks and kernels of dried corn and then transferring the mixture to another pan to cook. She carried with her, much of the time, her measuring spoons and a big wooden spoon—imitating one of her mother's chief activities. She told her first stories—remembering several months later the woodchuck she had seen by the lilac bush the previous spring or recalling the departure of her uncle Don and aunt Vickie in their van a month and a half earlier, insisting the van was a "truck, not a car." Through it all, she claimed the world around her as a place to explore, a place where she had freedoms and capacities and her own point of view.

WHEN I DESCRIBE our life on the farm now, I can almost see it as an idyll, a nearly perfect balance of work and family, of mind and body and emotion. It was not quite that, for even as Lawrence and I shared in this intense commitment to the land and to Kara, it was clear that he governed the land—and my labors there—and that I was to be primarily responsible for Kara's care. It is certain that Kara was thriving, sensing her place on the earth, among growing things. But it is also certain that we were not finding comfortable ways to be a family. Lawrence and I increasingly went our separate ways. More and more, Kara was becoming my whole emotional world, the real locus for my integration of mind and body and emotion.

IN THE DECADES SINCE, I have resisted the romantic view of that life, have usually adopted a tone of ironic distance, even disdain, though with a touch of pride, for the life I then lived—a mother, sensuous, nature driven, physical and sweaty and of the earth. Nor, I suppose, do I now strike most people as the earth-mother type. When I call that life to mind, I feel not romance but detachment, almost scorn: I have not gardened for years. Indeed, I profess to be so scarred by those years entangled in growing cycles and external directives that I cannot even manage a small herb garden or patch of lettuce outside my back door. Yet when I rely on body memory or when I fully image the hills and the barn and the wagon wheel and Kara moving joyfully through the grass, I can still return to that nerve center of sensory alertness:

my pulse races, my breasts tingle, my stomach tightens. I yearn for some lost piece of myself.

THAT IS THE YEARNING that overtook me four years ago, 1994, when I revisited the farm, long since sold. I drove slowly up the hill, saw the barn against the hills and fields, and felt the old pang of loss and grief for the sheer beauty of the place, even in bleak November, even after the nearly twenty years since I had left it behind. I turned in past the mailbox, drove up the winding driveway toward the modest house beside the still gleaming garage. Two men were working at something on a rack across sawhorses in front of the garage. I stopped the car—noted in surprise that the English walnut trees had actually survived, though the almond trees had not—and then turned to greet the man who came over to me.

"I used to live here. Would you mind if I looked around, walked down the hill toward the barn?"

He looked puzzled. "But—the man who was here last spring, *he* used to live here. He had a young woman with him, wanted to show her around."

"Yes. He was my exhusband. We lived here together. That was his girlfriend with him. He died this past summer."

"That charming man? *He* died? But he was so full of life. Such good humor."

"It was a sudden death." I was speaking in code of his suicide for anyone who cared to decipher meanings. But this man did not know the code.

"Too bad. He was so charming, such a nice man. Well, you take your time looking around. Or I could show you the house first. Do you want to see the house too?"

Ambivalent, I said yes and followed him into the house, looking around at what was both familiar and strange—and what was strange in its familiarity. Admiring the changes made by the subsequent owners, especially the whole new second floor with skylights and a second bathroom, I also sought evidence that this was the place where I had lived during what I now sometimes called my "previous life." I paused in complicated grief over the fireplace that had been our last addition to the house nineteen years earlier: the cherry mantle, the carefully selected blocks of cherry wood perfectly butted up against the marble surround, the marble hearth, the bookshelves we had built in to cover the entire wall around the fireplace. The rest of the room seemed alien: knickknacks, not books, on the bookshelves. No antique Kazakhstan rug, no Danish modern couch, no carved mahogany library table, no Chinese jade scepter with its ironwood stand set on the low Chinese table alongside the jade scholar's brush-washer in the shape of a peach.

After expressing my appreciation, I walked on alone, heading down the hill toward the barn. I inhaled the bracing fall air, breathing in the landscape. I passed the barn on my left, wound my way over to the pond (shrunk beyond recognition), looked up at the hill above me, recalling blackberrying expeditions, picnics, hikes, grazing cattle, newborn calves.

As I headed toward my car, I waved my thanks and good-byes to the two men back at work in front of the garage. When I passed the mailbox, I could not suppress a wry smile and a twinge of grief at the sign that told me what work the men had been about: Bill's Taxidermy.

3

Dealing with Bodies

L ast night I wakened from a dream with the weary assertion echoing in my head: "Once again I am going to have to wrest my story back from him." In my dream, Lawrence was a secret corpse, my responsibility; I was lost in a swamp of judgment. I am so given over to this revisiting of the past that Lawrence and the quicksand of our early married life threaten to suck all thoughts and words from me. My dreams merge with my waking hours, pushing me into a past I must understand before I can go on with my story, the story of my life with my daughters.

My story, this is *my* story, I keep reminding myself. Though I lived the first part of it in Lawrence's shadow and I must tell it in the shadow of his death, I will wrest it back, making it my own: that is my purpose in this current solitude in New York. But my story is reluctant, and my dreams are filled with ancient jade objects, with babies and cows, with cars and chickens, with dead bodies, with words in pursuit of form.

I AM REMINDED NOW of how much I felt the shadow of death even in those early days on the farm. I saw it at every turn: in the underbrush as I walked toward the barn, in the stains on the barn floor, in the chicken coop with its cracked planks and feathers matted in bits of shell. When I walked down the hill or out across the back fields, I scanned the ground for new evidence of mortality.

Like many new mothers, I kept thinking about how fragile a new baby is—how vulnerable the flesh. Seven years earlier my own sister had lost her first baby to sudden infant death syndrome when he was only two and a half weeks old. Though I tried not to think so directly about mortality, the grief and the fear remained just below the surface as I tried to settle for the more

37

abstract recognition that birth bears within it the seeds of death, that life has its cycles. But moving to the farm in that state of mind, I couldn't rest comfortably amid abstractions: here I had to confront all the real death that pervades the natural world as well as the human one.

I RECALL MY FIRST SHOCK at this reality of farm life: six dead rats fell onto the ground when I, oblivious, dumped the bucket of water that needed to be refreshed daily in the chicken coop—six large gray-brown rodents with naked tails and inert bodies. Lawrence was at the university, Kara in her crib. This confrontation was mine alone. Not that I really needed to do anything: just make that sharp intake of breath, remind myself to exhale and then keep breathing.

I'm not inclined to the classic shrieking response to rodents. I had half-befriended a resident mouse during my first year of graduate school when I lived in a rented room in a house with another graduate student and the house's widow owner. That mouse would sometimes come into my room in the evening, climbing up my lamp cord and arriving on the desk at which I sat working. I would put my pencil out to nudge it away from my immediate work, but I wasn't one to panic.

This pile of rats, however, was no mere mouse, no quiet visitor to my solitary life. This was the palpable intrusion of death and ugliness into my new life premised on birth, growth, fruitfulness. Breathing in and then out, finally in a rhythm, I carried on, leaving the stiffened bodies where they lay, at least for the moment. I carried the emptied bucket to the faucet by the garage and filled it before putting it back in its place in the coop. I scooped the laying mash from the feed barrel into the feeding trough. I approached each of the ten nests, one by one. Most of the nests were empty—all of the chickens had gone to the trough for the grain I had put out—and few of them were actively laying at that season of their lives. I gathered the few eggs—two here, one there, mostly none—not having to be furtive or aggressive since none of the hens had remained behind to guard her progeny.

My heart still pounding from the surprise of it all, the newness of it all, I retreated from the coop, carefully turning the small block of wood attached at the door to serve as a quasi-latch. This coop was no great pride of the farm: gray, weathered wood, gaps opening where it had rotted away from moisture and sun, squeaky hinges barely holding the door in place. It was a small space, smaller by half than the newly built double garage, which stood nearby, flaunting its sparkling white siding and glistening windows. That garage *was* the pride of the farm, as the realtor had been sure to tell us. The coop, by contrast, had only naked wood slats and windows that opened to air and sunlight—really just blank squares during the day, with open mesh chicken wire haphazardly tacked over them. These windows we were told to close off at nighttime, using the ancient shutters latched by that same make-do mechanism that served the door—enclosing the eight hens and two roosters each evening at dusk after they'd had their day of pecking in the yard outside. The chickens were free range and not particularly productive, but the few brown eggs they did produce—with their deep yellow yolks and their rich earthy flavor—were a part of the sensory pleasure of farm eating.

Having closed both the door and the shutters, I left the coop behind me, no doubt still permeable to the trespasses of rats and who-knew-what other intruders, nonetheless closed up for the night. I also left the six corpses behind me, lying stiffly in the grass where I had dumped them before I even knew they were in the bucket. Lawrence would have to deal with them later; I needed to get back to Kara.

THE RATS—the living ones—became a daily focus of distress during the evening feeding. Sometimes we would arrive home late—after sunset, the chickens yet to be fed. For those days when I needed to feed them after dark, I developed a strategy. Before entering, I opened the door noisily, reached just inside the door to the light switch, and waited for the scurrying sounds to stop before actually stepping into the coop. That way at least I didn't have to actually *see* whatever creatures were sharing the coop with the chickens.

I came to dread going into the chicken coop. Though I loved the sounds and sight of the chickens pecking in the dirt and the earthy taste of their brown eggs, I wasn't actually fond of the chickens up close. They had an unpleasant way of pecking at my ankles and an even more aggressive way of pecking at my hands when I tried to retrieve their eggs. I couldn't really blame them since they were only protecting their young, but I still didn't like it. Even less did I like the thought of being greeted by rats, dead or alive.

Although Lawrence didn't admit it, I don't think he much liked going out there after nightfall either. But he was intrigued by the obscure threats hiding in the dark. And I wonder whether this intrigue in some way differentiated his and my relationship to the farm.

One day he came up with a plan of attack. After Kara was in bed, he and I were to go out to the coop together—quietly finding strategic locations, he at one of the windows, gun in hand, I at the door. At the agreed-upon moment, I was to open the door stealthily, switch on the light, and pull quickly back. It was his task, rifle pushed through the wire mesh in the opened window, to shoot whatever scurrying creatures showed themselves. He must have seen this "attack" as a sport, really, for how *could* it rid the coop of intruders when all of the gaps and holes remained, ever open to whichever predator or rodent happened by? More to the point, though, I now wonder how I could possibly have stood across a small chicken coop with a loaded rifle pointed nearly at me. And how could I have calmly incorporated guns into my daily life, including this idea of killing—even just the hateful rats—for random sport?

The rifle and the shotgun, both in Lawrence's study, were largely confined to his domain: Why can I not recall when or why he acquired them? I certainly never handled them, and I have to assume that they were just part of our new life choices as we moved to the farm and, even more, that I am right in my confidence that Kara could not possibly have had access to them, even later when she gained increasing mobility. But how could I have ignored the fact that they were there and, as I now know, the fact that they remained in my children's summer home each time they spent the requisite vacation months with their father? How could I have suppressed the knowledge of this potential for violence in their lives?

AT THAT POINT, though I felt quietly estranged from Lawrence, I knew little of dark undercurrents. But my vague disquiet sharpened toward misgiving a few months later when atypical clucking disturbed our quiet several nights in a row. Each evening we had done the usual closing up of the coop, the ritual end-of-day feeding, water changing, turning of the latches on windows and door. Each night the chickens had quietly gone to roost after eating their evening laying mash, the supplement to whatever they garnered during their daytime pecking for insects in the yard. But recently they had begun to start up noisily after their first hour or so of quiet. And the next day the egg supply seemed diminished. As novices, we did not know whether to assume possible predators, egg thieves, or some other mysterious disturbance to their usual equilibrium.

On the third night, we went to investigate. Kara was asleep in her crib; the chickens had begun their disturbed clucking. Lawrence carefully took down his rifle, told me to follow him. When we opened the door, reached into the dark for the light switch, what we found seemed benign enough. And yet there was the disturbance, the reduction in egg production, the urgings of the life of the farm: the docile possum that had somehow squeezed its way into the coop and then between the wires in the feeding trough apparently could not be tolerated. In that brief second, it looked up at us, undisturbed, grain dripping from its mouth as the chickens continued in panicked cackling. In that brief second, the gun in Lawrence's hands exploded as I stood just behind him in stunned silence. The panicked cackling continued; the blood oozed into the trough.

"I did the hard part," Lawrence turned to me. "You can deal with the body." He spoke with his usual mixture of sarcasm, humor, command. I responded with my usual mixture of protest, acquiescence, entrapment. I did not want to fail to do my share, to seem ill natured in the life I had signed on for. Even in my own ears, my protests were futile. In some sense, I agreed with him: he *had* done the hard part, the part I could not have done.

Together we decided where to dig, took our turns with the shovel until the hole was deep enough. But the removal, the burial—that part was for me. I turned the feeding trough over, slid the heavy inert body toward the end where the gap between the wires was larger, scooted the ungainly corpse out onto the newspapers I had brought for the task. The flesh felt unpleasantly yielding, still soft and recently alive, even through the obscuring layers of newspaper. I nudged the body around into a more manageable position, lifted it with distaste, and carried it to the prepared spot. I tried to joke, to join Lawrence in mordant humor, about this impromptu burial ceremony, but in fact I just wanted this task to be behind me.

The chickens were already calmed as we passed the coop and headed back toward the house where Kara slept peacefully. Lawrence returned the gun to his study, top shelf, out of reach. But increasingly I felt some sense that it was reaching into my life—and Kara's too—even if neither of us ever touched it.

BY THE SPRING before Kara's second birthday, I had settled into the life on the farm with all its ambivalence and uneasiness. I was devoted to Kara; I was committed to the growing season; I thought I had made my accommodations to the shadows of death and uncertainty and even potential violence.

One Saturday afternoon, filled with the tasks of early planting season, we all were in the yard, Kara in her outdoor playpen, Lawrence and I working in different parts of the garden, when we heard unusual commotion on the other side of the house near the chicken coop. Dogs were barking, chickens screeching and flapping wings that could not take them more than a few feet off the ground. Tofa, inside the fence for now, barked in urgent response. Lawrence went to investigate and then into the house for his rifle. I waited with Kara and Tofa, our view blocked by the house. We all three startled visibly when we heard the two gunshots.

"Mommy!?"

Not sure whether to be frightened or merely curious, Kara looked up at me, waiting to take her cue from my response.

"Don't worry. You play in your playpen while I go and check." I gave her a quick hug and tried to obscure my worry as I chained Tofa to the fence and went to look.

But what I found was not so reassuring: the chicken yard looked ravaged, and Lawrence was nowhere in sight. Feathers were strewn everywhere; three chickens lay mauled to death, a severed wing off to the side. Two dogs—interrupted in their pursuit of prey—escaped down the hill, their pack broken into by Lawrence's gun. They barked their fury and fear. One dog lay dead in the yard.

When I entered the chicken coop, I found Lawrence, shaken but determined as he stood over another dog, seriously wounded. It was small and unthreatening, with droopy ears and large spaniel eyes that pleaded its pain and its wish to live. Lawrence looked even taller than usual in that cramped space. I momentarily envied him his size and confidence as he waved me back toward the door of the coop, but within the envy lay the seeds of dread. Like him, I knew it would be intolerable to allow this sad spaniel to live; unlike him, I did not have the fortitude to carry out this mercy killing or the wish to be confident with a gun. And it was an act of mercy when Lawrence reluctantly turned the gun again toward the immobilized dog and shot once, carefully: that particular suffering at least would end.

When animal shelter workers responded to my phone call, they confirmed that Lawrence had taken the necessary action. Pack dogs were a threat to the whole farm community, even potentially to children. They could not be tolerated.

"You can't let them run loose," the man reassured us, "especially once they've tasted blood."

This time neither Lawrence nor I had to deal with the bodies. The two men from the animal shelter took them away in their truck. By then, I had returned to the fenced-in yard to attend to Kara and our own dog, very much alive though clearly distressed.

I THINK THERE'S SOMETHING ELSE that I tried to suppress in my initial idyll of life on the farm: my own misgivings about my life as a woman in this family that we were constructing. I truly did love my physical bond with Kara, with the land, with growing things. But this feeling did not take place in isolation.

Even my simple pleasures in breastfeeding were not so pure as I have suggested. I was lucky: I had none of the mastitis or physical problems that I know many women have. But I did have the usual leaky breasts and perpetually milky clothing. I had cut up Lawrence's old T-shirts to provide extra absorbency in my nursing bras, but these rags were simply stop-gap measures against all that fluid and the accompanying fear that I might be somehow mired in the flesh. Several years later, when Kara watched me feeding her baby sister and then inserting those same, much laundered, pieces of tee shirt into my nursing bra, she would ask, "Does Adriane's milk need to be covered so it won't spoil?" In her own way, she already comprehended this nexus: flesh and decay, nourishment and concealment.

Also to the point: it was only when Kara and I were alone that I could claim the sensory alertness that I have described. When Lawrence was home, I felt called to a different alertness: Was I nursing her "incorrectly," too long perhaps? Might I be paying insufficient attention to her? Or maybe I was neglecting her proper degree of warmth or perhaps distressing her by indulging in my own preoccupations. And if we were among people, Lawrence reminded me to leave the room when I fed her lest the distractions be too much for her comfortable nourishment or my breasts be too publicly displayed. What *was* at risk—through concealment or decay, through dominance or insincerity—here in this life we were trying to make?

PERHAPS I didn't really so much dread what is fleshly as I feared that I would be locked into a gender role I had tried to elude in choosing to go to graduate school. In this new life as a mother, I *had* come to an awakened sensuality, a new (for me) love of what is bodily beyond the sexual. And I was groping toward different connections between mind and flesh than I had ever felt. But I didn't know how to do this in my life with Lawrence, and I still shuddered at the risk of being identified as exclusively female: a body rather than a thinking person.

I recalled reading *The Second Sex* in awe and trembling recognition when I was a wide-eyed college student. In Simone de Beauvoir's voice, I had heard a crying out against this miring in the flesh, a powerful intellect at work to redefine what we had been told a woman is: body, property, subordinate creature.

Even now I can recall the cover on that early paperback edition: a naked woman, all resonant flesh, gold toned, and sensual. But in my new life of the senses, I did not know what to make of my earlier uncritical acceptance of Beauvoir's disgust with women's bodies, women's reproductive capacities.

Was Beauvoir right that giving birth is somehow *merely* of the flesh, without its own consciousness? That the act of *taking* life is a more consciously constructed and hence more *human* act? And that, by association, *men* are more human as people who kill than are women as people who give birth? I would later hear phrases from local hunters—"A man's not alive until he's killed something" or "I never felt so alive as when I had that buck in my sights." But at that point I was still ignorant of Beauvoir's odd alliance with "good ol' boys" and their sayings.

I only knew that on the farm I felt betrayed by Beauvoir and by my own younger self as I struggled against the taint of death and possible violence, the pressure of Lawrence's demands, the threat of a life constructed for me by others. And I held tightly to my daughter, to my own sense of self, and to my fragile attempt to deal with bodies in my own way.

4

Reading *Redbook,*
Needing Feminism

I f I look out the window of my fifteenth-floor apartment, straight down, I can see the stream of traffic, dominated by bright yellow cabs, headed down Seventh Avenue through the Village toward exciting destinations farther south. I do not suppose this same view would have been any more visibly feminist twenty-six years ago than it is now, but I feel a vicarious thrill of the early movement in those years. I am, after all, now living in the sublet space of an acquaintance, a much revered New York feminist of the 1970s. When I browse her bookshelves, I find treasures of early second-wave feminism; when I look out the window, down into the traffic, I imagine the vibrancy of activism in the streets.

Turning inward, I look for evidence of my own early feminism and take pleasure in a few signs of gender rebellions in college. I recall a story I often tell: having signed out of the dorm illegally, a college senior, I had tucked my hair into a cap, pulled on jeans and a flannel shirt, and met three others at the local freight yard so that we could hop an overnight train out of town just for the experience. When the railroad bulls apprehended us in Toledo and threatened to phone our parents, I merely shrugged. That was the same year that I resisted my major professor's advice to choose a job that would accommodate the children I didn't yet dream of having and instead chose to go straight to graduate school to study literature, living independently on a small fellowship.

But I did not yet have feminism to assist in rebellion. How could I have worn a girdle under my jeans on that freight-train excursion, making it that much more difficult to pee in the field during a brief stop and then having to

run frantically to recatch the box car when the train began to gather momentum—grappling all the while with jeans and girdle around my knees? Not
for me—yet—the sensuous pleasures of unconstrained flesh or the straightforward resistance to peer expectations, though I had grown up in critical
resistance to makeup and high heels and false deference to boys' wishes and
had never even learned to flirt.

SEARCHING FURTHER, I turn to the unsorted documents in my box in the
study. Here I find the draft of an essay I wrote in 1972, typed on the back of
a mimeographed copy of James Baldwin's "Stranger in the Village," remain-
dered from handouts to composition classes. In the detritus of my former
life, I find at least a persistent thread, a small continuity with my present
thinking. Clearly, I did not then see myself as a part of the "women's movement." Equally clearly—at least by my own definitions now, twenty-six years
later—I was trying to think as a feminist.

The essay was my response to two questions that *Redbook* magazine
had posed to its readers sometime in 1972: "How do you feel about being
a woman? How has the Women's Liberation movement affected your life?"
I was at the time a reader of *Redbook*. My mother, always a reader herself,
had given me a subscription to this "women's magazine," recognizing that I
needed further guidance in filling a role that did not come naturally to me,
but also recognizing that *Redbook* was, for the time, a women's magazine
that pushed the boundaries. The question the magazine posed in 1972 could
well have been an invitation to reject what was then called, often derisively,
"women's lib." But it could also have been an opportunity to examine honestly my own life at that historical moment.

I took it as the latter.

Redbook, after all, had given me my first opportunity that very same
year to read Kate Chopin's *The Awakening*, a novel I did not then know and
certainly not one that I had encountered in my graduate school courses.
When I first read it, I had no idea who Chopin was, only that *Redbook*—in
its newsprint pages at the magazine's end—was offering me this full printing
of a novel first published in 1899 and now presented as part of my instruc-
tion in being a woman. When first published in the nineteenth century, the
novel had been quickly labeled "improper." It had also had a working title

that would have been resonant for me, "A Solitary Soul." But at that time I had no idea of its background, only the instant thought that I should pay attention to this novel: it portrayed a troubled "mother self"; it noticed that a woman might have an "artist self"; it ended in Edna Pontellier's ambiguously chosen death by drowning. And it had a lyrical quality that reminded me of Virginia Woolf, ending, as it does, with a dog barking in the distance and echoes of memory and desire.

That same year *Redbook* had also published—or, rather, reprinted—"A Challenge to Every Marriage," an article by Alix Kates Shulman on a contract that articulated an equitable division of labor between husband and wife and affirmed marital equality as a real possibility. Surely such a relationship was among my most ardent wishes.

Redbook's question, then—"How has the Women's Liberation movement affected your life?"—seemed legitimate, inviting my response.

And respond I did.

My response began with a three-part answer. First, I said, "I am mad" and went on to elaborate that I did not know at whom to be mad, only that I was angry at feeling, simply because I was a woman, "on all sides—and inside—a tacit assumption that certain activities, certain characteristics, certain perspectives are mine." Second, I said, "I am glad"—that "I do not need to expect others to serve or submit to me," that "I can work creatively while sharing with and caring for my daughter," and that "I do not have to prove my worth through aggression and external performance." Third, I added, "I am frustrated" at my inability to resolve a "tension between personal and professional desires" and an uneasiness "with my present life."

I went on to express my appreciation of "Women's Liberation" for the changes it had already wrought and my expectation that those changes would continue to develop. And I ended with the hope that both men and women would eventually be able to find a way to balance the multiple capacities that reside in each of us, "without making any painful amputations of interest," thus fulfilling as many "of our individual human possibilities as time permits." My concluding sentence voiced my wish "to live positively toward all my human values in a life determined by my own personal choices, not by a frustrated juggling of sexual roles."

Redbook did not select my response to include among those it published, but the question had tapped a nerve in me. After my opening assertion that "I am mad," my next sentence was, "I am not mad at my husband for assuming that my role is subservient." I think the essay as a whole was honest, but in this sentence I acknowledged implicitly what I could not yet confront directly: I *was* mad at feeling subservient. And I most definitely needed a feminist movement to help me further articulate that feeling and determine my own response to it.

So much was happening in the early 1970s, so much that I needed to be part of, though I didn't know how. On August 26, 1970, for example, New York feminists marched down Fifth Avenue, marking the fiftieth anniversary of women's right to vote. They called the march "Women's Strike for Equality." Not yet on the farm, not yet even pregnant with Kara, I had nonetheless felt both very far removed from this action and very committed to its goals. There in Bloomington, Indiana, married to Lawrence, I had made my own meager strike for equality by insisting for the first time that I be allowed to drive the only car we had between us, Lawrence's imported Porsche 911S. Granted, it was his car, acquired at great expense during a trip to Germany before I knew him. Granted, I had not even known its prestige value when I first started dating him: my roommate had to look out and exclaim before I knew that this sports car convertible, with its shiny roll bar and understated sleekness, was something to be stricken by. Still, when I finally made my claim, we had been married for two years, and I had *no* car at all.

That, then, was my "strike for equality": to drive his Porsche—to the grocery store. It suggested in any case that I was very far from having a life premised on equality. The grocery shopping was very much my "job"; the allocation of how much money I would be allowed to spend was Lawrence's. At least I would make this drive for myself.

Not a part of any explicit feminist movement, I had continued to feel the currents of change. I shared excitement with my friend Dorie over the publication of the first official issue of *Ms.* magazine in the spring of 1972 and discussed regularly with her our ongoing difficulties with graduate school and life as faculty wives and new mothers. We talked about the congressional approval of the Equal Rights Amendment and, the following year, about the Supreme Court decision in *Roe v. Wade*. Motherhood, equal rights, and definitions of womanhood were our mutual concerns, as they were among the ongoing concerns of the women's movement.

But in solitude, I worked to understand my marriage, my own particular motherhood. Dorie was much more forthright than I, ready to demand of her husband his equal participation and fortunate in having that demand received graciously. With Lawrence and in my own life, I could not make direct demands without causing enormous friction. If I resisted always being the one who washed dishes or changed diapers, his temper flared. When the kitchen floor needed cleaning, he sneered that we would soon have rats in the kitchen, not just in the chicken coop, if I continued to neglect my cleaning chores. When he arrived home from campus, he looked around the house and asked: "What did you do all day?" When I sat alone at my desk, studying the imagery of Virginia Woolf's novels—having put Kara to bed for the night—I heard him muttering in the living room about my "selfishness." I had resisted giving him a backrub after his long, hard day.

Still, I knew that we had made this deal: that I would be primarily responsible for Kara, and he would be the primary income provider; that I would cook our meals and feed the chickens and harvest the vegetables, and he would plow the garden and dig the holes for fence posts and tend the property.

IN ANY CASE, the problem wasn't just about Lawrence. There was something in me that needed to be resolved. And Kate Chopin's "A Solitary Soul" was relevant. I was very drawn to this novella when I first read it, but I was also distressed. How could Edna possibly have ended her own life? I did not then know all of the nuanced critical discussion of the novel's ending—including multiple defenses of her "selfhood" as somehow what she was protecting in her final drowning. But I was uneasy with the recognition that she could literally swim away from her children, leaving them with a parent who had shown himself to be fully defined by his own version of masculinity, not at all ready to take on responsibility for parenting tasks.

I couldn't yet formulate my concern. But as much as I was drawn to Chopin's lyricism and to Edna's need for a self, separate from wife and mother, as well as for sexual expression, I could not align myself with her choice of that "solitary self." I do not recall what I actually thought at the time—only that

I was disturbed by her final swim out to sea and unsettled by the suggestion that this act had to do with being a mother.

But I also knew that I did not want to be *only* a mother and that I would not accept the idea that as a mother I had to relinquish my "solitary self"— or my sexual self.

IT WAS DURING this same time period—when Kara was about a year old and I was disaffected with my marriage and struggling with my dissertation—that I somehow found an hour of afternoon solitude. Lawrence was certainly away, and I can only assume that Kara was sleeping. This was the salvaged hour or two that I spent every afternoon working on the unfinished dissertation while Kara napped.

But on this one undated but very specific afternoon, I went alone into our marital bedroom. The windows were wide open to the sky, piercingly blue and cloudless. The hardwood floors gleamed beneath the Bergama carpet on which sat the Chinese low table that held the ancient jade that both Lawrence and I treasured: the scepter on its ironwood stand and the scholar's brush-washer in the shape of a peach, carved jade, pale green and slightly mottled.

I ran my eyes over these precious objects. But when I lay naked on our bed, I opened myself not to this room or to these objects, but to the sky. Touching my breasts, my navel and belly, my thighs, my vulva and clitoris, I reached toward sensual alertness. For the first time in my life, I brought myself to my own orgasm, alone, drawing the sky into me as I felt all of my nerve endings alert to my own pleasure. I had read that a woman's vaginal vasocongestive responses are intensified after childbirth, and since Kara's birth I had experienced a new intensity in lovemaking with Lawrence, however emotionally fraught our relationship was. But this was something different. This was an awakening to something in me. Still, there was no possibility that I would swim away, that I could simply leave behind the life with which I struggled.

5

Making Lists

I have long been a list maker. An obvious way to keep track of things, lists are also a way to tame a chaotic reality: the multiple pulls on time and energy. I especially like to find old lists by chance, lingering in a book, misplaced in a discarded purse, hiding in a stack of unfiled paperwork. Even in recent years I have occasionally found lists from Kara's babyhood, left like time capsules between the pages of *Mrs. Dalloway* or *To the Lighthouse*—hardback editions no longer current for classroom use. Because old lists provide a shorthand diary of what my past life was like, I have learned to set them aside: physical reminders of that earlier time. When I turn again to my box of unsorted papers, I find a small handful of such lists.

HERE'S ONE LIST. I found it a few years ago, tucked away in an old edition of *To the Lighthouse* (the topic for chapter 3 of the dissertation): *wash diapers, bake pie, write chapter 3, bathe Kara, grade papers, cultivate tomatoes, harvest beans, feed chickens*. As with all such lists, there is no sense of proportion among the tasks; large and small are jumbled together. But at that point the graduate work—"write chapter 3" and "grade papers"—was barely surviving. The papers got graded, as they always do, because students waited for them. But chapter 3 was not only buried among other endlessly reproduced tasks but also regularly pushed to the end of that list, carried over to the next list, never prodded forward.

The mother work, too, is scarcely evident on the lists from 1971 and 1972—other than "wash diapers" and "bathe Kara"—though increasingly it was as a mother that I engaged with life. The needs of a growing child are, after all, immediate, prompting what Tillie Olsen calls a mother's "instant interruptibility." But there were other reasons at work as well: as a student,

I had lost all clarity as to what my goals were; as a wife, I was increasingly only a shell, a role played out in a series of tasks. My mother life expanded to fill these other vacuums, giving me a more vivid sense of purpose. But like my less rewarding gardening tasks, it, too, was tied to seasons and growth, external exigencies, and future possibility.

As the seasons progressed, I would occasionally think back to my earlier afternoon alone—seeking a sexual self and a solitary one, too—but only with a kind of nostalgia. I could not conceive an identity that didn't include Kara. Regardless of what the lists said, she was woven into every portion of my life, my constant companion as I worked in the kitchen or the garden or hung the diapers on the clothesline in the backyard—strings of white rectangles pegged together in beautiful symmetry. She gave form and value to the time that had no presence on the list: the time cuddling on the porch swing, walking down to the road together for the mail, reading a story together, or sitting on the floor beside the low window in her bedroom looking out at the chicken yard, the barn, the dog.

BY THE FALL OF 1972, I was no longer eligible to teach as a graduate student. Though I welcomed the easing of schedule, I chafed at the increased domesticity. Kara, not yet one and a half, became a more insistent presence, charming and devilish—and always there. With a wicked gleam in her eye, she would snatch my glasses, pull my hair, tug on the phone cord, even (on rare occasion) scribble in one of my books—and then, just as my exasperation overtook me, she would hold out her hand, smiling softly: "Hi," as if a greeting served as ready redress.

Unable to carve out real writing time, overwhelmed by countless gardening tasks and an endless stream of colds and earaches and unremitting parental responsibility, I looked elsewhere for an expression of creative energy that would still allow me to be with Kara: sewing could at least provide projects of my own, not driven by demands of season or husband, yet yielding visible, even durable, products. I made Kara a big stuffed doll with embroidered eyes and mouth and brown yarn for hair; "Big Doll" wore a red-and-yellow patchwork dress designed to teach about buttons and zippers. I made multiple stuffed animals, for Kara and for gifts to other children: bright blue seals with attached fins and floppy tails, frogs with black button eyes and vivid multicolored bellies. I made hand puppets from felt, bronze with a gold mane, to enact *Dandelion*, a favorite picture book. I made simple little outfits for Kara to wear and even sewed a pair of lounging pajamas for Lawrence.

At Christmas that year, I expanded my craft projects and constructed a board game called *Going to the Farm* for my three nephews in Ohio. It had the usual pitfalls and setbacks tied to rolls of the dice, though the goal was forward momentum: a visit to their younger cousin and her surrounding plant and animal life. This project had its darker side: I yearned for my larger family ties as we prepared to celebrate Kara's second Christmas, her first holiday at an age of awareness.

I TURN AGAIN to the life materials I have brought to New York. In another box, I find a carefully collated set of handwritten letters that I wrote to my parents nearly weekly during those years on the farm. Amazingly, my mother had saved them all, organized them chronologically, and returned them to me as I began this writing project. I had thought I had no narrative record of my struggles then—my journal for that period is nearly empty—and even this record is partial, shaped by its audience, sometimes written in code I doubt they could understand. But as these letters attest, my parents, despite our differences, were there for me, still foundational, as I tried to figure out how I was making my life.

The letters show me endlessly hedging on holiday plans, providing excuses and explanations to hide my yearning: Lawrence is putting up a new fence around the pasture area, to hold the two heifers we have just acquired—ten-month-old Scottish short horns that we will eventually breed; Lawrence is finishing the semester, attending meetings, grading papers; Lawrence needs to work on the article he has under way; Lawrence wants not to drive on roads that might be icy. All of these reasons were real, and as a full-time faculty member myself now, I much more readily understand how the end of semester compels a schedule, but at the time I was struggling to determine just what weight my own commitments held: Would I ever find time and psychic space for the endlessly languishing dissertation or for some sense of myself outside the demands of others? And how would I ever connect to a community or my now distant family?

We stayed on the farm that Christmas, going out into the fields on December 24 to cut down a scrawny cypress tree, which we then decorated with vines of bittersweet—clusters of wrinkled scarlet berries, each cupped in an orange collar—and popcorn strung on thread. Belatedly, we mailed off the hand-made game, *Going to the Farm*.

IN FEBRUARY 1973, I voiced my pleasure in a letter to my mother when the Supreme Court ruled for women's reproductive choice in *Roe v. Wade*. Her work at Planned Parenthood had made her acutely aware of how important this ruling could be for women. In May, I honored her feminist convictions by giving her a subscription to *Ms.* magazine for her birthday. Meanwhile, I continued to look for a feminist community of my own, joining three other German department wives with young children for an occasional night away from our families: not quite a consciousness-raising group, but a time to refocus our personal energies.

Also that February, I made a schedule for myself: to write during Kara's nap—usually an hour, sometimes more, sometimes nothing—and again for three or four hours after she was in bed every evening. Finally, I initiated a new round of appointments with my dissertation adviser and began submitting draft chapters for his review. Though the work was halting, I tentatively renewed my commitment. I would explore the patterns of imagery and idea in Woolf's novels; I would persist in my plan, though I wouldn't yet consider that these compelling novels had anything to do with how I lived my own life. I would find a way to complete this task: "Toward a Form for Paradox: Image and Idea in the Novels of Virginia Woolf."

BUT AS SPRING CAME, the garden and Kara and, over it all, Lawrence again held sway. Nearly two, Kara had a bit more independence, could play in the sandbox nearby as I gardened, trail after Tofa, "help" me with the planting. Together we prepared the soil, sorted the seeds, put out the seedlings we had started in rows of small paper cups on the windowsill. And I anticipated with pleasure a June visit from my sister and brother-in-law, Eileen and Jim, along with their three sons, Doug and Matt and Steve: finally, their first visit to the farm.

AFTER THEIR DEPARTURE, I wrote to my parents that we had had "a really good visit, though a little hectic," and I remarked upon my special joy in seeing Kara and Steve play together. A year older than she—and the youngest of the three Burry boys—Steve was delightfully attentive to her, and she gladly did her best to keep up with him.

But I did not write to my parents what I have remembered all of these years: Lawrence yelling at the boys for any minor infraction—slamming the screen door or holding it open too long so that flies slipped into the house; leaving footprints on the edge of the garden or sneaking a taste of raw peapods, sweet and rare. I remained silent as well about Lawrence's insistence that my sister's family sleep in their tent—not only outside the house, but out by the old apple tree toward the road rather than within the fenced-in yard. I remained silent about his taking Jim out to his "shooting range"—where he had set up tin cans for target practice—and then never letting Jim take even one shot; about his taking the boys down to the pond to go fishing, but not letting any of them come back up to the house for the dinner I had prepared until he himself had caught a fish.

Nor did I write to my parents of conversations with my sister as we stood together in the kitchen, chopping vegetables. Puzzled by my life, so unlike hers, she wondered how I managed and whether I felt at physical risk now that Lawrence was learning karate—a new hobby he had taken up that spring—or at emotional risk from his volatile temper.

It had never occurred to me to fear bodily harm, but, regardless of what I was not yet admitting to my parents, I did fear emotional harm. And I knew that my tenuous attempts to find a space for myself in this life of ours—to work on my dissertation, to seek out other women with similar concerns, to act on values beyond the domestic—had not had much success. I could only assure Eileen that Kara remained at my core, the only touchstone I could hold to unquestioningly.

And through that summer of 1973, Kara *was* my constant companion, so much so that by her second birthday she became adept at sitting at the kitchen table with pencil and paper, busily making her own "lists." By the end of that summer, she was all I had. Any other meaningful life had drained away: no clear professional goals, no real marriage.

IN QUIET DESPERATION, I started making other kinds of lists, lists of possible apartments in town, lists of projected budgets if I were living alone with Kara, lists of concerns to sort through. One such list, elliptical and confusing, now seems as lacking in proportion as my lists of tasks: *lawyer—grounds; childrearing—only child; location—finances; property—concessions; effect on Lawrence—my complicity.* "My complicity": Where had I lost my sense of love and commitment? How had I come to the point where I had only two journal entries for all of 1973, both very brief, both shadowed in depression?

July 1973. Kara 2 years old—dissertation unfinished—garden overridden with weeds—the days, weeks, years go by.

September 1973. something clicked & I went dead inside—no more hatred even—just nothing.

The most suggestive lists I made were lists of pros and cons—to leave the marriage or to try harder to make it a real relationship—and even these lists now seem elliptical and lacking any sense of proportion. Reasons to stay: *home, land, father for Kara, fresh garden food, financial security, sex, beautiful objects, time with Kara.* Reasons to leave: *freedom, time, dissertation, house and garden work minimized, the right to spend small amounts of cash, dispersed anger, open lifestyle, professional development, remove Kara from stressed household.* And then there was the long list of my grievances, including *L's temper, intolerance, lack of communication, disdain for my family,* and, in a frustrated outburst, *I can spend no money unapproved; I can go nowhere unapproved and un-preplanned; I must justify everything to L.; I must always defend myself.*

The lists seem almost pathetic to me now, but I know how desperate I felt, how much in need of change. I had assimilated the truism of popular psychology that you can't change someone else, but I made a note to myself: *some emotional change in* me *by mid-October.* Another list casts its own shadow over all of the preceding ones: *L's smile—and twinkle, the sharing with Kara, the three of us together, working in synchronization, sense of humor.* Among photos of that period, one shows Lawrence holding Kara aloft, smiling up at her in pure pleasure; another shows the three of us sitting on the porch swing with Tofa at our feet. The photos, the lists, the abbreviated journal entries. In the midst of it all, I queried, half a journal entry, half a conclusion to a list, *How to weigh the benefits for me against the losses for all three of us?*

But I was serious. The notebook that has almost no journal entries for that two-year period has, instead, pages of such lists. Pages of practical concerns ranging from rental possibilities to phone installation to minimal household equipment (tea kettle, coffee cone, broom, dust pan). Pages of numbers trying to figure out how I would make ends meet on my own. It did not occur to me that I might be entitled to financial support from Lawrence. I saw this project as entirely my own to figure out, my responsibility, my urgent need. Nor did it occur to me that Kara—and her baby equipment— would be anywhere but with me.

It now strikes me as odd how little Kara actually figures in the lists of pros and cons. As with the lists of tasks, I suppose, she must have simply been the *given* for my life at the time, the essential continuity while I tried to determine which other continuities were essential, which peripheral. And though I despaired of the dissertation and felt no intellectual urgency to do the writing, the PhD seems to have taken on the burden of "freedom," a life that belonged to me. It was as a wife, not as a mother, that I felt entrapped.

One of the lists gave me if not freedom, then at least a possible strategy, a way not to feel numb, trapped. It was headed *"try": assuming 2 mornings/ week; counseling; refusal to serve; hard work on dissertation; stronger sense of self; spending money when important to me.* Money, self, dissertation. Money had never been particularly important to me, but, like the dissertation, it had come to represent freedom, self-definition. Without ever intending to, I felt like a dependent. A disproportionate access to money was my clearest indication of that dependency; a completed dissertation was my clearest claim on something that was mine alone. Together, money and the PhD had taken on some of the symbolic weight of a selfhood under siege. The motherhood commitment remained an unchallenged premise for everything else.

BY SEPTEMBER OF THAT YEAR, I was writing much more openly to my parents about my urgent need to leave Lawrence. I invited them, for privacy's sake, to respond to me at the English department, Ballantine Hall. Before I could yet open the subject directly with Lawrence, I told them—as I told my sister—of my plan to divorce him. I wrote to my parents—pages of questions and concerns and processes that I might undertake. And I said to them, "I know that this pattern could only have formed through the participation of two parties—but now that I realize what has happened and want to change *myself*, it no longer seems possible within the relationship."

As Kara now points out when she and I talk together about men and women and ways to live in relationship to others, these surreptitious conversations—seeking counsel elsewhere rather than developing genuine discussion with Lawrence—could not have been good for the marriage. But I did not know how to talk with him or to resist his controlling responses.

Nor did I find immediate solace from my parents, who indisputably loved me but did not approve of divorce. These letters, these thoughts and queries, put them to a test for which they were not prepared. They wrote back to me that I should reconsider my plans. Starkly, they wrote, "Remember, there is no guarantee you will be granted custody of Kara." I knew they did not mean to hurt, but my cheeks burned, as if stung by fingers slapping first one side of my face and then the other.

I continued to write my letters, though, even sharing emotional ambivalence that could not have helped them address their own doubts: "I harden myself in my decision—and then, maybe lying in bed at night all tense with decision, I hear L. cough in the living room and suddenly am fully aware that there is another *human being* involved in all this—and become again a jelly of indecision. Or I look out the kitchen window and see Kara and Lawrence talking about the leaves falling from the trees and wonder whether I can do anything that is fair to all three of us." I also discussed with my parents why I did feel certain that I would have custody of Kara and then the burden of guilt that followed—"because I don't think the system is fair. . . . And because I couldn't think of leaving without Kara—and know that automatically means depriving L. of a good deal of his relationship with her."

I finally did talk to Lawrence, making myself vulnerable to his persuasive powers. And by October, I wrote to my parents, in a total about-face, that I was ready to give further effort to the marriage, trying still to preserve our commitment to Kara—Lawrence's as well as mine—and to find a way to be the "me that I want to be." As a token of change, I got a new haircut and returned—again—to work on the dissertation.

AND SO LAWRENCE AND I did *try*. My lists became the plan by which we would make a change in our shared lives. Kara began a preschool program two mornings a week; I used those two mornings and her occasional naptime and postbedtime hours to wring the paragraphs from my pen. I returned to earlier thoughts about Woolf as a secular mystic, a seeker confronting death and possible meaninglessness. From a formless rough draft, I carved out a new version of the chapter on *To the Lighthouse*, hearing in my imagination the "monotonous fall of waves on the beach"—a drumbeat of mortality—and experiencing with Lily Briscoe the flood of grief after Mrs. Ramsay's death, "to want and want and not to have." Refusing to see Mrs. Ramsay as an "angel in the house," I insisted on her complex humanity. I tiptoed around the notion that the Ramsays might provide a possible critique of marriage and argued instead that *To the Lighthouse* portrayed a metaphysical balance between despair and affirmation, drawing profoundly on imagery from nature to render this balance.

Gradually, draft pages stacked up in the tiny study that we had created out of a closet-size dressing room. Gradually, some sense of a writing self began to build up, too. Though the pages looked like they belonged to a dissertation committee, this writing self *was* mine; it struggled into being in part through a subterranean conversation with Woolf. In cold New Critical prose, I analyzed the import of her image patterns and averted my eyes from her radical politics and sharp feminist insights. But my subterranean conversation continued, unacknowledged for now.

BY 1974—my third summer on the farm, six years into the marriage—much had changed, much remained the same. Both my lists and my letters again traced the seasonal rhythms of planting, cultivating, harvesting, freezing, canning. I had become fully attuned to the growing season: the first moment in spring when it might be safe to put out seedlings, the threat of the first frost in the fall followed by the imperative to bring in any salvageable tomatoes or zucchini. And all summer long the vigilance about when it might rain, about which vegetable or fruit was in most immediate need. But other items had disappeared from my lists: Kara no longer required that diapers be laundered; chapter 3 was finally a fait accompli. Indeed, the pages of draft manuscript had accreted into a full 339 typed pages with adviser's approval.

I wrote to my parents that my dissertation defense was scheduled for July 22; I had made an appointment for xeroxing and binding the required copies; before then, I had only to finish the final typing during Kara's naptime or after she had gone to bed.

This set of commitments was strenuous, and I certainly had no "wife" to help me with the typing and proofreading, amid the other tasks at hand. But Kara was thriving, full of her own joy of the seasons, her books, her friends; I had made some claim on my writing, my access to "freedom"; and I had stopped making lists of pros and cons. Indeed, by the end of the summer, I had weighed in heavily with the affirmations of the life at hand: I had not only successfully defended my dissertation; I was also pregnant again.

6

Placentas and Other Hungers

I keep circling back, reviewing the early years of Kara's life: turning the lenses differently each time, seeking the angle that will bring clarity. I write at night, in the hours that can't be interrupted, hoping that the shards of memory will form a pattern in the darkness. In the daytime, I revisit old questions, squinting my eyes against a light too bright, trying to push the story forward.

Often, I begin the morning by standing at the window, sipping my coffee, gazing out at the river that peeks between skyscrapers and then looking down at the streets below. I test out phrases to describe what I see, as if practicing scales in anticipation of my more arduous pursuit of language for thought. With words running silently through my head, I watch the amusing dance of cars trying to claim parking places at precisely 9:00 AM, when the legal side of the street shifts for street cleaning, or I watch the patient maneuvering of a solitary car into a spot I could have sworn would not accommodate any vehicle without right-angle steering. I watch an ambulance make its final sprint toward the wide driveway at St. Vincent's Hospital. And I watch the slower buses, lumbering from stop to stop, heading south on Seventh Avenue among white delivery vans and blue and red and black cars and yellow taxis, as pedestrians with baby strollers and briefcases and shopping bags push along the sidewalk and on into the day's commitments.

In the midst of this bustle, I appreciate the more leisurely pace of the ritual opening at the Taquería de México, a small Mexican restaurant over on Greenwich Avenue. From my perch at the window, I watch the server arrive on his bicycle—which he chains to the parking meter—and then wait for him to unlock the front door and return with the metal crank to unroll the awning: another mark of the city taking up the activities of a new day. This morning I watch with special interest, having last night for the first time been a customer at Taquería de México.

ADRIANE AND I had planned an evening for just the two of us, a movie and light meal after her day at work. She chose the movie—a romantic comedy, at which we both laughed, our spirits lifting; I chose the restaurant, wanting to shift from observer to participant in my neighborhood eating spot. At the restaurant, we munched on chips and beans and guacamole; the server hovered, watching us and exuding benevolence all evening. Finally, he refilled our water glasses one last time and queried: "Mother and daughter?" His sentimental observation was not unusual: we are known to have a marked physical resemblance. But I think he was noticing more than that: as we talked, we tossed words back and forth easily, leaning forward and speaking and pausing in comfortable rhythms, mirroring each other.

In that same conversation, I told Adriane about my halting progress in writing of our lives, especially the piece I had just finished: "Making Lists"—the story about, as her sister puts it, how Adriane almost wasn't born. She seemed intrigued and then said, "I'm going to have to read this book. There's a lot I don't know."

But growing up in a family open to questions and given to talk, she has already learned most of it in bits and pieces. She has certainly long known the obvious: that less than a year after her birth, I left her father. As a child, she had even heard her sister ask the question: "Why did you have Adriane if you were going to leave Dad so soon?" This had not been a hostile question, only a need to understand. That, of course, is what much of this writing is about: trying to understand, for myself, for them.

Now I suck in my breath, desperate for oxygen at the inconceivable thought that Kara and I almost missed having Adriane in our lives.

BUT WHAT NOW SEEMS ESSENTIAL still does not yield to easy explanation. It is true that I had a plan to leave Lawrence before I became pregnant with Adriane or completed the dissertation; it is also true—as I have told it here— that I suffered a "jelly of indecision" and then succumbed to Lawrence's persuasive powers and to my own guilt at the thought of depriving him of Kara's daily presence. Perhaps, too, I had some latent hope that if only we tried, we could become a family in which Kara would feel as secure and nurtured as I had felt in my own childhood.

But my staying had another motive that I'm not certain I could even acknowledge to myself at the time. I understood that Kara was at risk of becoming my whole world—a strange echo of Jane Eyre's words before she nearly joins the conniving Rochester in a bigamous marriage: "My future husband was becoming to me my whole world." For Jane, the threat is that her potential husband might loom too large, casting a shadow over her relationship with God, "as an eclipse intervenes between man and the broad sun." I was no longer religious, but I understood the problem of having any one person loom too large. I especially understood the hazards of making my whole life around Kara: surely one of us would be smothered; surely I would risk losing sight of who else I might be, besides her mother.

I was not at all convinced that I could, with Lawrence, make a relationship that would work for me, but I did not think I could make for Kara a family of just the two of us. And so I stayed in the marriage in order to provide a sibling for Kara?

That conclusion, of course, is far too simplistic and gives to me an excess of singular agency. After all, the decision that we would stay together, have another child, took two of us. A simpler hypothesis is that both Lawrence and I understood that our staying together suggested the next logical step in family making: another child. In any case, simple calculation reveals that I became pregnant almost simultaneously with defending the dissertation.

ADRIANE'S PRESENT QUESTIONS echo those we have addressed throughout her life. When she was younger, she would periodically ask: "What was it like when we lived with Dad?" She would suddenly want to know, as if some crucial piece of knowledge had been left out of her story. Because she had been too young to form her own memories of our life as a nuclear family, she has always had to rely on my stories or her sister's to try to understand. My first impulse, then, was to tell her of her birth.

As she now knows—as I have been struggling to reconstruct—her beginning caught the rest of us in medias res. She was thrust into a family already fragile, unsettled by angers and yearnings beyond her. Perhaps that's why, when I try to recall the time of her birth and my pregnancy with her, I haven't usually turned first to my life with her father and her older sister, but rather to the life I shared with our cows.

That was 1975, and the two cows and I were growing large together, all three of us anticipating spring births. These Scottish short horns—one an inexperienced heifer and the other a second-time mother, having given birth the previous spring—seemed more placid about pregnancy than I. Still, I felt a kind of commonality with them, a shared rhythm of the seasons. So I watched them and tried to learn from their calm.

Each day began with the effort to stabilize my stomach, to rouse myself from lethargy. I needed to perform the many chores of the household and farm, even in winter. But it was hard to care about much other than the awaited spring. Time slowed unbearably as nausea and fatigue cast their shadow over everything. My face broke out; my hair fell out. When I cried—as I often wanted to—my nausea only intensified. I snapped and snarled and quarreled in the effort to push the weight of depression off my chest. I could not tell whether these emotions belonged to pregnancy or to me.

One journal entry traces my struggle with numbness. Kara and I were in town for purposes of our own, groceries or some social gathering of mothers and children. Driving down Bloomington's Seventh Street, midcampus, surrounded by morning traffic and roving students moving carelessly among cars and bicycles, I could not suppress the need to vomit. Barely managing to pull out of traffic, I opened the car door and retched onto the pavement. From the backseat, I heard Kara's voice: "Mommy, what's wrong? Why are you coughing?" Students on the sidewalk cast a casual glance in my direction, then passed by. Flecks of vomit, badly aimed, landed on my suede coat, a remnant of the elegant wardrobe acquired so long ago in London. When I glanced in the mirror, I looked colorless; dark circles of my own eyes stared back at me. For the rest of the morning, my voice was hoarse, my stomach queasy. When I finally made it home, Lawrence responded with his own distilling comment: "So, you left a mess on someone's street."

AS THE MONTHS WORE ON, Lawrence and I were finding it increasingly difficult to sustain our renewed commitment to a mutual life—especially now that I had completed the PhD and no longer had any clearly defined external goals: no job in sight, no visible writing projects. He had inevitably stepped up his expectations about what I would do around the house and farm, and I had complied, wearily agreeing that it was only fair. Kara alone had the capacity to call me out of my isolation. With her stores of warmth and joy, she remained at my center. But she was thriving and seemed to need little from me. Now nearly four, she still had that integrity, however odd that sounds for a child so young—a self-possession that had been distinctly hers from her earliest days of toddling around the farm.

To keep some sense that I had purposes of my own, I read whenever I could, seeking parallel lives in literature, as I had done for as long as I could remember. At the time of Kara's birth, I had been reading *War and Peace;* it had distracted me well and kept me from a close examination of my own life. During my pregnancy with Adriane, I spent much of the winter reading women writers and had responded keenly to Doris Lessing and her insistent truth speaking, especially about pregnancy, childbirth, and women's lives in general. As my due date approached, I was reading Zola's *The Earth,* a perverse choice for a pregnant woman, given the crass value system it portrays: the birthing livestock so clearly prized above the birthing woman. But I did look forward to the cows' and my parallel birthings in the spring—resisting the notion that I, too, was primarily property.

The calf born the previous spring had been male. We had named him "Persimmon" for his rich reddish brown color—the color of the pudding I regularly made from the persimmons gathered from the ground after the first autumn frost. We had then neutered him and scheduled him to be butchered, as one did with male calves not destined for breeding purposes, so we still had only the two cows. But with one of them in her first pregnancy, they needed daily attention.

I loved walking down the hill each morning to feed them, the seasons making their inevitable transition even when it felt that time stood still. This was the one daily chore that was pure pleasure to me. Once I reached late pregnancy, no longer perpetually nauseated, I would sometimes even take my morning coffee with me into the barn and a book to read while I waited for them to finish eating, drawing together my small horde of pleasures: soli-tude, the land, stories and words and tastes and smells and images.

The March morning that the first calf was born, I left behind the book and coffee. Snow blew in my face as I set out—late false snow, an air bliz-zard that would not stick to the ground. The air cut sharply, but I felt oddly exhilarated. My nausea had lifted; I had had a real night's sleep. Kara would soon need my attention—and I felt that this time I would be able to give it cheerfully. But for now the rest of the household slept; I could enjoy my morning's solitude, my morning's pleasure.

The gate squeaked as I closed it behind me and headed down the hill, looking out over the rolling fields for the location of each of the cows, though they were usually together. I liked seeing where they were before they saw me. I liked visually taking in the land around me: the pond against the hill of blackberry bushes that rose behind it, the woods beyond that, the scattered wild rosebushes and early spring flowers, the fences and the barn and the gravel road named "Lee Phillips Road" after the very people from whom we had bought the farm. I liked the sense of place and possibility and history, though it wasn't quite my own history.

Both cows came immediately that morning, following me into the barn, breathing clouds of vapor in the snow-blurred air, calling out their hunger for the feed I would put before them. They found their designated places, seeking the taste of grain I put out first; I stanchioned each of them in place and measured out the amount that we'd been told was optimal for a gestat-ing cow. I sat in the chilled barn, watching my own vapor breath. I felt my baby bounce briefly on my pelvic floor and the sharp pain that ran quickly down my thigh when the bouncing struck a nerve. Thinking and watching. Despite the physical discomfort of late pregnancy, I savored the moment: the chill warmth of the barn, the snuffling lips gathering in the grain, the circle of solitude around me, the stirring of limbs within me.

Later that same day, as Kara took an uncharacteristic nap and Lawrence worked in his study, I went out again—to enjoy another moment of solitude, to claim again the landscape as my own. But this time something seemed amiss. The two cows were not together, and the landscape felt out of balance as I headed toward a lone cow that seemed lost and aimless, wandering the field. It was odd to see her alone, odder still to note that she was chewing on something. That's when I realized that she'd given birth to her calf and left the newborn to fend for itself. She seemed unable to grasp her situation, to take on her new responsibility. Instead, she chewed distractedly on what I now saw was the placenta, taking for her own bizarre nourishment what had so recently been the calf's source of sustenance.

People doubt me when I tell of this incident; indeed, the veterinarian argued with me, saying it wasn't possible and would be "unnatural" because cows are herbivores. But that is what I saw: an unnatural mother, I suppose, in several ways. For she was not only wandering calmly across the field, chewing on the new placenta; she had also deserted the calf. We found him in a ditch on the other side of the field: a healthy roan, again a male. It took our human intervention to bring cow and calf back together: Lawrence lifted the newborn from the ditch, carefully carrying it down the hill to its mother. It left its mark on him, peeing on the leg of his jeans before we got to the barn, but it knew its mother once they were reunited. She, too, seemed to return to her sense of appropriate attachment, offering the necessary nurture once the calf was actually there to suckle.

I'VE HEARD that whoever has possession of a newborn's placenta will hold control over that child's destiny—that the placenta must be burned or thrown into the sea in order for the child to claim control over its own destiny. Do hospitals here in the landlocked Midwest burn all those placentas, the smoke from used-up nurturance rising in celebration of the newborn babies' independent destinies?

Or perhaps they bury them, return them to the earth, as I've also heard is the practice in cultures where the placenta is seen as the child's twin, a kind of alter ego designated to act as guardian angel as the child grows to maturity.

And if the mother eats this symbolic piece of fleshly life? Does she then take into herself the responsibility to act indefinitely as alter ego, guardian angel, protector, and infinite source of nurture? Or does she conversely become the monstrous devourer of the child's right to an independent destiny? And what becomes of the mother's own independent destiny or, for that matter, of her needs to be nurtured, protected, watched over?

In my cherished moments of solitude at that time, I gave no particular symbolic weight to the cow and the calf and the placenta. And I certainly had no plan to engage in a rite chosen by some new mothers of the era: the ritual ingestion of my baby's placenta. But I thought a great deal about what my needs were and how I might meet them. And I recalled the straying new mother, distracted, hungry for what the placenta might provide her. Even now, it is the hunger of the mother I remember—that and my solitary straining to make sense of my life.

TWO WEEKS after the birth of the first calf, Adriane was born. When I tell her about her actual birth, I like to tease a bit and insist that I wasn't really like the cow: I had no urge to chew on the placenta or any desire to leave my baby in the ditch. Despite the lure of solitude, I welcomed her with relief after the long trial of pregnancy and with the nameless pleasure in recognizing that, even from birth, she was distinctly herself. I would not have called this presence a destiny, nor would I now. But I treasured her singularity and felt strongly that she would have the resources to meet what lay ahead of her.

In any case, I liked her from the start and was even pleased by the birth process, though this claim is something else that people often doubt. As with my first pregnancy, I had prepared for this birth, read all I could, practiced breathing, done exercises. I was definitely glad to have the pregnancy part coming to an end, and once again the whole process of giving birth made me feel active and able after all that passive waiting.

As with Kara's birth, I knew that this birth was imminent when my water broke in the middle of the night. As before, I rose from bed, laundered the bedding, restlessly awaited the actual birthing. Again, I did this alone, having chosen to stay home when Lawrence had joined a party of colleagues that evening. But this time I knew that I needed to be patient, and I was used to taking care of most physical matters on my own. The next day I went ahead and served lunch to Kara, Lawrence, and a visiting friend—a former colleague of Lawrence's passing through town briefly. I watched the others eat, picking at the Jell-O I allowed myself, as I timed mild contractions until there was no doubt it was time to make the half-hour drive to the hospital.

By the time I was checked in and ready, I no longer needed patience or much help from anybody. In fact, I hardly had time to use any of my techniques or to call on Lawrence for assistance. And the doctor hardly had time to get in off the golf course, where he was interrupted in his Saturday afternoon game. He didn't even change his clothes or shoes—only put on the outer layer of surgical green that the hospital required. After I pushed Adriane out, I pushed some more and delivered the placenta, followed by a late and innocuous clot that splattered blood all over his golf shoes. He was good-natured about it, but I could tell that he wasn't too happy about what this new baby, her placenta, and I had done to his shoes.

That's how Adriane and I first met each other: in a room full of people, bright lights overhead, me still flat on a birthing table, and a doctor just off the golf course with blood on his shoes. She had emerged blood smeared and blotchy red, crying out heartily against the shock of arrival. The doctor held her up for my first look at her, but—still flat on my back—I could barely see her white hands waving just on the edge of my vision. Finally, the nurse laid her briefly on my chest so I could actually *feel* her presence. Her face was still blotchy, and her eyes squeezed shut, but her body was warm and damp against mine. Then they whisked her away from me, off to the nursery and the incubator that her pediatrician liked to use for the first few hours of all his patients' lives. So we had to wait a while before we could really get acquainted.

I didn't like this separation, but it did give me some time to try to get reacquainted with my own body. At first, I lay in a so-called recovery room, feeling the emptiness inside me, the slack flesh of my abdomen—a soft rounded mound sagging between my hip bones where the skin used to be pulled taut across the strainings and kickings that went on within. I was angry that they had taken her from me, and I felt betrayed by my body, especially by the continued contractions that periodically and unpredictably turned the sagging mound into a hard ball. Why did I keep having these fruitless and arbitrary contractions when the birth was over, the task accomplished? I did not recall them from Kara's birth. And no one had warned me that a second birth was likely to differ in this way from a first: the uterus no longer needing to be the highly developed muscle required for birth, straining to return to its earlier discreet pear shape; the body having to work so much harder than the first time to restore its own equilibrium.

My body felt alien in other ways as well. Once again I had been told that an episiotomy was necessary; painful stitches were now an irritating reminder that a male doctor had decided what my vagina was capable of. My breasts, not yet engorged, not yet ready to yield sustenance, were nonetheless uncharacteristically large—alien mounds of flesh on my chest. Nurses massaged my abdomen every hour or so to release any remaining blood clots. My stomach, unfed since the night before, rumbled with a ravening hunger. Lying there in the recovery room, I felt myself only as flesh, leaking fluids in all directions, still laboring, deprived of the fruit of that labor, and desperately hungry.

For a while, I succumbed to the hospital routine and my alienated body. But soon I roused myself and walked down the hall to the nursery to peer through layers of glass and into the incubator at the back to make sure that Adriane was real. And I gathered enough energy to insist to the staff that this was supposed to be a "rooming in" arrangement, that at the very least I was "supposed" to get my baby for the evening feeding.

That's when Adriane and I finally met for real. She was too newly born to nurse yet, so we made our acquaintance with eyes and voices and touch. She lay against me, just looking—those newborn blue-gray eyes that might become any color later on—and I held her and looked back. The lights were low, the curtain pulled around us; we had no distractions. We mostly just looked into each other's eyes—they say that babies' eyes seek out human faces right away, seek out anything that looks like two eyes in an oval—and I needed to take her in visually for myself now that she was really here.

Her face was still blotchy red. Her ears were dented and bright pink, and her hands and feet were now purplish and pruney. Her head was still slightly elongated from her chin to the back of the head and her nose flattened from her passage through the birth canal, out of my body. But I could see and touch all her fingers and toes, the red birthmark on the inside of her right ankle, the bend at her knees and the curve of her nearly naked skull that just fit the palm of my hand. And I knew the simple *wholeness* of her.

We just looked, but there was a real recognition in her look as well as in mine. And I talked. I told her about the grass and the hills and the cows and the pond and the woods, about the books she would read and the places she would go. I told her how lucky she was to have a sister, how much they would come to rely on each other. I told her how glad I was to know her and how she would have to help me know what was going to be best for her. With our bodies touching, our eyes focused on each other, my voice murmuring to her, I began to feel the return of my own body, the renewal of a sense of purpose.

"WHAT ARE YOU WORKING ON THIS SUMMER, MOM?" Adriane asked a few years ago when I visited her at college at the time of my early attempts to write of her birth in fictional form.

"A story about you, about your birth, the farm," I answered, invoking her complicity.

"But I'm not fiction," she insisted, smiling.

"You mean I didn't make you up?"

When Adriane actually does read this story—now already years later—she may well insist that I couldn't possibly remember what I murmured to her in that first real meeting between us and that I wouldn't likely have told her her future anyway. She may insist that that part really is fiction. And I suppose that's true. But it's the sort of fiction to which a mother is entitled as she thinks back on her own and her children's intertwined destinies.

And it's certainly not fiction that she went home to the farm, that the second cow soon gave birth, that I was wakened one moonlit night several weeks later by a plaintive mooing. Leaving a sleeping household, I walked out to see a second newborn calf, pure white, already licked clean and standing on wobbly legs, its mother watching over it in the moonlight. Within a few days, it was dancing on the hillside like a lamb in springtime.

It isn't fiction, either, that during the summer of her infancy Adriane spent many hours lying in a carriage outside while her sister played nearby in the grass or the sandbox as I hoed and weeded and sweated in the garden. And it isn't fiction that both calves and their mothers prospered in the barn down the hill. Nor is it fiction that many of my pleasurable hours were now spent sitting on the porch swing, sometimes just Adriane and me, sometimes Kara, too—the three of us, reading or talking or making up stories, nursing and cuddling. Sometimes we just looked out over the hills, the pond, the woods, the barn—imagining lives to come.

Or maybe it is fiction. It cannot, in any case, be a very truthful account. It leaves out the sleep-deprived weeks that lay ahead, the bronchitis that Adriane acquired from her sister before she was two weeks old, the many adjustments large and small that a new baby brings into any family.

And Adriane may still need to remind me that I've scarcely given her father any role in her story. She may ask, teasing me and recalling other stories I've told her, "Do you think I was conceived by artificial insemination like those calves?"

From other stories I have told her of our farm life during her infancy and before she was born, she knows about the insemination process. I have told her how—the same year I became pregnant with her—I checked the young cows' taut pink vulvae every day for signs that they were ready and then how the man came in a truck with semen on dry ice. I have told her how he used a long glass tube, working it in through the kinks and turns of the cows' vaginas, delivering the sperm to their eggs.

She might remind me of all that and then prod me further, still teasing: "You can't act like that's how *I* got started. I really did have a dad, you know."

NO. EVEN THAT CONVERSATION IS A FICTION, a reasonable fiction that I first thought of in 1993, when it was still possible to anticipate joking and teasing about the absence of her father. Perhaps it is now once again possible, but such teasing can never again be without its somber undertone.

For the cows, in any case, it seemed easy, despite their wayward hungers: not a bull in sight and no real choices to be made anyway. For me, it was much more complicated: I had yet to figure out how to make my life in the midst of its surrounding demands, how to address my own hungers and how to nurture my daughters well. But I swear I didn't deliberately set out to write their father out of the story. I swear I didn't mean to destine his exile from our lives or foreordain his death.

7

The Presence of the Father

M y calm felt so fragile—and so necessary to me and to Kara and Adriane—that even now I guard it assiduously in this construction of our lives. The easiest protection was to draw the circle of solitude around the three of us, to try to pretend their father wasn't really there. And in a way he wasn't. But in another way his presence shaped everything in our lives, even within that circle of solitude.

Well, then, what about the father? What happens when I try to write him back into the story?

WHEN WE CAME HOME from the hospital, I was relieved to *be* home, out of the rigidity of the hospital schedule. I looked forward to our making our own life, our own schedule, together. Each of my three mornings there, the nurses had wakened me at 7:05 to take my temperature and blood pressure. The routine that followed had been similarly attuned to bureaucratic regulations rather than to human hungers and needs: breakfast at 7:20, lunch at 11:30, dinner at 4:45; babies in rooms from 9:30 AM until 2:20 PM, again from 4:00 PM until 7:20, and once more for a 9:30 PM feeding and then twice during the night at 1:30 and 5:30. The latter schedule was for "rooming-in" babies, not exactly what I had anticipated and certainly not guided by Adriane's own hungers or mine. Now at home, I hoped that she and I could begin to find our own rhythms for eating and sleeping. At last I could again gather Kara into my embrace. I hoped, too, that Lawrence would be a part of these new rhythms, drawn in through the indulgent smiles and gentle touch with which he had first greeted his new daughter.

Even so, this return was not simple. For one thing, Kara was ill and needed loving attention herself at the same time that she had, as much as possible, to be kept away from her new baby sister. For another thing, there was still no one to attend to my hungers. Indeed, when we walked in the door—having left the hospital on the third day and retrieved Kara from a friend's house—Lawrence's first words were: "I don't know whether to go out to the fields or into my study."

And it's true: neither the imperatives of the spring planting season nor the demands of the semester had halted simply because we had a new baby. Even so, I felt abandoned, taking this comment as a reminder that Lawrence expected his life to proceed uninterrupted—that it was up to me to attend to my daughters and myself, that his schedule would prevail here. When he went out to the fields, I wearily turned to Kara's and Adriane's disparate needs and then prepared that evening's dinner.

It's not that anyone else could have helped. I had long since learned that any other presence in the household made Lawrence even more difficult to live with. And I even believed that those early weeks of a new baby's life should be a turning inward, a bonding together of parents and children. It is possible that out of sheer self-preservation I instead turned away from Lawrence, gathering these two daughters to me, closing him away from the circle of new nurturance. But I know that I felt decidedly closed out myself, thrust upon my own resources and increasingly focused on these two daughters, who were my primary emotional resource, but also my primary responsibility. As Lawrence withdrew into his world of masculine responsibility, I withdrew further into this world of mothers and children: of necessity struggling on, alone.

MY BODY SEEMED TO MIME my emotional condition as I dragged through those first days home. I felt exhausted, feverish, and weak, alternately suffering chills and waves of heat. Painfully large and hard, my breasts looked grotesque and were now too full and taut for Adriane to get a good grip on; the visible conduits of milk, like white veins just beneath the surface of the areola, both fascinated and repulsed me. My slack abdomen and painful perineum—the consequence of the episiotomy—made me feel cumbersome. When I thought of Lawrence's responses, I became even more irritable, wavering between a chill hardening toward him and a smoldering anger.

Within the framework of his presence, I was consumed by the material realities of early motherhood. But when I look back at my journal of those days, I find that I wasn't just living those realities; I was also keeping a place for myself among them: the journal entries were my own small attempts to document the experience of pregnancy and childbirth, a small claim on observation, if not yet on story. I had almost forgotten just how much I always meant to write my own mothering experiences.

Coming upon those pages now—written haphazardly with dashes and garbled syntax, mixed in among reading notes and old lists, not in consecutive order as are my later journals—I discover a tenuous resolve nearly lost within the welter of physical and emotional demands. I recall that I had especially treasured Doris Lessing's *A Proper Marriage* because she wrote about pregnancy and childbirth and early motherhood in concrete terms, avoiding the sentimentality I had seen elsewhere. I recall that I, too—already then—yearned to tell the truths of my own life.

BY APRIL 9—our second day home from the hospital—I was aching for sleep: Adriane nursed every two and a half hours during the night and every three to four hours during the day; there seemed to be scarcely any pause between feedings. That night I was also wakened by Kara's vomiting all over herself and her bed. Fortunately, she soon drifted back to sleep. Having changed her clothes and sheets, I put in a load of laundry, sighed deeply, and crawled back toward my own bed, hoping at least to rest my eyes before the next feeding time. Lawrence slept on, worn out from his long days divided between the fields and his academic work.

I got up the next morning, an automaton in a nightgown, yearning for the sleep I could not recoup. As I emerged from the blur of postbirth days, when I had seeped liquids in all directions, I seemed to harden into a mechanical being: cooking, washing dishes, doing laundry. I tried, as well, to pitch in on the urgencies of the season; the Friday after Adriane's Saturday birth, I dug twelve pounds of carrots to store—salvaging what had been preserved in the earth over the winter—so that Lawrence could plow the garden. I couldn't do my share of the planting because Kara's illness—a deep bronchial cough and upset stomach—kept me mostly in the house with her, though I did manage to feed the cows and chickens and to do some vacuuming, an inside job in any case. The least mechanical parts of my day were nursing Adriane—my breasts had finally settled into a softer, more comfortable shape—and reading to Kara.

Every spare minute of Lawrence's time seemed devoted to the fields—organizing seed and fertilizer, doing the preliminary plowing, and preparing the garden for planting. Though these tasks were not really farming—indeed, he had taken on this work as a kind of hobby—they were still a major commitment on top of his full-time commitments at the university. He, too, became tired and irritable. I yearned for him to make some concession to my need for "recovery" and rest, to show at least a few signs of affection, consideration, pride in our new baby. Feeling this lack, I could do little else but proceed, though I, too, became almost uncontrollably irritable.

Kara had her own insatiable hungers, mostly for my undivided attention, which I could not easily give her. I spent more time than usual with her—both of us confined largely to the house—but I felt that I was constantly telling her "don't" in an attempt to keep her germs away from her baby sister. Almost certainly she could also sense the tension that flared around her.

As for Adriane, she was just learning how to be a body in the world around her. She paid no attention, on her ninth day in this family, when the stub of her navel fell off, a strange, black, charred-looking piece of flesh–non-flesh. But she definitely responded when a week after her birth we took her to the hospital for a routine PKU test: she screamed violently at the intrusion of pain when they stuck a needle in her heel. Then, when she was merely two weeks old, I took her to the doctor with congestion and cough, a deep rasping in her tiny lungs. The doctor labeled it bronchitis and put another needle into her little bottom with scarcely any flesh on it. I could hardly complain since she clearly needed this penicillin, the wonder drug of the twentieth century, but she, of course, had no way of knowing why she had to sustain this new assault on her fragile body.

GRADUALLY, we all emerged from these weeks of physical frailty. Both Kara and Adriane recovered from their bronchial infections; Kara regained her access to the land outside; Adriane began to sleep almost through the night—by six weeks she was waking me only once during my own seven-hour stretch. All of us were relearning how to smile and sometimes laugh.

Even Lawrence developed a smile of sheer beneficence when he gazed protectively at his new daughter or engaged his first daughter in conversation about the lilacs or the new calves, the birds that settled in the trees in noisome flocks or the dog barking and barking in the distance.

AND SO IT WAS: in fits and starts, the four of us became a family in the months that followed Adriane's birth, at least in the visible structures of our lives as we worked toward a schedule that could accommodate all of us. But the structure was fragile: suppressed angers seemed ready at any moment to leap into rage. Much of the anger was Lawrence's—a barely contained rage that simply overtook him, often without visible provocation, often directed at me. But the anger was increasingly mine as well, creeping out of obscurity more and more frequently. The sense of danger, barely hidden, frightened me. I knew that the early weeks of a baby's life are hard on all families. Perhaps this was simply the unromanticized truth of early motherhood—something I should learn to deal with or at least a temporary aberration, simply to be gotten through. I tried to be clear-eyed in my examination of my life, but I did not know how to gauge the degree of difficulty I felt.

Though Kara and Adriane sometimes seemed preternaturally attuned to stresses that were not their own, they fortunately seemed oblivious to the simmering moods around them. As my journal attests, Adriane, in her early weeks, quickly learned to smile in recognition, especially in response to Kara. And she developed a contagious laugh, a high, uneven squeaking that spread joy in its sheer exuberance, extending up into her eyes and out to elicit response from Kara or me and to prompt a rare gentleness in Lawrence's face as well. In reasonable time, she learned to reach and grab, to roll over, to make things happen in her still small universe.

Kara could hardly keep her hands off her younger sister, usually with her own attentive joy, though occasionally with the jealous pokings of an older sibling. At this, Lawrence would lose his beneficent smile, yell at her to stop, and turn to me, angry and loud: "Can't you control her?" But Kara usually attended happily to her infant sister's needs even as she maintained that potent sense of who she was. When the nursery school teacher asked each of the children what they wanted to do when they grew up, Kara answered,

"Drive a car." And when asked what she wanted to *be* when she grew up, she responded even more decisively: "A big Kara."

For now, we moved on with our lives, as must be the case in most young families, exhausted by interrupted sleep and conflicting demands. I worked in the kitchen and the garden, sent out tentative feelers about employment—copyediting prospects, an adult-education course at the university, whatever seemed possible as part-time or at-home work—and increasingly focused my life on my daughters.

We had put in a half-door to the large kitchen eating area so that it now served as a child-proofed play room in which Kara and Adriane and I could have our mutual lives. They shared a bedroom off the living room where they could also play safely, though this choice was rarely as successful because Lawrence preferred to spend his time sitting in the living room with the television on and a book in front of him, not wanting to be distracted. If they became at all insistent, he would call out to me in the kitchen: "I'm ending up *babysitting* in here."

I LOOK THROUGH MY PHOTOS of that era. Sadly, I note that I find very few of Adriane as an infant, none of me holding my new baby, though I do find a handful of Adriane and Kara together. In one of these, taken in October, they are together in the field by the barn; Kara is poking at something in the grass, and Adriane is sitting independently, her feet in white baby shoes, straight out in front of her; behind them is a young steer, Albus, named for his color, stark white—the Latin choice being Lawrence's. In this photo, Albie, as we called him, looks both stalwart and benign, unaware that he would eventually be slaughtered, his shimmering hide preserved and displayed in Lawrence's house in town. In a second photo—also taken in the field down by the barn—Kara holds her tongue out as if tasting the air; she sits on the ground, holding Adriane firmly on her lap. In the background, not far away, stands one of the mother cows, her roan calf a step or two behind her.

Of photos taken earlier, in the spring or early summer, when Adriane was only a month or two old, one shows her lying on her stomach in the grass in the yard, holding her still nearly naked head up with her newly strong neck, an attentive look on her face; Kara is again with her, gazing unself-consciously toward the camera with a small smile on her face. And then there is the one of them with their father, next to some flowers in the yard, almost certainly taken the same day since both children wear the same clothes: Lawrence is at his most charming, his own small smile looking unusually kind; he grasps Adriane firmly around her chest, propping her on his right knee as Kara sits demurely on his left knee.

But photos reveal so little: random images snatched from the ongoing currents of life. The journals are more explicit, suggesting not only that I am missing from my own life, but also that I am not finding any rhythm in my days. Increasingly, I document my rising angers, angers specifically directed at Lawrence. I want more from him, and I wrench against the framing power that he continues to claim. The pages enumerate a series of "situations," building in a kind of crescendo to an unsustainable frustration with this life in which I feel myself to be a function rather than a genuine presence.

ONE OF THOSE "SITUATIONS" took place early in an afternoon of Adriane's first few weeks of life. Lawrence left behind the television and his books to pursue his other major preoccupation: the farm. He said he'd be mowing pasture, putting in fence, but he also took his gun in case he felt like doing a little target shooting. He said he'd be back soon. Kara and Adriane, still fighting their respective illnesses, stayed in the house with me, all of us settled into our kitchen and bedroom quarters. But by dusk and no sign of Lawrence, I could no longer suppress my worry—about how he *really* was, how *we* really were. Anxiously, I piled the two sick kids into the car and drove out on the rutted car tracks to the back field.

No doubt my query was shaped by my own anger at having been left in uncertainty about his return: "Why were you gone so long? I was worried."

And Lawrence responded with *his* anger: "You weren't worried—you were mad. If you were really worried, you would have come looking sooner." His additional anger that I hadn't left the kids alone in the house in order to give the cows their evening feeding aggravated me further: How was I to leave a sick infant, a sick almost four-year-old alone in the house? Why was that even a possibility in his mind? And just below the surface: Must it all be my responsibility—cows, chickens, children, house, garden, and his volatility as well?

And still I looked for work, not wanting to spend my limited time in an unrewarding job but knowing that I needed some focus beyond my daughters. To take on this search, I needed to take the girls with me, riding to town with Lawrence on days when he had classes, leaving him at the university, and then proceeding to juggle their activities and my inquiries.

One such day when Adriane was about four weeks old, we all spent the day in town—what Lawrence liked to call my "day off." Having left him at the university, we did errands, went to story hour at the library, made initial contacts about my hope to teach an adult-education course on novels by women: George Eliot, Virginia Woolf, Doris Lessing. I was coming down with my own cold and sore throat and felt exhausted by the end of the day. Dinner was over; Kara and Adriane were finally settled in bed by nine; I paused to look at the newspaper before gathering energy to wash dishes.

"I don't feel good. I need a backrub. I haven't had a rub for weeks." This was a not uncommon request from Lawrence, and he was likely right that he had not had a rub for quite a while.

But I was exhausted and ill myself: "I'm sorry. I'm just too tired, and I still have to wash the dishes and clean up the kitchen."

"But you had the day off today. You should *volunteer* a rub. Anyway, you're just reading the paper." He tussled with the newspaper, teasing and tickling.

We managed to elude the rage this time. He was still laughing, joking, when he pinned me down until I agreed to give him a rub as soon as I'd finished the dishes.

That time it was easier to quiet my own anger. He was, after all, in good humor, not raging at me. And I didn't really mind giving the rub, a safe enough way to touch with our bodies when we were otherwise so dangerously separate emotionally.

But the angers still smoldered, and I was not always so willing to suppress my own. One Sunday morning—this time *he* was reading the paper—I simply told him he needed to stay with the kids while I went out to the back woods to look for mushrooms. It's true that this task was hardly necessary, but it was one that I enjoyed and even one that had its evident usefulness. From Euell Gibbon's *Stalking the Wild Asparagus,* I had recently gained confidence that I could recognize at least the most basic kind of edible mushrooms. And they were like found gold to me, a mushroom lover who was given only a set amount of money each time I entered the grocery store for the weekly shopping. So I insisted to Lawrence that he could sit at the butcher block in the kitchen to read the paper while Kara and Adriane played safely in the child-proofed play area right by him.

"You really know how to mess up a schedule!" he shouted at me, drawing from his list of frequent responses. "You're wasting *my* time," he would say. "You're spoiling *my* morning, interrupting *my* schedule."

And I knew that I was. And I knew that I had to.

As I headed out toward the back woods, I felt an odd elation in releasing my own anger. "*Your* time, *your* morning, *your* schedule," I chanted at the sky, full voice. Again and again, louder and louder: "*Your* time, *your* morning, *your* schedule." With each repetition, louder and louder, I felt my spirits lift. By the time I got to the woods, I gloried in the cache of mushrooms I could gather, exulting in my own voice raised to the sky.

NO, I DO NOT KNOW HOW to fit him into a workable story. It is a narrative problem—I can't find a way to credit and include his point of view—but it is also a personal problem and a cultural problem. I cannot easily assess just how much our stresses were specific to us, how much I can legitimately hold Lawrence accountable for what seems self-centered, how much I was myself guilty of closing him out, and how much our experiences were simply what most young families must grapple with in relative isolation. Even so, I know that the angers in our lives could not be ignored. And I knew then that I needed to value my time, my morning, my schedule—for myself. By the fall of 1975, my journal ends with a list of problems, asterisks carefully identifying the ones that were most crucial. It now reads to me like both a sigh of despair and a dogged resistance, a final attempt at telling my own truths.

problems: Can I fight on so many fronts at once?

television (constant)—I can't respect this

**lack of generosity toward others.*

my lack of money control

lack of respect for my "housewifery"—yet demand that I cook, bake, garden, etc.

little involvement in child care (feeding, diapers, playing—tho some good
spontaneous play)
   need to account for my time
   inflexibility of schedule
   *lack of affection
   *lack of communication
   intolerance
   *frequent raging—uncontrollable temper
   service demands on me—disdain and sarcasm when unfilled
   dislike for my family—control of my visiting
   life style—work orientation
   farm—cuts me off from what I consider most important
   attitude towards kids—Kara's reaction

At a new emotional precipice, all I could do was return to making lists. I could not really push the father to the periphery, but I didn't see how to tolerate his looming over everything. I can see now that I was increasingly leaving out the beneficence of his smile at Adriane, his sharing of the world with Kara: I couldn't find a place for those details in the story that was running forward, almost beyond my control. I couldn't make those pieces fit into an emotional whole or a livable whole, either. We did not feel like a family.

8

Fire

Ladybird, ladybird, fly away home
Your house is on fire
Your children will burn

In her childhood writings, Adriane—in London when she was nine, back home in Ohio when she was ten—wrote dramatic stories of a fire she could not have recalled. She wrote, from a baby's point of view, of flames licking around her, her terror colored a vivid mix of orange and red. A few years ago she found those stories among the many books and papers she has stored in her third-floor bedroom in Wooster, salvaged from a more recent fire. Like her mother and her sister—also like her father, I suppose—she saves her writings.

Like her mother, she holds on to thought and feeling as well. During the infancy she cannot recall, she and her sister were surrounded by the volatile emotions that I have described here, but that I tried to keep to myself at the time. Indeed, for many years I continued to keep them to myself, thinking I was protecting my daughters from hostilities they need not feel. This is what books on divorce usually advise: do not involve the children in adult angers. But if she knew how to imagine a fire she could not remember, how much more likely that she sensed the power of her parents' emotions, threatening, like the flames in her stories, to engulf her?

This was the real question for me throughout Adriane and Kara's childhood: Where did the worst threat lie, and where the best course of action? How might these two children most fully grow into the richness of their capacities?

For many years, I retained the confidence that I had acted well on behalf of my daughters, extracting them from a burning house. And I have not changed my mind. But decisions made in the past do not always remain so clear and still.

IN THE FALL OF 1975—perhaps coincidentally, though perhaps not—the smoldering emotions in my marriage leapt from metaphorical to actual: the real fire that later would haunt Adriane's dreams and imagined stories. It was an October afternoon, and Adriane slept peacefully. I went out back with the refuse from the house—out behind the fence where the rusty barrel stood in readiness. Off on the other side of the yard was the compost pile. Thus we disposed of most of our debris—burnable or compostable—no garbage disposal, no regular arrival of weekly trash collectors. We recycled glass where possible but weren't alert to the air pollution we were creating, real though scarcely noticeable there on the farm, twenty miles from Bloomington and much farther yet from any industrial center.

I lit the fire, tended it briefly, then returned to the house, anxious for the social contact the phone could afford me in my isolation: miles from friends, alone with my six-month-old daughter, our one family car called to service for the trip to town. I was grateful for these few minutes of adult conversation, while Adriane slept, before Kara returned from her afternoon nursery school and her father from his afternoon at the university.

The phone conversation provided social contact but no real respite. With my own marriage in jeopardy, I responded readily to my friend's marital distress. I attended to her sorrows and grievances, rapt but with split consciousness as I silently ticked off the parallels with and distinctions from my own marriage. Though Adriane was barely half a year old and Kara just over four, I too had reached the stage of marital crisis where fleeing with my daughters—whatever the hazards—seemed preferable to staying in this house that so rarely felt like home.

"Wait," I interrupted Alice abruptly as a strand of smoke blew past the kitchen window. "I've got to go."

By the time I stepped outside, an acrid smell burned in my nostrils and smoke gathered against the house. Flames had begun to lick along the foundation, following the path of autumn leaves pushed there by the wind.

Gasping now, I ran back inside and snatched Adriane from her crib.

"Fire!" I shouted at the top of my voice. "Help, fire!"—calling to neighbor farmers at work in the field across the road and then returning to the phone to call upon the volunteer firefighters who served our rural address.

Was Adriane then straddling my hip this whole time? Did she cry in shared fear or grow wide-eyed in amazement? When *did* I grab her from her crib and when realize and then assuage the sense of danger?

Try as I do, I cannot quite recall. I only see the stored images of myself standing first in the kitchen talking on the phone with Alice and then standing helplessly in the yard as flames prodded at the house immediately outside the girls' bedroom. In one other image, Adriane is reaching happily up to me as I retrieve her, though I'm not sure just where this image fits. Is it possible that Adriane, never really in danger, stayed peacefully in her crib as the flames merely surface-licked the leaves and grass outside her window? No, that at least cannot be possible: I could not have stood by and watched the flames with my daughter still inside, no matter how small the risk.

BY THE TIME Kara and her father returned, the only remaining evidence was a pathway of burnt leaves from the burn barrel to the house, the charred siding on the back of the house, a relieved gathering of farmers and volunteer firefighters.

Singed by the near miss—the "What if?"—I know I now held Adriane closely, gathered Kara to me as well, and joined the general sense of merriment and relief, while underneath the burning fear persisted.

Fly away home.

Fly away *from* home?

How to save the children from the burning, the persistent rage and fear and worry?

Six weeks later I did flee, snatching two children from the rage that threatened daily to singe us. By then, that burning seemed a more real danger than the wispy flames the wind had lifted from the burn barrel toward the house.

IN MY EARLY WEEKS here in New York—through much of February—I was visited on an almost daily basis by a raging fever. I would waken comfortable in the morning, ready for a new day, but by afternoon my temperature would start to rise. I finally purchased a thermometer and was shocked to discover a genuine fever at work, 103 degrees, before it slowly subsided, only to return the next day. During those afternoons—several of them before I finally managed to obtain antibiotics—I lay on the couch, allowing my mind to range over thoughts and images, words and stories. This, too, was part of my work.

Lying there, burning with fever, I moved tentatively toward the understanding I am now claiming: that decisions made in the past do not always remain so clear and still. Sometimes, the present reshapes the past, not just once but repeatedly, as events echo one another, calling out across time, reverberating with inchoate meaning. All these years later, I continue to grope for understanding.

IN MY FEVERED MUSINGS about our last weeks on the farm, I am aware of a more recent echo: a fire at our home in Wooster in the summer of 1993, when Kara was settling herself in New York after her college graduation that spring, and Adriane was on her usual summer visit with her father. This fire was caused by an electrical malfunction in a fan that Ron and I had set up in Adriane's third-floor bedroom to help us cool the lower floors for a small dinner party we were having in her absence. And we were lucky: though the fire sent flames shooting from the upper windows, a vivid orange against the night sky, we were able to intervene; two fire trucks came quickly, bringing local firefighters who were not only prompt and professional, but also unusually careful, even managing to minimize water damage. Our only role was to deal with the blackened stairwell up to the third floor, the charred walls and burnt windows, the smoke-filled clothing and infiltrated drawers and closets with stacks of notebooks and papers, smudged but salvageable. The damage had been contained; insurance would help with the reconstruction. Most crucially, no one had been hurt.

The next afternoon Ron and I suffered a lingering grief as we anticipated Adriane's return home, the loss that she would face. Numb from our own trauma, and mute, we sat on the front porch awaiting her arrival and staring at her burnt mattress, which lay in the front yard, thrown there by firefighters. My own eyes kept returning to a stuffed animal sprawled among the debris thrown haphazardly onto the mattress: a monkey with blackened skull, the "daddy" monkey now with empty Velcro arms. Just the previous day, when we had set up the fan in Adriane's bedroom, that monkey had sat, oblivious, on her bed, holding its matching baby in parental embrace, a lingering remnant of my daughter's childhood. Now, upstairs in the charred bedroom, the baby monkey sat alone on a handcrafted child's rocking chair, unattended by the discarded father. The firefighters—apparently alert to a child's feelings as well as to urgent interventions—had carefully salvaged the baby.

When Adriane and Lawrence drove up to the sight of the scarred mattress in front of the house, Ron and I tried to greet her with a joke: "Welcome home. We burned your bedroom down since you're about to go off to college." It was a silly joke and ineffectual, but it did at least bridge her arrival. Even with the sense of loss that awaited her in her bedroom, I think she was glad to be home. I knew I needed her in my embrace.

Now, too, the joke falls flat, and the embrace begins to look exclusionary. I cannot at this point pretend to be oblivious to events that followed. But surely we were all oblivious then: when Lawrence and Adriane and Ron and I stood together in the front yard, taking in the scorched mattress and the "daddy" monkey with blackened skull and empty Velcro arms, none of us considered the meanings that might lie beneath the surface. We were just grateful that, so far, we had avoided the what if's and survived the if only's: no child had been in that bed, no home had been burned to the ground.

But now, as I emerge from my fevered musings, the metaphor compels me. I, too, responded to the first necessity: to put out the fire, to salvage as much as possible. I, too, sacrificed the father with burning skull, pulling the children from hazardous embrace, wrapping my own arms around them. If only it were so simple.

9

Mythic Self

My decision to leave *did* seem simple in the fall of 1975. And in the years that have followed—especially in times of weakness or timidity—I have relied on the image of myself at the moment of departure in its vivid simplicity. In this image, I am bold, determined, fully competent. I cannot be derailed by trivial circumstances or other people's judgments. I am doing what is necessary, and I am strong.

I see myself walking across the large open space of the Indianapolis Greyhound station. The place is hardly mythic, but I am oblivious to my surroundings: I hold my head high and keep my eyes forward. On my left hip, I hold Adriane, seven months old, and with my right hand I hold Kara's hand. I am using my right foot to push an empty car seat across the large open space to meet our connecting bus. Our suitcase is not visible in this image; perhaps it has been checked through from Bloomington. I do not know what will come next. But I have left Lawrence, fleeing what I was convinced I could not change. And I am strong.

For many years, I have cited this image as the centerpiece in the tale of my great escape. As the protagonist of the tale, I unite a protective maternity and an assertive independence; I am heroic in a state of emergency. This self-image is both extravagant and true. In it, I am not only larger than life, but also stronger than I was before or have been since. In it, I am doing what I know to be necessary for my own self-preservation; in it, I am strong on behalf of my daughters.

But, of course, the truth of this image also encompasses its falsehood and covers over its fissures and contradictions. I *am* strong on behalf of my daughters, but my strength cannot be mythic except in my own imagination. Not superhuman, this strength is snatched from a life under way and founded in less savory realities than any mythic strength, whether maternal or heroic.

FRAGMENTS OF THE DAYS that immediately preceded the bus trip now resurface, suggesting other realities, differently refracted. Here I am not so much strong as simply stolid. I resist grief—my own grief and Lawrence's, too. Mine has been suppressed; his has come too late. I am impervious to it.

He had cried the previous night when he finally realized that I meant it this time: great sobs roiled up in him, tears welled in his eyes as he stood in the kitchen, leaning on the counter for support. I had never before seen him cry, not even when his mother died, so I ought to have been moved to reciprocal grief, as I recall having been when my high school boyfriend and I cried together when we broke up. But not now, not with Lawrence. Two years earlier, when I was trying to determine what to do, how to heal my pain in this frozen relationship, I had cried my own wrenching sobs as I lay across the bed. But his only response, called from the other room, was: "Stop that. Control yourself." Eventually I had learned to staunch the grief.

Now I was hardened. I could not allow myself to feel that his pain was real; I could not risk my resolve. This hardening, of course, is not strength; it is desperation or perhaps even cold selfishness.

Strength, desperation, selfishness—whatever the foundation of my resolve, it became momentarily vulnerable when Lawrence gave in to it and took us to the bus station. I felt nothing when he kissed me good-bye. But when he held each of the girls, lifting each up into his arms, pressing each in turn close to his heart, my resolve almost broke. The rain fell lightly; the wipers on the bus went back and forth. I clenched my jaw in silence.

I somehow managed to get the three of us into our seats, to resist the plea in his eyes as we waved through the glass. In the car en route to the bus, Kara had precociously pointed out to him that this separation would be best for all of us—mimicking what she had heard me say to her in preparation for our departure. Seeing her father's face now, she suffered anxious afterthoughts. I reassured her that we would return, though I couldn't reassure her that things would ever be the same for any of us. She pressed her face up against the window, calling out to her receding father, "I love you, Daddy. I love you, Daddy." But he couldn't hear her. The bus pulled away, and I pulled her closer to me, grasped her sister more tightly still, sealing away my vulnerability long before we reached the transfer station in Indianapolis.

In normal times an anxious traveler, I cannot remember being frightened or worried, and I was not even vaguely regretful by the time we made that long walk across the Indianapolis bus station. By then, I felt whole and strong and certain. It was November, a week before Thanksgiving, and I was as clear in my overall purpose as I was on my immediate destination: South Bend, my parents' home, the solace of family. I could not be certain that they had even received my letter letting them know I would be on my way. Nor could I be certain that they would support my decision. It was, after all, not so long since they had written to me, "You cannot be sure that the courts will grant you custody"—words that seared me, but the only words they knew that might make me reconsider the divorce I had set my mind on.

Perhaps that's why I hadn't telephoned them. I needed simply to act, not to risk any attempts at dissuasion. I knew they would not turn me away, but I knew they did not want this divorce.

Ironically, part of my certainty had developed during a recent visit from my father. I had learned something crucial about myself as he and I worked together in the garage, sanding, measuring, putting finish on the shelves that were cut to fit in around the newly constructed fireplace. Working side by side with my father, I had remembered that shared work could be a pleasure, that the constant tension of judgment and rejection was not a necessary component of shared tasks, as I had come to assume in working with Lawrence. What I had thought were similarities between Lawrence and my father—a sense of certainty, a claim on unexamined masculine privileges and priorities—did not hold true in the atmosphere in the garage. My father and I worked as partners—talking together, sharing plans and strategies, working in comfortable rhythm—something that Lawrence and I had long ago ceased doing.

Just recently—more than two decades later—my mother told me something else about that time I spent working in the garage with my father, something she had never told me before. After that visit, he told her: "I never thought I'd advocate divorce. But now, for this marriage, I don't see any other way." He grieved, but he, too, had apparently come to accept the inevitability of this next step. Perhaps that's something else I had learned as we worked together in the garage: my father's capacity to empathize with me even though his own worldview differed radically from mine.

In any case, it wasn't the risk of my parents' disapproval that opened another possible fissure in my resolve. I knew at my deepest levels that I could count on their fundamental love and support. But I did keep hearing the threat: "You cannot be sure the courts will grant you custody." What if I was strong on behalf of my daughters and then lost them to legal challenges? What if this separation really wasn't the best thing for them? And if it wasn't good for them, how could it be for me?

Stereotypes make strength and independence contrary to femininity: women are expected to focus on relationships, to pursue attachment. But which relationships? Which attachments? I knew, at least, that this move was not a return "home." I would not be living with my parents, only visiting them. But I did rely on their being supportive of me in this moment of crisis, despite the implied judgment in their earlier responses. I needed my attachment to them to be *real,* my welcome into the family to be assured. But my urges now were not toward traditional dependence: my children provided a source of strength, not a yoke of subordination. The other impetus: my own need for independence.

When I tell my tale of escape, I usually omit all of these questions and uncertainties. I emphasize, instead, my invincibility. I especially like to note the presence of the car seat. I hope that its ordinariness will undermine the pathos—a mother and her two young children escaping the domineering husband and father—without diminishing my overarching strength. But the car seat did have a very pragmatic purpose: I was going for the holiday, but I was also planning to buy a car. I would need the car seat for Adriane when I made the drive back to the life we had left unresolved in Bloomington.

All these years later Kara remembers almost nothing of that week in South Bend. But she does remember buying the car, an act of symbolic importance to her as to me: I had never before owned my own car. The Datsun station wagon, to which I had had limited access on the farm, was the closest I had ever come to that form of autonomy. Even then, I had been subject to Lawrence's choices about where I would go and when. So it was significant to Kara as it was to me that I was now buying the first car I had ever owned in my own name: another green Datsun, a coupe, used and cheap, no doubt selected not only for its price, but also because its handling felt familiar to me.

I had to borrow money from my parents for this modest purchase, but it represented a seal on my reach toward new freedoms. I could no longer tolerate being a dependent; I would drive myself and my daughters to our next destination.

During that Thanksgiving visit, however, I rejoiced in feeling not alone, not thrown too quickly upon my own limited resources. Kara and Adriane and I felt the comfort not only of their grandparents, but also of their aunt and uncle and three cousins, all there for the holiday. The pleasure deepened in contrast to the tensions of past holidays, when Lawrence had been openly condescending toward the bonds I felt to parents and siblings, harshly domineering to my young nephews. Now Kara could play freely with her three cousins, no one being yelled at; Adriane could fall asleep across her sleeping grandmother's chest, beyond the cloud of Lawrence's disdain; I could relax into the calm of sustaining love.

TWO DAYS BEFORE THANKSGIVING, an unexpected letter from Lawrence broke into my calm. Actually, it was not a letter but a note accompanied by four single-spaced pages of journal entries. In the note, Lawrence said, "This is not a letter—but you may read it anyway. . . . It wasn't written with any particular purpose in mind. If I think it should have one, it would only be that we begin together again." *Begin together again*. The thought exhausted me, as did the journal pages in which he acknowledged a hunger for the morning smiles he had always rejected grumpily, a grief and guilt for the tears he had ignored two years earlier, a sense of failure in his denials and impositions. "God, how stupid," he says of his own behavior. And "J. was right"—something I couldn't recall his ever having said to me in our seven and a half years of marriage.

In the journal pages, he also spoke of the partially completed fireplace wall: "Polishing furniture into late in the night. Unfinished wall, irony again as if so designed: monument to the incomplete and unfinished. Why else was it started? Polishing for whom? Just something to do? who will see it? as if tidying up for own funeral."

I couldn't at that time hear the depth of his potential despair. Impervious to the grief, the self-accusation, the loneliness, the plea to begin again, impervious even to the covert hint at suicide, I simply honored his request that I return the journal pages to him and enclosed them in a letter I sent him the next day, a letter we were to find in his filing cabinet after his death years later.

This week I have pulled the letter from the boxes I brought with me to New York, rereading it obsessively as I try not only to reconstruct my own mindset but also to discover a greater empathy for Lawrence. I am haunted by his metaphor of incompletion, the fireplace we had planned together, the hearth now added, too late, to the home I had left. But I know that I did not, then, feel that this was a hearth to which I could any longer belong or a home to which I could return.

Perhaps I had been wrong even to attempt this marriage. Certainly I had long known that I could not be an angel in the house, an angel of the hearth—that compelling image that Woolf had slyly pilfered from Coventry Patmore's idea of Victorian femininity: "She was intensely sympathetic. She was immensely charming. She was utterly unselfish. She excelled in the difficult arts of family life. She sacrificed herself daily." If Lawrence had qualities in common with Woolf's father, Leslie Stephen, and his fictional representation, Mr. Ramsay—the irrational rages, the autocratic behavior, the charismatic intelligence—I could not claim a parallel similarity to her mother or to Mrs. Ramsay, a compelling Angel if ever fiction gave us one. I could not match that icon of Victorian domesticity, nor would I try.

What, then, was I to do? I had long since given up trying to be the dutiful daughter: I loved my parents and trusted their love for me, but I had chosen my own undutiful path by diverging so pointedly from their religious heritage. I had tried and failed at my own version of the sympathetic wife. What I clung to, despite questions and contradictions, was that idea of a larger-than-life mother—a questing, independent self. But this idea was really two versions of selfhood, and, by most accounts, these versions were incompatible with each other.

Driving back to Bloomington, with the car seat and my two daughters secured in my new car, I relied on a resurging certainty. A job would be the essential first step for both my requirements as a mother and my independence: I had to support myself and my two daughters. In this regard, at least, motherhood and independence had no war with each other. On my drive toward my future, I clung irrationally to my idea of a mythic self and the unfounded certainty that I *would* get a job.

10

Outlaws and Conspirators

Women sometimes hint at the pleasurably unstructured lives that they have with their children when husbands and fathers are away. They speak in conspiratorial hushes lest the men discover their possible treachery. So, too, with the memories that women and children occasionally call up from their oddly pleasant lives while their men were away during World War II or with recollections of planless days at summer cottages when men showed up only for the weekends. In *Of Woman Born,* Adrienne Rich describes such a time in her life—a summer in Vermont when she was on her own with her three young sons—as a period of "delicious" freedoms lived outside the rules. That summer she and her sons became "conspirators, outlaws" from the usual structures of family life. Also that summer, she says, "I felt enormously in charge of my life."

In charge of my life, living beyond the rules: that's how I felt during the first few months after Kara and Adriane and I left the farm and found our own conspiratorial life away from their father.

When we returned to Bloomington after Thanksgiving, we did not return to the farm, but we did not yet have a place to live. Hence our first concern: to find an apartment. My standards were minimal: a place to sleep, a basic bathroom, a kitchen of some sort, immediate availability. But finding a place was no small task for a single mother with two small children and almost no money.

The ads were sparse. It was, after all, December, and Bloomington was a university town. Everything was guided by the academic calendar. My friend Alice helped me look at the few listings that seemed remotely possible. We took heart when we saw one on Tenth Street, the lower floor of an older house—which meant not only a porch (shared), but even a small backyard.

Then we lost heart when we saw the layout: though the listing said "two bedrooms," one bedroom was a passage from living room to kitchen, and the other was a kind of large hallway between the back door and the bathroom. There was no bathtub, only a shower, and it was hard for me to imagine Adriane submitting to a shower when she was still in the crawling stage. Anyway, the place wouldn't be available until January.

I said no, regretfully, and motioned for Alice to follow me out as the landlord opened the door to the next prospective tenant. The line of waiting college students outside aggravated my desperation, but I still couldn't see how to make this work. Alice and I stood briefly by my car—consulting in shorthand—before rushing back inside with open checkbook. By being quick with my deposit, I barely managed to preempt the next interested party. Kara and Adriane and I would not have a home of our own until January, but at least we could count on one then. Meanwhile, we would make our vagabond lives with Alice and her husband, Jon, and daughter, Katherine. Their generosity overcame the biggest hurdle; come January, we would find a way to make a home of our own without a bathtub, without the privacy of real bedrooms—an outlaw home, but *ours*.

Of course, it wasn't exactly easy to feel in charge of my own life while camping out in someone else's home, especially the home of friends who were themselves in marital stress. During our first week there, I witnessed the first of several violent arguments between Alice and Jon: voices rose in dispute and lamps crashed to the floor as one chased the other through the house, knife in hand. This sight shocked me—indeed, it still shocks me when I recall it—but it hardly dispelled my sense of direction in my own life. I somehow knew they would not do physical damage to each other; for whatever reason, I trusted their relative good intentions—or maybe I was just that desperate for a place to stay and friends to count on.

In any case, this was our home for the month of December, the season of Advent: peace on earth. I talked regularly to Lawrence; Kara, Adriane, and I visited the farm; Lawrence and I took our first steps to find a divorce counselor and shopped together for modest Christmas presents for our daughters. Though we weren't yet talking to lawyers, everything was changed; my freedoms could hardly be called "delicious," but I no longer lived by the rules. I was learning how to be in charge of my own life a little at a time.

APART FROM ALICE AND JON'S unforgettable arguments and incredible generosity—all mixed together in contradictory images—I recall little of that month. I remember that I tried to do my share of cooking and household tasks and that Alice somehow found that contribution a reason to be grateful to *me*. I know I did my best not to intrude on their lives any more than our very presence made necessary. I know it cannot have been easy for them or for us. I can only figure that on the whole we did our best to help each other ease the stresses of our changing lives.

The only really specific memory I have from that time comes from the fact that it was the holiday season. Katherine and her mother had a tradition: every Sunday evening of Advent, Katherine would put out her shoe for the Christmas elf, who would in turn leave her a treat to discover in the morning. Because Kara was sharing Katherine's life and her bedroom this Advent, Alice and Katherine naturally assumed that Kara would participate in this tradition.

I was game, too, until the first night that we tried it. Unable to sleep, Kara called out to me repeatedly. When I tried to calm her, she whispered to me, being careful not to wake Katherine.

"I can't sleep, Mom. I'm scared about that strange man coming in here tonight. I have to keep my eyes open and watch for him."

"But he's a friendly elf—he won't hurt you."

"I just don't like strange men coming in while I'm sleeping."

What could I say? Her whole world had been shaken by recent events, and I was not willing to allow this new tradition to frighten her further. But this tradition was important to Katherine and her mother, and I knew that Katherine's world was vulnerable, too.

Trust was all I had. So I clung to that and to my sense that language was an important basis for the trust that Kara had in me; I would have to be honest with her and at the same time count on her capacity to protect Katherine.

"We'll need to keep a secret, Kara, just between you and me. Can you do that?"

Kara's eyes opened wide, not sure whether to be more afraid of this responsibility or of the strange elf that might arrive if I left.

"Okay, but I don't want anyone coming in during the night."

I told her, then, that the elf was a story, a special story, for children at Christmastime—like Santa. Because I had always tried to speak the truth to my daughter, I had never been able to play the fantasies that some parents do so well, not even the Santa fantasy. So Kara already knew about Santa: a story about giving, but one that was important to lots of children—not a lie, just a story that children and parents had fun with, believing for a while. When her friends got older, she could share with them her own way of enjoying that story, but for now she needed to keep her version to herself.

"When Katherine grows up, can I tell her about the elf and about Santa, too? Can *I* tell her that it's really her mom?"

"Not until she grows up, though. That's really important to Katherine and her mom."

"Okay, Mommy. You're *sure* that no strange elf will come in the night, just Katherine's mom?"

"Yes, and I'll come, too. I'll be your elf while we're staying here—to help Katherine have her story."

"Good night, Mommy. I think I'll sleep now."

Kara did sleep then, but her sleep was haunted by elves in the night, strange men that might come in.

That night Kara and I formed a conspiratorial bond that was the first of many I would have with my daughters. I was not consciously constructing that alternative society of women and children only, but as we forged our new life together, we had very little to hold on to but each other.

THE BOND STRENGTHENED once January came and we moved into our own space: no more secrets, no more terror of intruders in the night. Now we had our own place where we would set our own rules. And we gradually found in that world an increasing sense of the delicious freedoms of living on our own.

One of our first concerns in the new place was to fill in around its sparse "furnished" look. We had little but needed little since two beds, a kitchen table, and an old couch and chair for the living room were furnished. But we did need curtains to hang between the bathroom and the girls' bedroom. In the liberty of our new access to choice, Kara and I happily selected a set of

Woodsy Owl sheets—"Give a hoot, don't pollute"—one to hem and hang in the doorway, the other to act as bedspread for her. The choice may not have been so different from one we would have made while with Lawrence—he, after all, liked me to find ways to save money—but when he cared about how things looked, the choices were singularly his even if the work was to be mine. And when he chose to care, his taste was impeccable, his disregard for price was formidable, and his further disregard for his wife's and daughter's preferences was not to be challenged.

The only piece of furniture we had to provide for ourselves was Adriane's crib, which we had of necessity taken with us from the farm to Alice and Jon's house when we had made the first move. Now, in making this move, we had no station wagon for the transportation of crib pieces, nor was I in the mood to disassemble and reassemble it. My innovative response was—whimsically, with that sense of new freedom—to walk the crib down the sidewalk the ten blocks from Alice's house to the new apartment. In this decision, I showed great lack of foresight since the crib's wheels were not made for concrete. By the time I completed the journey, what had once been round and mobile were worn to nothing and locked in place. Always thereafter when I wanted to roll the crib from one spot in a bedroom to another and had instead to lift and struggle, I felt a surge of perverse pride in my foolishness, a signal, I think, of how I had felt denied the option to be my own kind of foolish in my previous life.

OTHER FREEDOMS seem equally trivial now but felt very real at the time. I bought none of the designer clothes that Lawrence had liked me to buy, always under his supervision. Instead, I freely bought the jeans and T-shirts that he had told me we had insufficient funds for. Our meals were no longer the expensive specialty meats that he had preferred and that I had prepared with the vegetables gathered from the garden or set aside in the freezer. Kara and I ate simply and casually, occasionally even feasting on peanut butter and popcorn if that's what we were hungry for, and Adriane happily participated in our simple mealtimes as she gradually grew ready to choose her own foods.

Our outings, too, were simple but pleasant: to the public library for story hour—a leisurely walk of a few blocks—and to the laundromat nearby. On the farm, where I had had a washing machine but no dryer, I had taken a perverse pleasure in hanging clothes on the line, even in early winter—letting the diapers freeze as they dried, then thawing and folding them. In the laundromat, I recalled standing in the wind and sun, gradually filling a clothesline with a long row of continuous white rectangles, pinned at their corners with old-fashioned wooden clothespins. But the lost pleasure succumbed to a new relief: not to feel the resentment that I had had no choice, that it had been Lawrence's decision that we had no dryer (let alone no diaper service), even though it had been my responsibility to do the laundry. Now I had neither washer nor dryer, but I also had no one to oversee when and how I did the laundry.

And so the laundromat became a place of fugitive freedom, where Kara, Adriane, and I went together when we felt like it and amused ourselves in our own way while water sloshed in several machines at once, and clothes spun and dryers whirled. Here too—or so it seemed during the daytime in 1976—was a place where women and children gathered in temporary community, a miniature version of those secret enclaves formed in the absence of men.

THAT EASTER was our first holiday alone. Easter had never been a real holiday for me; in my childhood it had been a religious holy day—sunrise services and singing in the children's choir—but not a holiday for children's pleasure and indulgence, as seemed to be the case for the culture at large. Once I became an adult, no longer a practicing Christian, Easter fell out of consideration entirely. But that year when Kara, Adriane, and I were so recently on our own, I felt a new need for ritual. It was still not to be a religious ritual, but I also did not want to make it all about chocolate and childish indulgences. I needed simply to mark the day for us as a family: the three of us developing our own ways of sharing in cultural rites.

Without knowing that this Easter would be a marked memory for all of us, I echoed a desperate gesture I had made the previous spring—when Adriane's birth had been imminent and I had been trying to resist the numbness that threatened me. With a hungering inside me, I had wanted to mark this cultural holiday for Lawrence, Kara, and me: calves being born, eggs to be gathered, new life all around us. And so I had searched through cookbooks for some special culinary treat that might reach toward celebration for the three of us—anticipating our new baby's birth, celebrating spring and generation and hope.

Even then I knew I should by tradition have chosen to make hot cross buns, but the ingredients seemed too ordinary. I settled instead on a recipe that had nothing to do with Easter except the commonality of "buns" in the name: cheese buns, in the Hungarian section of the *New York Times International Cookbook*. That's what I had made that Easter—six days before Adriane was born, when Kara was not yet four years old, when I still thought there was hope of resurrecting this nuclear family, soon to be four of us: Lawrence and me, Kara and this yet unnamed new baby of ours.

Only a year later there we were, a different family of three, and we needed a holiday, whether it was a real holiday for me or not. This yearning was my first experience of what I came to understand as "single-parent holiday fervor": the need to make this day all the more special precisely because we were not a nuclear family, not up to a "normal" celebration. Even if I wanted to avoid making it about chocolate and indulgences, I still wanted to make it memorable for Kara and Adriane. Thus began our own Easter traditions, a way to value the turning of the earth, the changing of the seasons, the need for my daughters to have some ritual dimension to their lives.

Our first Easter on our own, then, I baked cheese buns in our outlaw apartment. We dyed Easter eggs together and arranged to hunt them in the small patch of grass in the back yard by the gravel parking space. And I gave each of them an Easter basket filled with inexpensive toys and art supplies— no chocolate in sight, no Easter bunny either. It was lucky for me that this was not a holiday that particularly interested Lawrence: hence our leeway to forge our own first holiday traditions.

IN THE YEARS THAT FOLLOWED, I kept my pledge to this holiday of our own even in the midst of spring-semester pressures at work: baking cheese buns; dyeing Easter eggs; preparing a modest Easter basket for each of my daughters; waking Easter morning to hunt for eggs, usually in the house because it would still be too cold and damp outside in northeast Ohio. The joy here was in fair measure the joy of watching my two daughters attending to each other and to their environment, searching around with eyes wide open, sharing with each other the pleasure of discovery. A special joy: Kara would regularly help Adriane fill her own basket with brightly colored eggs, even as she loved to discover the hard-to-find eggs, too high up for Adriane's shorter stature and younger eyes to descry. We would follow the egg hunt with our distinctive breakfast menu of cheese buns and hard-boiled eggs.

Over time, cheese buns became an essential component of our way of honoring the arrival of spring, so much so that merely on a whim I once indulged in the extravagance of shipping them to my daughters in distant locations—straight from our freezer with next-day delivery, for they are made with eggs and cream cheese and subject to spoilage. When I mentioned this gesture to my mother, she was puzzled at my willingness to pay the shipping costs, but my daughters understood just what it was that I was honoring years later: the rituals and celebrations of our lives together.

THIS YEAR, when all three of us are actually in the same city at Eastertime, we won't honor this holiday when others do; each of us has our own plans and commitments on April 12. But I will still bake cheese buns in my narrow New York kitchen, though it will be after the fact. This time I will walk from one part of the city to another, carrying them in my own hands, for a celebration that we will have on our own schedule. No matter. By now, we are quite used to deciding for ourselves when we have our holidays. What we celebrate is not the day itself, but our distinctive bonds.

When Kara phoned me late last night, we did not even mention the imminent holiday. We talked about the paper she is working on and then about the one that she wrote last fall, investigating maternal infanticide. We ranged over the complex issues—cultural and historical—and discussed possible writing strategies. At this juncture in our lives, we celebrate our togetherness most potently through conversations about books and ideas, about reading and writing. We discuss at length the ways we made our lives together in the past and the ways each of us is making her life now. But we do remember the cheese buns.

IN THAT SPRING OF 1976, I gradually read my way through all of Jane Austen's novels and then the contemporary women writers I discovered at whim on our many trips to the public library, reading voraciously to fill in the tradition of women writers that I felt as a void in my education. But I was really trying to discover how women, regardless of the era, had made their lives. Meanwhile I persisted in trying to make my own life, frugally paying bills out of a temporary support payment from Lawrence and looking toward the future. I doggedly typed letter after letter, working my way down a list of more than one hundred academic job openings, nationwide, that I had correlated with my credentials, however tangentially. Though this was hard work, I could barely suppress my excitement at the world of possibility that lay before me, framed by a new liberty, full of quirky freedoms that few others might appreciate: a life of our own for Kara and Adriane and me.

I must have known that to construct such a life I had to close the boundaries around the three of us, deliberately fencing off Lawrence as I celebrated my own newfound liberty. In the decades since, I have witnessed the grief of newly divorced fathers when mothers and children move on to make their own separate lives; I have felt my own grief for these grieving fathers. I have even occasionally felt grief for the daily interaction that Lawrence lost with his daughters. But all I can recall of that period for myself is a sense of narrow escape, a willingness to act as outlaw, a need to celebrate small pleasures within a life of my own with my daughters.

11

No Longer a Daughter-in-Law

T hough I had claimed outlaw status that first spring on my own with my daughters, I was still technically within the law of marriage. But I did not feel myself to be Lawrence's wife. So I was uncertain of my family status when Lawrence's father came for a visit in late April: Was I still his daughter-in-law? Harry wanted to meet his granddaughters, whom he had not yet met; he wanted to see whether he could mend this nuclear family that he saw as broken but not beyond repair. He wanted, as well, to mend his own relationship with his oldest son, from whom he had been estranged since Harry had remarried following Lawrence's mother's death: both father and son had been unyielding, unable to see the other's point of view. And though it seemed that this estrangement resulted from the new marriage, I was convinced that years of previous dissension had made the breach irreparable. Now here was my father-in-law, paying a family visit, reaching out in apology to the son who had rejected him, reaching out to the granddaughters he wanted to know, reaching out to his daughter-in-law, who had no ill will toward him but who was rapidly exiting the house of law.

I HAD ALWAYS LIKED HARRY well enough: he had been kind to me, welcoming me into the Frye family when Lawrence had first taken me home to Rochester, New York, for introductions. It's true that I had felt inclined to side with my mother-in-law, Hildie, when it seemed necessary to take sides; I had loved her as a kind of angel in that house—she did always seem to give and give, to me as well. She had died very early in my marriage to Lawrence, and although I had grieved her loss, I certainly had no ill will toward Harry and no reason to think he was wrong to remarry within a year of her death. He had written that his sense of himself was as a married person, and when he met Marie, it had felt right to carry on with that sense of his identity. He meant no dishonor to his children's mother, but marriage was what he needed for himself. And he clearly cherished it, almost as a value in itself.

Old histories had erupted for Lawrence when his father sent word of his new marriage, and I had not been sufficiently invested in repairing emotional damage to maintain contact with Harry once Lawrence backed away. At that point, in any case, I had been preoccupied with trying to salvage my own marriage: those were the years in which Lawrence's volatility was taking a toll on me as well as on many of his relationships, not just that with his father. For the previous five years, we had tacitly accepted this estrangement from his father, perversely coincident with Kara's birth and early years. It had taken a crisis to bring Harry to Bloomington for this visit; with this crisis, Lawrence, too, was apparently ready to welcome his father into his house that was no longer quite a home.

HARRY SPENT HIS VISIT at the farm with Lawrence and Kara; I remained in our apartment in town with Adriane, too young to leave her mother for an overnight visit. He also stopped in town to see us—indeed, he helped me to deal with my car, which kept stalling out in the damp southern Indiana air that spring. He was gallant in the way that I would have accepted only from a man of his generation; he visibly doted on his granddaughters; he was unusually patient with his son's astringent comments. Leaving behind his wife of five years, he had come alone on this futile mission to repair the irreparable.

Shortly after his visit, I received a letter from him, addressed solely to me, pleading the case that his son had failed to plead successfully. The letter was fraught with his grief for our ruptured lives; it spoke to me more poignantly than his son's letter had the previous November when I had first left the marriage. But I could not respond to this one any more than I could to its predecessor. I had placed myself outside the family home; fleeing the law of father, I left behind the father-in-law as well.

May 17, 1976
Syracuse, N.Y. 13205

Dear Joanne:

I have thought of you all many, many times since my return home, and I can't begin to tell you how very much I valued my chance to see you all—even though it was perhaps a rather hurried visit. I simply cannot get over those two beautiful grandchildren—how bright and alert they are—and pretty fond indeed of their Mother and Dad! It bothers and troubles me no end, to realize their home is divided; it surely would seem that some sort of compromise could be made, to keep the home as one. *But then, I do not know the circumstances that have given rise to the divorce—I was not told, and though of course most interested, if only to know if I could perhaps help reconcile,—I did not ask. Larry has always seemed to resent questioning—at least by me,—(although ever ready to question* me)—*so I did not pursue the issues, feeling that if he wanted me to know, he'd tell me. I did not think it proper to ask you, thinking it perhaps too personal that you might not care to discuss it.*

Friday morning, I was up early, well before Larry and Kara were awake, and I had an opportunity to walk around outside and reflect on the situation. I could see the tremendous size of the garden, the house, the isolation without benefit of a car, the back-breaking work a continuing growing "farm" operation would entail, and the demand for funds required without immediate evidence of a "return"—all these things, coupled to an impatient and demanding and uncompromising husband—and I thought to myself—if I were a woman, refined and educated and well qualified to utilize my talents and academic abilities—would I want that sort of life in relative isolation and "Old World" labor and subservient to the driving whims, ambitions or what not of another?—and my definite and overwhelming decision was NO, *I would* not—*maybe for a year or two at the most, for experience or self-discipline—but beyond that—*NO. *There is* much *more to life than that.* . . .

What I've written about, Joanne, is simply my *feelings, derived from the aura that seemed to permeate the house and grounds that Friday morning, in the misty rain—and is not necessarily coincidental with your situation. It is what I "sensed,"—in addition to a feeling of loneliness and frustration (maybe that is not the right word to describe it) from the house—no longer a "home."* . . .

Joanne, I truly hope you will keep in close touch with us—please! I know I consider you as a daughter, and my regret is that I haven't kept in contact with you and Larry these past 5 years. I must confess that my failure to do so was prompted perhaps largely by Larry's seeming reluctance—or failure to express—acceptance of Marie as my wife. Of course Marie was hurt by that, and I too—and that seemed to make a coolness between Larry and me. But

that is now water over the dam, as far as I'm concerned—and I am very anx-
ious that we keep track of each other. Be assured I will help you in every way I
can. You are a wonderful Mother to two beautiful children—and I am sure
you were an equally wonderful wife to Larry.

Please kiss Kara and Adriane for me—and tell them Grandpa loves 'em,
and looks forward to seeing them again soon. Please write us,—we want very
much to hear from you.

With Love,
Dad

Harry had begun by trying to convince me not to leave this marriage, but the odd thing was that he ended by validating my decision. I do not know how conscious he was of doing this. When I read the letter, even now, I can see him moving from his original position in defense of marriage to an empathy for his daughter-in-law: the understanding of the need to escape from the drudgery of the land, the loneliness, and the frustration; the recognition that the husband, at least in this case, was often impatient, demanding, and uncompromising. I do not know if, in writing this letter, he came to some belated self-criticism of his own early behavior as a young husband and father; I do not know how fully he understood what it meant to be a woman, expected to be subservient.

I HAVE TURNED TO HARRY'S LETTER in my effort to puzzle out the relationships among law and love and family. In these months of intensive focus, I am spending most of my days alone, walking along city sidewalks, staring out of windows, culling memories from old notes and papers, constructing new understandings in notebooks. But I do not feel lonely, which he rightly saw that I felt as a wife and mother of young children on the farm. My reasons for not feeling lonely now are obvious—though I am mostly alone, I have those tendrils of affiliation out to Kara and Adriane, to Ron, to people central in my life. But in my life on the farm, I had been nearly closed off from my own family of origin as well as from Lawrence's, and I felt eclipsed by Lawrence's towering presence. I had tried to make the attenuated emotional connection to Lawrence match the legal bond we had formed; I did so grudgingly, trying to convince myself that it would be better for my daughters. But at that moment in time the emotions and the law were not congruent.

Still, I realize that many of the commitments I now have to other people are codified by law. I eventually did make the choice to marry Ron, though I know that the history of marriage is woven through with injustice toward women as well as toward gays and lesbians. And there are laws standing guard around my relationships with Kara and Adriane—constraints that are invisible until a mother steps out of line or someone else transgresses—though the legal bonds cannot speak to the power of the emotions that bind us. Regardless of the law, I have come to understand that I could not simply excise Lawrence from our lives even when I severed the legal bond of marriage. In what sense *was* he still "family"?

I HAVE ANOTHER REASON for having turned to Harry's letter. Though I am not lonely, I do not wish to succumb to solipsism: as if my own is the only valid perspective. In including Harry's voice, I am seeking a different angle on my experience—someone else's view. I can see that in finding echoes of my own view, I also risk self-justification. But, despite Harry's empathy for my position, he did not truly join me in seeing this divorce as necessary; his central wish was that I find a way to continue being a "wonderful Mother" and "an equally wonderful wife," and that would have required that I reenter the old house of law, controlled by a dominant father. That I could not do.

I cannot help recalling Adrienne Rich's path-breaking poem "Snapshots of a Daughter-In-Law," which she claims to have "jotted in fragments during children's naps, brief hours in a library, or at 3 A.M. after rising with a wakeful child"—not unlike the circumstances in which I did my own more pedestrian dissertation writing. The poem itself does strike me as a series of fragments—thoughts and images and confused, overlapping pronouns: *you* and *she* and *I*. I place myself in the poem—as the poem invites me to do—with the "Nervy, glowering . . . daughter." But this daughter is also a daughter-in-law, as is her mother—indeed, as mothers usually are. The structures of law and masculine privilege surround each of these women. And the directive of the "angels" in the second fragment—*"Save yourself; others you cannot save"*—comes to the woman only in her near numbness. But here's what I now confront: saving yourself is not so easy. At the very least, you must be attentive to harm done to others even when you are convinced of the imperative.

I DO NOT REMEMBER what response, if any, I sent to Harry. But I do know that I was grateful for his empathy as I severed my bond with his son, and I was grateful that—with Kara's help—he was a grandfather to my daughters in years to come. This continuing relationship would in fact be largely Kara's doing as she grew older—sending letters to this near stranger who was her grandfather, even when his son continued to bear his own ill-defined grudges against him. And when Harry died years later, it was to Kara that his widow wrote in her grief. In some obscure sense, not legal and not immediate, he was still family, even though I was not his daughter, even though I was no longer even his daughter-in-law.

12

Celebrations

Though my marriage to Lawrence had ended months if not years earlier, it was officially dissolved on May 15, 1976, two days before Harry sent his ineffectual letter. We had done the legal work very civilly, relying jointly on one lawyer between us and hardly wrangling over any of the details. The divorce books, a common item on self-help shelves of the time, advised strenuously against such an arrangement, arguing that the lawyer is certain to be in the hire of one side or the other and cannot be expected to represent both parties. And it's true that this lawyer—who had drafted both of our wills in 1972 and had taken care of whatever minimal legal business we had had during our marriage—was in Lawrence's hire. But I didn't care. I wanted only two things: my freedom and my daughters.

When I went to court that May, I went alone, acting on both our behalves. I don't recall how we reached this decision, but I was pleased to be the active agent in the proceeding. I wanted to go before the judge myself, to be present at the act of dissolution. By Indiana law, only one of us needed to be present, and so I assume that for once Lawrence simply acquiesced to my preference. Perhaps it was his preference to be absent as much as it was mine to be present. Or perhaps he was glad to spend the morning with Kara and Adriane while I took care of this mundane business.

In my memory, the judge is imposing, male and white, sitting behind a large oak desk set above the rest of the courtroom, paying little real attention to the routine cases before him that morning. This was not a court date on which he would face difficult issues or real decisions. I stood before him, below him, as he went through rote procedures, my heart pounding despite the fact that this process was both routine and desirable. I recall feeling bizarrely gratified when he praised our settlement as unusually fair: this was

111

the only moment in which he stepped outside his role as disengaged signer of papers and looked me full in the face. He seemed genuine in his approval, and he spoke directly to me. My gratification was also genuine because I, too, thought it was very fair. But I can see now that what he probably meant is that the agreement simply honored gender priorities that were both his own and those of the culture: the property, though divided "in half" by standard Indiana state law, was really Lawrence's domain; the children (to my infinite gratitude) were largely my domain.

I left the court with my heart still pounding but also with a lifting sense of newly claimed freedoms. I got in my car—itself a symbol of those freedoms—and promptly backed it into a telephone pole. New liberty, I concluded glibly, could not be claimed without some wreckage. But I was confident that the wreckage, like the inconsequential dents in the car's rear bumper, would be minor.

When I arrived back at my apartment, I joined Lawrence, Kara, and Adriane in a mood of careful festivity. Young as they were, Kara, nearly five, and Adriane, thirteen months, were most likely to mimic whatever mood they observed in one or both of their parents; and Lawrence and I had made that studied choice: we would celebrate the occasion regardless of whatever ill feelings may have gone into producing it.

That evening I cooked a spaghetti dinner, a menu probably selected to respect both my limited budget and Kara's food preferences. Lawrence brought a bottle of champagne—Taittinger Brut—not exactly matched to the menu but clearly matched in his mind to what the occasion required. Never much of a champagne drinker, I had insufficient respect for the choice at the time, but for years afterward I would respond to Taittinger ads in the *New York Times Magazine* with a disjunctive sense of identification.

Throughout the meal, we retained that same sense of civility that had mostly gotten us through deciding who retained which household item and how we would prepare for college costs for our daughters, a distant but not hypothetical concern for either of us. As I consider that occasion now, it seems to have the same strained feeling of good will that Lawrence, Adriane, Ron, and I would work to construct years later, in 1994, Lawrence's final visit to our home. But at the time I felt it as a true mark of our ability to cooperate, to wish each other well in our new and separate lives.

A FEW WEEKS LATER we planned a more elaborate celebration, again honoring our newly separate lives, but this time at the farm where Lawrence still lived. This celebration was Lawrence's idea, a more decisive closure to our attempt at both marriage and rural life. He would soon move to a house in town, purchased in the recognition that he could not sustain the arduous life on the farm without a wife to assist him.

The freezer was nearly empty of the numerous labeled packages of fruits and vegetables from the year before, but it still held a package of particular significance: a beef tenderloin, the last remaining meat from Simmon—short for "Persimmon." The first male calf born on the farm—the year before Adriane was born—he had been slaughtered the previous fall. Most of the meat had been sold, but Lawrence had kept selected pieces for his own freezer. This tenderloin was the last of them.

Lawrence liked this kind of ritual event, and it did seem appropriate for the four of us to gather at the farm for one last time. I felt odd being back in that kitchen as both a guest and not a guest, but—though it seems almost cannibalistic to me now, having since become a vegetarian—I did look forward to tasting this carefully raised and cared for piece of prime meat. Although Lawrence had rarely cooked during our marriage, he wanted to prepare this special meat, and for me his cooking now called to mind my pleasure in his cooking skills when we were first dating. With attentive skill, he roasted the tenderloin to perfection; I offered a potato salad chopped and mixed ahead, presented attractively in a special blue crockery bowl that had been my grandmother's; together we steamed last-minute vegetables from among the few remaining packages in the freezer; the girls played quietly with each other in the still childproof area beside the kitchen. The preparations felt like a model of our postdivorce spirit of cooperation, similar to our spaghetti and champagne dinner.

But our amity was too fragile to survive. As I loaded a tray to take out to the picnic area in the yard, the tray tipped, and the spirit of cooperation dissipated: the pan of steaming green beans added too much weight to the collection of drinks and condiments and corn and beets and the heavy bowl of potato salad. I reached desperately to catch flying pans of food, feeling the sharp sting of steam and hot metal on my fingers and wrist before simply looking helplessly at the floor before me: I had managed to rebalance most of the pans of food but could do nothing to retrieve the heap of potato salad and broken blue crockery with juice and milk dripping over it.

Perhaps we could have sustained our friendliness if this mishap hadn't intervened. Perhaps we could have gone on through a deceptively amicable evening out under the picnic shelter in the yard, sitting together, enjoying the food we had grown together, watching the children we had produced together as they played in the grass.

But old impulses die hard: Lawrence met this accident with his habitual fury and hostility. In contrast to the calm just minutes earlier, he now paced the floor, shouting at me, spitting out words such as *stupid* and *clumsy* and *ruined* and *fault*. I waited briefly to see if the fury might pass, but my own impulses were new to me; instead of allowing myself to be pelted by this emotional hailstorm as I cringed in silence, I rose up in resistance—something I had not been very good at in our days together—and responded with a white-taut hysteria. My voice was thin and high and colorless, unused to expressing anger in this way, but embracing the force of my own pent-up emotion: "I can't stand to be yelled at like that. All right, we'll leave right now—that's why I left this house in the first place."

I remember feeling both irrational and stifled by my own anger, shocked that I would shout like that and unfamiliar with my own raised voice. Yet I was also liberated in my sense that this wasn't my real situation: I could just walk out, no longer bound to weather the storm, to listen unresponsively until the vituperation came to its own exhausted end. In some ways, I even felt cleansed by my responding fury, a catharsis for someone who had spent too many years always expecting that my careful calm would soothe Lawrence's rage.

But my catharsis was not without a price: Kara's terror at this unfamiliar mother's rage. Her father's rage she had seen before, though we had tried to keep it from her as much as possible, but she had never seen it matched in this way by her mother's. Her first response to the situation was: "Oh, Mommy, you spoiled the food." And then: "Daddy, why did you yell like that?" But finally, with mommy yelling, too, she went out onto the porch, taking her sister with her, and sat on the porch's edge, crying and holding Adriane on her own young lap. Adriane, in perplexed sympathy with her sister, began to cry as well, the two of them a picture of childhood grief.

Self-protectively I held on to my sense that I needed this emotional release and even hoped that the experience could be cleansing for Kara, too, though clearly not for Adriane, who was yet too young for that to be even a possibility. Perhaps it would be valuable for Kara to experience more directly the actual tension between her parents and thus to comprehend the need for us to live separately. I recalled having discussed some of these possible consequences when her uncle and aunt, my brother and his wife, had visited us three years previously, in my period of nearly leaving the marriage the first time. I recalled having told them that I didn't want Kara to grow up thinking that Lawrence's abusive rages were an appropriate model of behavior. Her aunt had responded that Kara ought not to see my toleration of such rages as an appropriate model either.

Now here I was rejecting the model of quiet toleration, justifying the model of equal and responsive raging. My own catharsis felt clear to me, and I felt certain that I was acting in my daughters' best interest. But I was still nagged by my earlier view that raging was not the model I wanted to offer any more than I wanted to suggest submission—and I was stung by the image of my two children clinging to each other in their circle of grief.

THE DINNER THAT FOLLOWED returned us to a subdued celebration. Lawrence, in uncharacteristic apology, kept patting me on the head and shoulder and inquiring: "Are you feeling all right now?" His anger had come primarily from my "spoiling" the perfect dinner that he had planned; his apologies were a genuine attempt to restore equilibrium. My anger had swelled from an untapped store of anger; I accepted his apologies but felt no reciprocal wish to apologize. I do not recall what the last tenderloin tasted like or what kind of meal we actually ate.

As Kara and Adriane and I departed for our own home, Lawrence approached the car window on my side. Reaching through the open window, he tentatively touched first one breast and then the other, his touch testing the hardness and fullness caused by the milk left unused as I weaned Adriane. Straining away from his touch, trying not to make an issue of what felt like an intrusion and trying as well not to sense any sexual overture, I simply pointed out to him that I was experiencing the discomfort of taut, overly full breasts.

LATER THAT EVENING after the children were in bed, he phoned me: "You wouldn't be interested in sex, would you?"

I floundered for an appropriate response: "I don't think it would be wise."

"Wise?" As usual, his sarcasm foreclosed any real discussion.

"No, I wouldn't be interested." Then, trying to be flippant, I added, "Besides, I won't keep this shape for long."

After hanging up the phone, I tried to sort out the day: Lawrence's anger, my anger, the children's grief, his apology, his sexual overture, my refusal. We were decidedly divorced and yet the disconnection still had its raw edges. At that point, I could not have known how we would continue to rub up against each other's raw edges or what might yet be the costs of my claim to freedom, but those were not the terms in which I was prepared to think at present.

I turned on WFIU, the classical music station, took off all my clothes and lay on my bed, trying to clear my head and find relief from the summer heat. I soon realized, however, that I could not yet welcome my solitude in peace: flies buzzed around me, zooming up to the ceiling and then swarming down. As Wagner's *Flying Dutchman Overture* played in the background— horns swelling in romantic emotion, strings paced by the occasional drum roll—I pranced naked on my bed, striking wildly at the flies, dancing my release from the day's turmoil. With the flies mostly dead or dissipated, I lay back down, finally joining the sleep of my daughters.

THE FLIES remind me bizarrely of Sartre's tormenting flies in *Les Mouches*, a play I had read in college, exploring revenge and guilt and freedom and responsibility—an echo of my younger explorations of existentialism, though mine was a feeling of liberation, not torment. And the Wagner—a composer I've never been particularly fond of—seems too neatly to articulate a German romantic anguished search for love, especially given Lawrence's scholarly devotion to German romanticism and his own anguished search for love, still active at his death.

But my journal entry of that day makes clear that I didn't make up this last catharsis with its overly literary possibilities, nor did I make up the events and emotions of the day that led up to it. These events are as I recorded them, before I thought about import, before I knew what kind of life I would go on to make. Anyway, if I try to examine the possible symbolism, it doesn't quite work out: I did feel liberated, not tormented, and my pursuits were neither vengeance nor romance. But one piece of Orestes' final speech is apt: "All here is new, all must begin anew. And for me, too, a new life is beginning." A new life. A new life premised, for me, on the central motives for my divorce: my freedom and my daughters.

Sorting It Out

Reprise, 1994

With my New York writing time nearly gone, I decide to venture out of my solitude on a sunny spring afternoon—a rare foray into a more public space, beyond the personal relationships that have otherwise sustained me during this period of introspection. I walk through the city streets with a clear destination in mind, though it has no primary import for me: the Asian Art Fair at the Armory. Crossing Union Square, I eavesdrop on random conversations about jobs and upcoming weddings; I watch the pigeons peck in the path and rise in small flocks into the trees. The sky is a glorious blue. The hum and bustle of the city invigorate me.

But once admitted to the Armory, I feel my energy drain away. I wander aimlessly from booth to booth, not sure where to place myself among the collectors and aesthetes. I do not seem to belong here as I had belonged among the pigeons and pedestrians. But I do not mind even this alienation, at least not until I stumble upon an object in a display of ancient Chinese jade that throws me again into my past: a small column of white jade. My fragile public self dissolves. Against my will, I am unexpectedly thrust even more deeply into my intimate self: in anger and memory and desire.

I stand mesmerized as my eyes try to follow the intricate carving: mice—or are they rats?—climb over one another, separate and intertwined, tails and mouths moving in all directions. In this small column of white jade—a mere three inches high, an inch and a half across, delicate, precise—I try to trace the relationship of rodent legs and tails, mouths and ears and noses, reminding myself to breathe as I move farther into the interior of this booth at the Asian Art Fair, away from other passing visitors, my eyes fixed on the jade carving. My knees threaten to buckle, but I steady myself by moving my feet apart. I have to keep looking, waiting as the fissures within me spread like cracks in a windshield hit by a rock.

When I was married to Lawrence, I lived a daily life with such an object as now seems to shatter me: a miniature column of white jade, though the carving was of herons and lotus blossoms, not rodents. I have long known that my daughters' father was a man who craved possession and regularly acquired Chinese jade, oriental rugs, wooden masks from Africa and leather ones from Italy. When we were together, I saw this desire to collect as his acquisitiveness, his wish to control what he loved. But now at the Asian Art Fair, still half within the umbra of my intense introspection, I stare through this small jade column into my past, gripped by alien emotions: a desire to possess, an anger at possession. All of this immersion in the past has left me newly vulnerable. I am not certain who I am.

MY WRITING TIME IS NEARLY GONE, and I have not yet even come to what I thought was my real story: the story of my life as a single mother, premised on my freedom and my daughters. Daily I pace along the windows overlooking New York, trying to move forward into the story of the life I meant to celebrate. But that will have to await my return to Wooster. I see now that I must use these last few weeks of solitude to revisit the grip that Lawrence has had on me.

Still alone, suspended in time and space—fifteen floors up, neither in the city nor of the city—I again look to documents to help me stabilize. I spread out the insurance papers that my daughters have generously shared with me. They provide a starting point: descriptions of the objects that the Asian Art Fair has called to mind, in particular the two that Kara and Adriane kept in the aftermath of their father's death: a scepter and a bowl, both jade. Kara and Adriane did not keep the small carved column of white jade that used to stand beside the other jade in our living room.

Their father's insurance papers describe the scepter as follows: "CHINESE JADE: IRONWOOD AND JADE JU'I SCEPTER, S-CURVED DIAPERED IRONWOOD SHAFT OF THE CH'IEN LUNG PERIOD INSET WITH 3 JADE PIECES PROBABLY OF THE HAN DYNASTY (206 B.C.–220 A.D.); PALE CELADON GREEN WITH BROWN MARKINGS: OVAL SHAPE, WITH DRAGON AT THE EDGE AND CARVED WITH T'AO-T'IEH MOTIFS;

A SCABBARD BUCKLE CALLED SUI WITH CARVED CRAWLING CHIH DRAGON; AND
A BAT OF HAPPINESS." The bowl is described more simply: "CHINESE JADE:
SCHOLAR'S BRUSH-WASHER; IN THE SHAPE OF A PEACH, CARVED AND UNDERCUT
DESIGN, WITH CORAL PIECE; MING (1368–1644)."

I do not fully comprehend these descriptions, but I remember the shapes
that are integral to my life as well as the value derived from the designa-
tions "Ming" and "Han." The scepter is raised up on an ironwood stand. It
consists of three pieces of mottled pale green jade, carved and embedded in
ironwood—which is also carved—fifteen inches long, rising in a curve in the
middle for the grasp of the hand of power. Reading the insurance papers, I
recall the crawling dragon and the bat of happiness as vivid claims on symbolism and authority. I can imagine this scepter being lifted up regally; sometimes
I wish for that kind of power. The bowl, too, is mottled and pale green, a gently rounded oval, five inches in length, smooth on the inside, carved on the
outside, with a small red-orange coral embedded on the piece of carved jade
that juts out from one end of the oval. I recognize its graceful utility and yearn
to cup it in my hands. I can imagine dipping my own scholar's brush into it.

Calling these objects to mind—now safely packed away until my daughters are ready for them—I also yearn to reach out and touch Kara as an
infant, to lift her into my arms and protect her from much of what lies in
store for her. I can almost see her: clear-eyed, a faint tinge of pink on her
cheeks, lean and tender fleshed, with a nearly naked newborn's head. She is
lying on the floor next to the low Chinese table that held these and other
jade objects; beneath her is an oriental rug, in tight geometrical patterns of
burgundy and black and ivory, with small touches of deep azure. She wears a
yellow baby gown, drawstring around her feet, her knees bent slightly open.
Her fists close gently; her eyes open wide onto the world.

In another memory, from nearly five years later, I see Adriane as a one-
year-old, standing upright in a light-green jumpsuit, casting her eyes mis-
chievously over her shoulder as she reaches toward objects she knows she is
not allowed to touch. By this time, she and her sister and I no longer live in
the house where their father lives with these precious objects. With me, she
is a visitor at the farm to which she was born.

There is a much earlier memory, too: of Lawrence and me together
before we had any children. We are in an elegant shop in Chicago, hushed

and dimly lit, not far from the Water Tower. That day, struck by the beauty around us, we purchased two antique objects: the scepter, a symbol of power, and the scholar's brush-washer, a tool for writer's work.

WHEN WE DIVORCED, I did not want possessions: I wanted only my daughters and my freedom. As the judge had seemed to recognize, most of our possessions, in any case, belonged to Lawrence. But it is not easy to leave possessions behind and so much harder to leave people behind. For many years, I rarely saw the scepter and the brush-washer, but they persisted as vestiges of the life I had once had, the life I might have continued to have, the alternative life my daughters lived when they were with their father for summers and holidays. I could not excise him from my life and disappear into an autonomous freedom: he was my daughters' father. My life remained entangled with him, and even with his possessions, through our daughters: Kara and Adriane.

AND SO I MUST RETURN to Lawrence's death—to examine that experience more closely, more fully than can be done in small echoes—not because it is central, but because it threatens to take control of the story. Even in his death, he took that power. But I need you to know that this story—the story I came to New York to write in solitude, in caring, the story of my life with my daughters—is not about him. This is the story I had already begun to construct years ago when the phone call came, tearing a jagged hole through it. Forgive the repetition.

WOOSTER, OHIO. July 5, 1994, 4:00 PM. I savored time alone on this quiet summer afternoon. Then the voice on the phone said the awful words that play again in mind and memory: "Lawrence took his own life yesterday. I'm sorry to call with this news. Yours was the only number we had for contacting Kara and Adriane. We thought you should be the one to tell them—as their mother."

As their mother, I received this news alone, standing in the empty space in the dining room, stunned, the late afternoon sun limning everything in the room. At first, I could only stare blankly at the sunlit outlines of the philodendron that hung in the window and at the softer outlines of the fern by the piano, still beyond the reach of the afternoon sun. Soon I would need to be angry at Lawrence, at what he had done to himself, to his daughters, and to me—even, pettily, at what he had done to my writing project. Allowing my bitterness to surface, I would call his suicide "the last selfish act of a selfish man."

But first I had to act as Kara and Adriane's mother. That identity had persisted through the divorce eighteen years earlier, through the building of my professional life, through my own remarriage five years earlier. Now that identity would have to bear the weight of their father's suicide: I stood alone, needing desperately to protect my daughters, to take this shock into my body, knowing that I could not deflect it from them, not knowing what its consequences would be for any of us.

I tried to say the word *suicide* when I called to cancel my plans for the afternoon, but my throat closed. Instead I said, "Kara and Adriane's father has died." Numb and aimless, I paced, needing someone else to come home: Ron, whose comfort I craved, Adriane and Kara, to whom I yearned to give comfort.

As I waited for Adriane to return from her job—an occupation for the summer after her first year of college—I rehearsed the words I might use to tell her the unthinkable. But when I greeted her at the door, my arms reaching awkwardly around her, I could only fall back on worn phrases: "Oh, honey, I'm so sorry. Your father took his own life yesterday. I just got the phone call."

I relied on the same phrasing that the formal voice had used on the phone, not quite a euphemism, but still not that word *suicide;* I was not yet ready to acknowledge self-murder. My voice and my words sounded cold, stripped of emotion. Adriane felt their import and leaned into me slightly, responding more to my touch than to my voice. Nineteen years old, tall and limber, she received the news with her muscles taut, her shoulders firm. She had been privy to some of her father's recent anguish about a difficult love affair, had seen in him a vulnerability that few others had witnessed, but she could not have been prepared for this news. I cannot remember any words that she uttered; I can only remember her firm body and measured breathing.

Holding our bodies in careful balance, Adriane and I moved together to sit on the couch. I kept my arm around her; she rested her head on my shoulder briefly. Neither of us had yet found our tears. I knew that my next task was to call Kara in New York. I did not want to deliver such news to her at work, but I knew that I might otherwise have trouble reaching her in a timely way. Wishing to ease the news for her older sister, Adriane helped me devise the phrasing: "Kara, I have some sad news, but I don't want you to hear it at the office. I need you to call me from home as soon as possible."

A FEW YEARS LATER Kara would tell me that my voice at that moment sounded like death. To me, it just sounded stiff, beyond grief. I heard from Kara a small gasp of recognition before she gave me the office-voice assurance that she would leave work right away, call back soon. In her voice, I heard, too, the competence that had served her so well throughout her childhood, on through college—learning three foreign languages, spending a semester in Russia, undertaking an interdisciplinary major in international studies— and now in her postcollege office job in international commerce. I heard the resilience that had enabled her as a child to move regularly between the homes of her divorced parents, the resilience that would sustain her through what would come next. At twenty-three, she had already demonstrated her capacities to perform new tasks, to face unforeseen circumstances, to carry forward responsibly.

LATER THAT EVENING the four of us were finally gathered under one roof. Ron had returned home at the end of his day; with astonishing rapidity, Kara had arranged to fly in from New York; the rest of us had retrieved her from the Cleveland airport. Now we were together on our front porch for a glass of wine, a cigarette for Kara and Ron. The night enveloped us in summer warmth and the soft shrill of crickets. Though it had to be at least midnight, there were still a few stray fireflies high among the trees on the college campus across the street, flickering elusively. We breathed in the night air, momentarily oblivious to clock and calendar.

I remember deliberately loosening my muscles as I propped my feet on the ledge in front of me. I crossed my ankles and cupped my hands around my glass of wine, resting it against my thighs. Kara and Ron and I wanted to talk, though we were not yet ready to pry open this unfathomable reality. Adriane—younger, more restless, and not drinking wine as were the rest of us—claimed a chair on the porch but frequently got up to pace, wanting to be in this gathering but not able to sit still. I do not recall any of us asking the obvious questions: Why? How could he? What could we have done to prevent this?

Those questions came later, slowly rising out of the emotional slough that at first restrained our minds and limbs. At that moment, all we could acknowledge was that we desperately needed this gathering on the porch. The only conversation we could yet stir into life was to list the urgent tasks: to talk to the coroner, to identify the body and retrieve it from the morgue, to arrange for cremation, to sort through everything at the house and in Lawrence's office, to talk to an attorney and sign papers. I did not yet know the full extent of these obligations, but I had been told that it was imperative for us to act quickly, to identify the body as soon as possible: it could not be left to lie there in the morgue, unattended. As Lawrence's immediate survivors, Kara and Adriane were the ones required to perform this task.

I remember relying on pragmatic concerns, speaking to Kara and Adriane through the habits of all my years of single parenting: "You can go to Bloomington yourselves, if you prefer, or I can go with you, or both Ron and I can go with you. We don't want to intrude, but we want to be of help where we can." I'm sure my voice was wooden but equally sure that it bore within it the trust and respect that have always been central to my love for my daughters. Throughout their lives, I had supported both their independence and their relationship with their father, however fraught it was, and I did not know what other resources to draw upon in this moment of crisis. But when I think back to that evening, I ask myself: How could I possibly have thought they could make such a trip alone?

Early on in our relationship, Ron had recognized and respected that Kara, Adriane, and I didn't rely much on parental authority. But in this moment he knew to speak decisively: "We'll all go to Bloomington. What we need now is to be together." And suddenly, gratefully, I knew he was right: this trip would only be possible together.

FRIENDS HAVE ASKED ME INCREDULOUSLY: "Did you and the girls really have to do that? Didn't Lawrence have any other family?" And he did: a brother and two sisters. But his daughters were his next of kin, his closest family, the family to be notified and in turn to notify his siblings. As their mother, I, too, became a kind of next of kin, regardless of the intervening eighteen years since our divorce. The ties that we had broken fell back into a linked chain, as his daughters—*my* daughters—took up the material and emotional detritus of his death.

WHEN KARA RECALLS OUR TIME in Bloomington, she most remembers the smell: the stench of blood and mustiness, of a house that has been closed around the dead. But smell is not my primary sense. My memories are mostly visual and visceral.

The body, for example. After all, officials had not waited for our arrival before removing it from the morgue. Our first task, after talking with the coroner, was to go to the funeral home to make the identification, though that would be pro forma; neither the coroner nor the police had any doubt about whose body this really was. We didn't either. At the funeral home, with the body still awaiting our official recognition, a soft-spoken, suited young man ushered us into an upholstered room, ivory and discreet maroon, a lamp glowing gently on an imposing walnut desk. The four of us sat clustered across from him, talking decorously about cremation, death announcement, death certificates for legal purposes.

After the paperwork, this careful young man led us into a different room, sterile and tightly confined—white walls, a stainless-steel gurney, bright lights overhead. On the gurney lay the body we were there to name: draped in a white sheet, mostly cleaned up, it lay there starkly. This was Lawrence and not Lawrence: a face drained of color, matted hair, a hole on the left side of the head—the side toward us, the side where the bullet had exited. We could only assume there was a matching hole on the other side where the bullet had entered.

After we had affirmed officially that this body was indeed Lawrence O. Frye, I whispered to Adriane, who stood beside me: "That's not your father." I wasn't quite sure what I meant by this, since I don't believe in an afterlife of the soul or the separation of mind and body. But it didn't really look like him. She told me later that for a moment she thought I really meant that what we were looking at was the wrong body. And in a way, that's also what I was feeling: How could this body, drained of life and color and complexity,

be the same man with whom they and I had struggled in our different ways
for so many years?

LESS THAN THREE WEEKS EARLIER, Lawrence had sat on the couch with
Ron and Adriane and me in our basement TV room, watching an NBA finals
game—Was it between the Knicks and the Rockets?—not, in any case, a
game any of us was invested in. The game was simply a way for the four of us
to be together on this overnight visit that Lawrence was making to Adriane
on his way to visit Kara in New York. Although this occasion was not the first
time he had visited us overnight, it was not a frequent or comfortable experience. Each of us always tried to be gracious—he brought wine, I cooked
dinner, we all talked more or less genially—but we were also conscious that
we were negotiating potential turbulence. Hence the NBA game: a way to sit
side by side, talk if we wished, remain quiet if we preferred.

But that was on Friday, June 17, 1994. As we watched, the game was
interrupted by a split screen: the infamous Bronco chase, O. J. Simpson pursued by police cars and helicopters as cameras and commentators captured
it all, moment by moment. Lawrence's caustic comment was something to
the effect that the journalists were hovering so that we'd have "the chance to
watch O. J. blow his brains out, live, on camera." Weeks later I would recall
the comment against the harsh substratum of his own suicide. At the time, I
took it as Lawrence's typical sardonic humor. We, of course, had no idea just
how much turbulence we were negotiating or how close to the marrow that
comment actually was.

Six days later, after a difficult visit with Kara, Lawrence had returned
for another overnight. I knew it had been a difficult visit if only because it
could not have been otherwise, given her small apartment, her three room-
mates, and his capacity to take up more space than any confined living
quarters would allow. I may also have known more directly from a phone
conversation with Kara that she would have had to sneak in during some
city excursion he made on his own. My memory may be wrong on this, but
it calls up with it the deeper layers of remembering: for many years I had to
rely on the girls' sotto voce communications or a secretive phone call when
they were visiting him. He had not liked for Kara and Adriane to talk with
me "on his time."

When he arrived this time, he seemed agitated. At the dinner table, he kept teasing us to ask him what was on his mind, why he was late, with whom he might have had an extended phone conversation that morning. Tired of the verbal games he liked to play, we were mostly quiet, unwilling to take the bait. Yet he seemed softer than usual, even kind in his expressions of gratitude to Ron and me, as well as deeply affectionate toward Adriane. When he said good-bye the next morning, he still seemed to taunt us with what we hadn't understood in his emotional riddles, but his departure was gentle, his words of farewell appreciative.

ALL OF THAT WAS PART—a very small part—of the complexity that seemed to have drained out of this cold body on the gurney at the funeral home. How could he have shrunk to this, the man who took up so much space, the man with the ready verbal jibes, the man committed to controlling those around him? How could he be just lying here, drained of life and power and language?

AT HIS HOUSE, we faced a greater sense of his complexity. If his body had not seemed to represent him when drained of life, his house by contrast retained his image in indelible markings. All of us hesitated at the door, knowing that our first obligation on entering his house was to take off our shoes, a behavior he insisted upon. When we then entered with our shoes on, we knew we had transgressed and felt the house itself chastising us.

The house *was* still his, even in his absence. Apart from the assertive transgression of not removing our shoes, we couldn't help behaving as guests. We spent our nights—with a fragile sense of relief—in a local motel. But for the next five days, most of our tasks had to be undertaken in this house—this house in which we were interlopers, this house that stank of death and bore the indelible markings of the newly dead.

The living room, marked by Lawrence, looked unmarked by death. On the floor lay the first oriental rug he had ever bought—before I knew him— the rug we had kept on our living room floor for the seven and a half years we were married. Here, too, was familiar furniture: the mahogany library table with elaborately carved end pieces and a glossy surface upon which we had eaten many dinners in our early years together; the same Danish modern couch with teak arms and legs, the same black leather chair (worn now into patterns by his buttocks and shoulder blades), the granite end table on brass legs and the elaborately carved Chinese low table—displaying antique Chinese jade pieces and made of what the insurance papers identify as "TZU-TAN" wood and "DANCING GRAPE" wood. Also here were additional oriental rugs, lithographs and photographs and an oil painting on the walls (some familiar, some unfamiliar), wooden African masks and leather Italian masks (all after my time), and a brand-new, state-of-the-art stereo system. And books— shelves full of them, stacks of them on the floor, library books and personally purchased first editions and new paperbacks—all ready to be taken up and read at any moment. Through the window, on the patio in the backyard, we could see the marble picnic table that Lawrence had personally designed.

Other rooms also looked familiarly in process: the "brown" room—a recreation room with chocolate brown bookshelves and ceiling tiles whimsically painted brown in alternating pattern—and the kitchen holding objects I knew: stoneware on which I had served many meals in an earlier era, the salt and pepper shakers (still jarringly familiar), the dish drainer. All looked innocuous, ordinary, even as they sent chills through me: nothing here seemed ordinary any longer. In the "brown" room, we found the butcher-block table, remnant of our life together on the farm, strewn with junk mail (the kind I, too, accumulate for weeks on end before finally sorting and throwing out), as well as the marble-top table with wrought-iron frame that he had had made when we lived on the farm so that I could make candy on its cool surface. The barber's chair and pinball machine—quixotic purchases made some years after my time—gave testimony to his capacity for ironic playfulness.

We moved through the house slowly, as if under water, noting objects, forestalling feelings—this house in Bloomington to which Lawrence had moved after our divorce. I mentally sorted objects into categories, eras of a life with which I had been entwined. And I kept reminding myself that this house—that smelled of death and had closed itself around Lawrence's body a mere few days earlier—was also my daughters' other home, where Kara and Adriane had spent many months of their lives.

It was here that they had had endless emotional wrangles with their father, had deepened their reliance on each other, had spent intensive solitary periods of reading and writing, withdrawing from conflicts that had imperiled their childhood. Here, too, they had played games, worked puzzles, eaten meals, washed dishes, talked and laughed aloud. This house was *theirs* as well as his. Yet it was now up to us—Kara and Adriane and Ron and me, in confirmed allegiance to each other—to arrange for the disposition of all of these objects, Lawrence's possessions.

When we got to the dining room—also dominated by intriguing objects, art objects distinctively arranged in counterpoint with whimsically chosen personal objects—we still resisted looking down the hallway, though we could no longer hold emotions at bay. Here, on the large birch table with glossy blond surface (acquired after my time), we faced the jarring reality of our purpose. Circling through the house, we had put off approaching this central object: the table with the note or, rather, series of notes—the suicide note that seems essential, but that I have since learned is left by only a small percentage of those who kill themselves. Here we also found much evidence of preparation and thoughtfulness: insurance information, retirement account, and, with especial poignancy, work to have been returned to current graduate students, now with a weary Post-it attached—"sorry, unable to complete. LOF."

I cannot recall reading the suicide notes immediately, but I cannot imagine *not* reading them either, even though we had yet another confrontation we were evading in our halting movement through the house: the physical place of death. I think we must have read the notes without really taking them in, knowing we would have to return to anguished words that we could not yet assimilate.

Finally, we were willing to walk down the short hall toward the study and two bedrooms. We knew that this hall was where he had spent his last lonely moments, gun in hand, positioned on a beach towel so as not to leave a mess. We knew that in those lonely early-morning hours of the Fourth of July, this is where he finally put the gun to his temple and pulled the trigger: the shot that had torn into our lives had first gone through his head and then into the wall in this ordinary hallway.

We had been in the house several sluggish hours before we were willing to venture into this hallway. We were even longer in the house before we knew that the blood that had drained from his body had—quite contrary to his meticulous preparations—ended up draining through the house's ventilation system and falling onto laundry hanging in the basement, splattering grotesquely over the basement floor. This spectacle, I must admit, I never did see for myself; it was Ron who first went down into the basement to investigate what might be stored there that Kara and Adriane would want to retrieve. It was Ron—of all of us, least entwined in Lawrence's life, perhaps most able to look directly at these realities—who first encountered this particular horror.

I think it was also Ron who helped us to venture on through the hallway and into the study, closing in on the most vital evidence of who Lawrence was: a scholar, a teacher, a poet, a lover, a father. Here we found an article virtually finished—"The Author as Liberating Seducer in Friedrich Schlegel's *Lucinde*"; we found photographs of women he had loved; we found books and papers, computer disks, a few poems, children's drawings sent to him long ago by Kara and Adriane. We had to assume that the computer held mysteries we would never unravel, perhaps poems and personal materials we would want to retrieve if we knew how. Instead, we chose to protect Lawrence's privacy; Adriane, committed to this goal, did what she could with this ancient IBM to delete files we could not open and did not want to leave for others' eyes. We took disks with us when we left, though none of us knew how to access these files from his archaic word-processing system. We left the computer itself behind, along with its lingering mysteries.

As we dug deeper into the filing cabinets—always trying to find what *had* to be found before we could escape from this purgatorial world into which we had been thrust—we found other objects, not just files. We found an elaborate choker of gold and amethysts—destined as a gift for whom? We found boxes of bullets, set aside for what purpose, for use in which gun? We found a will—after the attorney had already designated Lawrence's death intestate—a will bizarrely preserved from 1972 (but then so was my matching will), signed and dated February 8. In these paired wills, each of us named the other and our daughter as well as "any children which may be born to our marriage at a later date" as our legal heirs: Kara and Adriane. This wording (fortunately) coincided with the dictates of Indiana state law: in the event of divorce and no subsequent marriage, the children are the inheritors, though the specifics of the will and its hypothetical trust fund introduced minor complications in the disposition of property.

But, then, everything was complicated, a tangle of artifacts and emotions. Throughout those days, I retained my anger, but I also learned to temper it, interweave it with grief for the loss of this complex and lonely person, grief especially for the loss of my daughters' father.

NOW, NEARLY FOUR YEARS LATER, I return to the suicide notes that Kara has xeroxed for me. Yesterday I walked to meet her in the East Village to retrieve these papers, needing to hold the documents in my own hands, to contemplate them in solitude as I strive to make sense of our lives, together and apart. She and Adriane are generous in their willingness to share their thoughts and feelings with me, to hand on documents when I need the tangible.

Paging through the copies, I am shocked to realize just how many notes he actually wrote, how painfully they trace an anguish that I had failed to recognize inside this man so given to dominance and control. One is a literary quotation, from Kleist: "To give birth to that which kills me," which he had written in the original German. Another is also literary in tone, almost abstract, though deeply personal: "Circling like an animal, around one's own center, never found and ever shifting. Like the plunge into the lake, so cold; hovering over the surface, not deciding, saying no, and plunging when not watching one's self. The pointless act which will be done as soon as the hovering circle defines the inevitable. Save me from enigmatic movements of my self. To whom do I call, and who would hear?"

I am brought to tears by the palpable pain. In my own circling anguish, I must find a place to settle: I choose the note that bears upon my own life, addressed to my daughters. From it, I resurrect a small sense of gratitude that in doing this he has at least left them, among the notes and papers on the dining room table, a kind of absolution: "You know already how I feel about you, how I love you both. You are both wonderful and will do well. All I have is yours to share, divide—including disarray and debts." Also in that note: "Your mother will hopefully help sort out and order."

And that was my task in that awful week in July 1994: to "help sort out and order." I could do little there at the house with so much disarray and so many artifacts and no claim to be there *other* than as Kara and Adriane's mother. We did what we could in those five days, arranged to hire out what could be hired out: cleaners who could remove blood stains, a security system for a house that would stand empty; we made preliminary plans for the sale of valuable objects and of the house itself. Much of the decision making fell to Kara, the older daughter, though we all tried to pitch in where we could.

Kara and Adriane between them spent careful time, but there was not enough, trying to decide which objects each of them wanted to keep: the jade scepter, the peach-shaped bowl, thoughtfully selected oriental rugs, the small Chinese table. They didn't yet realize that they were also leaving behind memories they would not be able to retrieve—their great-grandmother's Christmas kuchen recipe, their father's recipe box—though they at least knew to take photographs and personal writings.

We finally drove away, taking with us a few select objects and, in a box, Lawrence's ashes. En route we dropped Kara off at the Indianapolis airport to fly back to New York; carrying her father's ashes, she faced yet another grim obstacle in the scrutiny by airport security, where X-ray discerned denser fragments of bone in this apparently ordinary parcel. What we couldn't take with us, we left behind, in much disarray and difficulty to be dealt with from a distance, over time. We left behind unnamed fragments of the life that Kara and Adriane had shared with their father.

I RETURNED ALONE FOUR MONTHS LATER to act as family representative at the small memorial service planned by German department faculty and students: the mother of Lawrence's daughters. On that same trip, I visited the farm where we had lived for the final four years of our marriage, Kara's early childhood, Adriane's infancy. I explored old places, resurrected old pieces of my life and my daughters' lives, too. I was, by then, no longer necessary to the material tasks of sorting objects. But the other task—helping to sort and order my daughters' memories and emotions—of necessity remained one of my maternal commitments. Indeed, by then, I was also making forays into this writing project, beginning serious immersion in my own sorting out and ordering, my own piecing together of memory and meaning. Isn't that, after all, what stories are—and what we use them for?

NOW, NEARLY AT THE END OF MY STAY IN NEW YORK, I am laden with meanings and memories. My presence at the Asian Art Fair was largely arbitrary, not chosen as part of any particular plan. But as I stared at the small pillar of carved white jade, with intertwined rodents scrambling each for position, I was impelled to think about design, to examine anew my relationship to possession and power and desire.

From beneath the burden of memory, my anger at Lawrence surfaces again: I do not like that he has made me change my understanding of the past. I do not like that I can no longer be the "good" parent balanced by a "bad" parent. But the old certainties no longer sustain me. I must find a new path through the thicket of duty and desire, love and family. And yet I have been doing this all along: picking my way through memories and events, breaking myself apart in search of new possibilities for understanding.

It is time now to return home.

PART II

A New Life

1976–1989

13

Entering Kauke Hall

June 1998: I am ready to be back in Wooster, but my return from New York leaves me estranged. To reground myself, I walk each day through neighborhoods around the college campus, circling old territories. Apart from research leaves spent in cities elsewhere, I have lived here for the past twenty-two years: it is home, but I need to think about how I belong. No doubt my stay in New York has prompted a new rupture in my sense of place as well as in my sense of who I am. And yet, walking through the old neighborhood today, I do not focus on the contrast; I try instead to reenter my early life here with my daughters, to find again that young mother seeking her unknown future. The quirky details I encounter on these familiar paths draw me back, not through big memories, but through small ones, rising with unexpected force.

I approach our first house circuitously. Four blocks from the college, this is where my daughters and I lived during our first two years here as we began to forge our new life. I had claimed it as home almost immediately upon getting the job offer at the College of Wooster: 1976 and I was ready to push forward. Now I come upon this house with a shock of recognition. The tree that Kara brought home from first grade on Arbor Day, our second year in Wooster, still stands sentinel in front of the house, though it is now dead; the brick sidewalk is barely visible, overgrown with grass. The porches are the same, the front porch where I so often sat to read or dawdle with the girls and the quirky little back porch from which Eileen and I watched a one-and-a half-year-old Adriane—ignoring the slippery leather soles of her high-top white baby shoes and scrambling up the jungle gym (now gone) in the backyard during our first weeks of making our home here. There, too, is the yard itself extending all the way to the back alley: I see it surrounded by the fence that my brother Don helped me put up that first September, but in reality the fence is long since removed.

If I were to walk up the side alley, I would pass the green duplex next door, still green, though faded to a pale reminder of its past. I can almost see the tricycles and bicycles that used to gather there and the children playing freely between the two houses. There's a new garage out back where the two alleys intersect, but the intersection itself is the same, still marking the place where I collided with a motorcycle in 1978, forever throwing out of alignment my one-year-old car, my second car ever and the first that I had ever bought new. And behind the garage, there is no longer an apple orchard where Kara and her next-door friend, Scott, used to play—only a large maple tree that must have also been there in the midst of the scraggly fruit trees.

Despite my caution, the ominous weight of events that took place there comes upon me anyway. And one house raises anew the vague sense of nameless danger. At present, I must avoid too close an encounter with this part of the neighborhood: I cannot yet tell you this part of the story.

So I turn away, walking on up the street and on past my second house in Wooster, a mere two blocks north of the first one and that much closer to campus. We lived in this house for ten years, the core of our life as a single-parent family. Here, too, is a porch where I used to sit and read, a smaller backyard, the garage that remains from our time in the house. I can spot in back the small shed that acted as a playhouse and even as a quasi-jungle gym for adventurous children who wished to climb up and find ways onto the garage roof. The swing set is gone, rusted into oblivion; the picnic table is gone—it now sits moldering in our current backyard—but I can recall our casual meals and comfortable exchanges around that table. Gone, too, is the giant tractor tire that served as a sandbox in the backyard and the other two trees we planted here on a later Arbor Day, one brought home by each of the girls from their grade school in 1981, Adriane in first grade and Kara in fifth.

I walk on, moving away from both houses and from the college. Attempting to duplicate old walks, I head out to the college golf course, where I would sometimes surreptitiously gather a few blackberries or Black-Eyed Susans and Queen Anne's Lace and lush Red Clover, cost-free festive touches for a rare adult dinner party while Kara and Adriane were with their father in the summer. I walk past the paper factory and back toward the first house again, passing the wooded lot that I used to frequent on walks in our early years—tangled brush and overhanging trees and children's pathways among the undergrowth. I enter it and meet two children, boys. Both are Black, and I am reminded of the rare but real hints of racial diversity in this working-class neighborhood, even when we lived here, in a town so marked by racial homogeneity. The boys are friendly, but we all are a little shy, so we go our separate ways. As they move on, I yearn for that old life when all was still new: that neighborhood, my daughters as children, the friendships they had, the friendships they lost, the time I spent with them, the times I could not be there for them. My own young self with my life ahead of me.

ON THESE WALKS NOW, I can no longer resist Hagar Shipley's phrase from Margaret Laurence's *The Stone Angel*: I, too, am "rampant with memory." But Hagar is ninety years old when she wanders through the places of her past; the phrase rightly belongs to her. I, in my fifties, am too young to claim it as my own. Still, Margaret Laurence understood it when she imagined that old woman haunted by the past. And how old was *she* when she wrote it? Still in her thirties? Much younger than I.

"Rampant with memory," I walk back toward the college, shocked at the thought that in my twenty-some years in Wooster, I have never lived more than a ten-minute walk from my current home—the third house into which we moved in 1988—or from my place of employment. What a narrowly circumscribed life that distance makes it seem. I pass the "new" music building, under construction when we left the second house for our current home, already ten years ago, and head toward Kauke Hall, the central class-room building on campus. This is the one consistent dwelling of my time here through these decades, though I have had different offices there and taken several research leaves, changing spatial relationship to my work many times. Now I relive my first approach, walking up the front sidewalk as I used to do, tracing the brick walk toward the landmark arch and its austere tower that mark the building for strangers trying to locate themselves on campus.

I LAUGHED TO MYSELF when the chair of the English department warned me, "This is a short-term position, a two-year contract." As if I wanted to stay any longer. At that point—in 1976, newly divorced and ready to make a new life—I felt that any more than two years would be a life sentence. Even now, my brother-in-law says to me, "I never thought you'd stay there so long." I didn't either. I was hungry for life, and I didn't think I would find it in a small town in Ohio. But it was a job and a perfect jumping off place for the life I planned to make.

The interview had gone smoothly. I had miraculously received an offer on the spot. I liked what I had seen of the department and was pleased at the prospect of teaching at a small liberal arts college; I repressed the thought that they were as desperate as I was and might well have settled for the proverbial warm body in the classroom so late in the hiring season. Never mind. This was the second of two offers I had received that July, and it was desirable in many ways: the location was close to family—my sister, Eileen, and her family would be only sixty-five miles away, excited to have us close by; the liberal arts context was familiar to me, the kind of teaching that I wanted to do; the town seemed a reasonable place for a single mother with two small children. Staying over for an extra night after the job was mine, I phoned my sister to rejoice. The next day I located a house to rent—from the person I would replace during his two-year leave of absence. The house felt right: oak moldings, three bedrooms, a basement, a front porch, a backyard, even a jungle gym. I quickly settled upon this path into my future.

My brother, Don, visited during those early weeks, passing through on the way to his own new life in California. But he was there to help me, too. First, we built a fence, working together to create a safe place to play in the backyard. Then I confronted childcare. In this, I had little choice since there was no available communal childcare for a child who was not yet toilet trained—like Adriane at age one and a half. So I ran a newspaper ad: *Childcare needed 20–25 hours per week. Two children, ages 1½ and 5. My home, good pay.* I had no idea how impossibly false this ad was—how many hours of childcare I would actually need for a job that regularly required at least sixty hours a week, even if many of them were at home, or what really counted as "good pay" when minimum wage was nowhere near sufficient. Childcare would be my biggest monthly expense, more even than housing. The pay I could offer was higher than minimum wage, and I insisted on paying into Social Security, but how could it possibly be enough? Still, just as I had known against reason that I would get a job, I also knew I would somehow make this work. I would set my house in order, make my children safe, and begin a life of my own.

DON VETTED THE EARLY PHONE CALLS from job applicants. I scheduled interviews with six women. I talked with Candy, nineteen years old, attending business school in the evenings, not particularly familiar with children. I talked with Lucille, garrulous, fixated on her pony, her step-grandchildren, her own mother. I talked with Sandy, who claimed much babysitting experience and spoke of the "necessity" of spanking the children sometimes— "only hard, not with a belt." I talked with Carol—African American, the only woman of color in the entire group—who had a school-age child of her own and wanted to do the childcare in her home; I was tempted but really wanted my children in our own home. Ollie didn't show for the interview.

That left me with Pauline, whom Don had liked on the phone and who pleasantly reminded me of a woman we had known on the farm. More crucially, she paid attention to my own views on child rearing—no physical punishment, a degree of freedom for the children, a mixture of nurturing and respect and caring discipline—and was apparently willing to tolerate my prohibition on candy, at least as part of any system of rewards. (Did I also make clear at the time my dislike of Barbie dolls and gun play? Or was that later? It's odd that I cannot recall.) As a forty-year-old mother of six sons and a daughter and as someone who had become a grandmother at age thirty-two, she seemed well prepared by experience to negotiate the demands of childcare. In any case, classes were about to begin, and she seemed like my best bet: silver hair, a warm face, a caring heart.

And Pauline turned out to be another of my miracles. In the five years she was with us, she was never ill, never unable to come to work. On her own, she took on light housekeeping tasks, believing—as I did—that children do not thrive under vigilant supervision. She seemed pleased to be in a house she could care for—larger and more sustaining than the house trailer in which she and her husband and teenage daughter made their own family home, her sons grown and on their own. And she was visibly devoted to Kara and Adriane and even to me. In the blizzard of 1978, when roads were closed and the college shut down briefly—something that has never again happened in the decades since—Pauline still came to work at our house, staying with Kara and Adriane while I trudged off to my office to grade papers and tried to maintain my professional life while the snow piled up around us.

BUT NOW the midwestern sky above the tower prompts a summer memory: my first approach to Kauke Hall as a new faculty member. Exhilarated to be starting anew—to be free of my past and entering a new phase, however temporary I expected it to be—I had walked boldly up the brick sidewalk, toward the building's landmark tower with the arch below, dressed in summer garb: jeans and sandals. Never mind the bee that flew between my toes and stung me angrily. Never mind the August heat, the hassles of getting settled in a new community—school registration for Kara's kindergarten, childcare arrangements, a new neighborhood, new people, new job. Never mind the severed strands of a life I had left behind me. Though it was 1976 and everyone seemed obsessed with looking back over a two-hundred-year US history, I was in no mood to be looking back. I was in no mood to fret over minor irritations. My mood, like the nation's, was euphoric, but my whole momentum was forward: to begin again, to move through the arch, through Wooster, and on into the life ahead. I had walked into Kauke as if I belonged, even as the red welt grew large and painful between my toes, marking my arrival.

14

Mommies and Monsters

N ow that I have resettled in Wooster after my New York sabbatical, my past and present seem even more entangled. Though it is 1998, a recent dream thrusts me back: the young mother who is me and not-me stands bare-breasted in a room with a nurse and my two children—both still young. The nurse looks at my breasts and challenges me: "You can't breast-feed any longer; your milk is gone." To make her point, she squeezes each breast firmly. From the left breast, she gets no result; from the right breast she gets a thin trickle. Desperate to prove her wrong, I squeeze the left breast even harder and finally get a thin trickle there, too. But by now both of my breasts throb painfully, futilely. I look over at my two growing daughters—Kara, a healthy preschooler, and Adriane, a thriving infant—and taunt the nurse: "But look. See how healthy they are. I must have been providing milk."

Peering into the past, I develop whole new anxieties that I couldn't afford to feel at the time: perils we evaded, ways we could have gone astray. I worry about all that I couldn't give my growing children. Then I look at them now: nourished and whole. And I, too: Can I find my wholeness and tell my own story?

SHORTLY AFTER FIRST ARRIVING in Wooster in 1976, I said to my sister: "Really, I think that children can almost raise themselves." And I meant it, believing in a kind of laissez-faire parenting, resisting the idea that I should constantly supervise their activities and thoughts. Even now I can see that each of them blossomed without the kind of mothering that the culture dictates. But I can also see that the situation was not really so simple: in those early years, I not only drew upon their own capacities to define themselves

143

and to give to others but also relied on Pauline as my surrogate. And I regularly turned away from hazards I could not handle.

Yet I was attentive in my own way. Surely, it means something that I made every effort to be there for them, that of those sixty work hours each week, I tried to put in as many as I could at home. During exam week, when I didn't have classes, I might turn on *Captain Kangaroo* and take a cup of coffee back to bed with me. I could at least be home while I graded papers: doing my best to meet these ever-conflicting commitments.

"Tell Mommy, tell Mommy" comes the little voice up the stairs. I am in my bed, still wearing my flannel nightgown, clipboard on my knees and student papers spread in an arc around me on mussed sheets, coffee beside me on my desk, which also serves as a nightstand. And here is Adriane, herself totally naked, "I wanna get up there. I wanna sit down there." She sits next to me on the bed, surrounded by student papers, saying assertively, "I sit up here. Kara did it. No, me did it."

"You took your clothes off?" I ask in my laissez-faire way.

"No," she asserts in her paradoxical twenty-three-month-old way.

WAS I THERE FOR THEM? I read to them, the one parenting activity I always chose when possible. And I talked with them. Reading Richard Scarry together, we would blend our reading with talk. I'd read, "Don't throw stones at another child. You might hurt him." And Kara, age five or six, would add: "Or her." Again reading Richard Scarry, this time about truck drivers—generically and most commonly "he"—Kara would add: "Or she." More poignantly, she would examine the Rice Krispies box and ask, "Are Snap, Crackle, and Pop he's or she's?" And then, challenging a privileging system that left her out, she added, "I know they're he's. Why are there more he's than she's in the world?" Surely they *were* learning my values, in whatever ways we had of sharing them? Surely, too, they were learning, with me, strategies for challenging the culture around them.

BUT I DID ALSO RELY HEAVILY ON PAULINE, who was our mainstay during our early years in Wooster. Make no mistake: she was my mainstay, too—not just my daughters'. She oversaw our household, nurtured Kara and Adriane, noticed when I was feverish myself, though still trudging off to work. Her kind face greeted me when I came home; her affection for my daughters was beyond dispute.

Still, I needed protective girding when Adriane wakened from her nap, climbed out of bed and came down the stairs, drowsy-eyed with red stripes of sleep on her face, asking, "Where's Pauline? I want Pauline." Even more, I needed protective girding when Kara, older and more invested in reasons, echoed Adriane's assertion with an additional twist: "I want Pauline. I feel like I know her better than I know you."

Grateful as I am, the sentence still chafes: "I want Pauline."

Children cannot, of course, raise themselves. In those early years, Pauline was an essential part of their nurturing. And in those early years, I needed to rely on some false notion that my vigilant attention was not required. What, then, slipped beyond my purview? What shall I now make of my laissez-faire motherhood?

ONE DAY, thinking I would take pleasure in drawing the parts of my life together, my college-age babysitter collaborated with Pauline to plan a surprise visit to campus for Kara and Adriane, including a visit to one of my classes, "Fiction by Women." Kara, five and a half, was up to the task, able to sit quietly and draw while I carried on. But Adriane, not yet two, ended up scrambling on my lap while the students and I analyzed George Eliot's *The Mill on the Floss*.

The discussion focused on the foreclosed choices for women in nineteenth-century novels: when self rises up, love is chastened, a woman drowns. In front of a classroom of mostly women—including my babysitter, who told me I was a model for her in her wish to make a life of her own—I needed to affirm that these either/or choices would not work for them, for us. There, too, were my two very young daughters. Could I be a model for all of them and also give to Kara and Adriane what they needed from their mother?

IT WAS DURING THIS PERIOD that Lawrence said to me on the phone: "How much time are you spending with Kara and Adriane? It cannot be good for them to have you so long at work." And he wrote to me in his usual mix of elliptical comment and abrasive judgment: "I could have told you, but you had to find out for self: now, Joanne, you have that frustrated feeling of full-time work plus home."

But how could he understand this life I was living, this full-time commitment to both my work and my daughters? Had he ever been the one who was wakened in the night to a daughter vomiting in her sleep? Had he been the one who cleaned the wall, gathered the pajamas and bedding, soothed the daughter back to sleep, started a load of laundry? I know he had often graded papers late into the night, but had he ever, once wakened to a vomiting daughter, simply used that time as an opportunity to work?

Lawrence's judgment grated on me when he was so blind to what my life was actually like, and yet it was a tremendous relief that this judgment at least resided at a distance. This, after all, was the life I had chosen: flannel nightgown, vomit, student papers, active daughters, caring babysitters. Unable to foresee the future that would come for any of us, I forged ahead, rooting myself in Wooster, disregarding external judgment, holding to the compass for this new life: my work and my daughters.

AS I STRIVE TO RECALL THOSE EARLY DAYS, I keep retracing old paths. Today, I again walk by the old house, but this time I make the turn up the alley. I pass the small back porch, the pale green house on the other side of our alley, the newly built garage. Breathing shallowly as I arrive at the other alley—running perpendicular to ours—I pause to recall the orchard that is no longer there. I never ate any of its fruit, but I still have a bitter taste in my mouth as I call it back to mind.

It was a Saturday in October, and we were newly settled in Wooster. The day seemed to glow around us: warm sun, blazing leaves, grass still green. The orchard had trees then, scraggly, but alive, and there were a few apples, most of them already wormy and rotting on the ground. Oblivious to the rotting fruit, I thought it a perfect day for children to play outside, for five-year-olds in one another's company to push just past the boundaries of their own yards and into a slightly more adventurous space.

The last time I had checked, Kara and her next-door friend, Scott, were dawdling under the single maple, among the aging apple trees, soaking up the autumn warmth. I felt confident in the safety of their explorations as I stayed in the house with Adriane, then a year and a half, the two of us comfortably playing on the dining room floor with Legos and wooden blocks and Fisher Price fantasy people.

But my emotional balance shifted the minute Kara came in from outside, though I could not immediately see why.

"What were you and Scott doing out in the orchard?"

Drawing on one of our most steadfast resources, we talked, together constructing the events of the previous half-hour. Those "big boys" had been there, too: teenagers unknown to me. They had teased these two young children, taunting them with possibilities both real and imaginary. And they had threatened to hang the cat from one of the apple trees. With that final taunt, they had tried to torment Kara and Scott into some sort of compliance. "Just put your mouth here," one said, "and suck on my penis. Or else I'll have to hang the cat from the tree." His friends had gathered around in ominous readiness to act on the threat, readiness to take their turn.

Kara knew about penises and vaginas, about rudimentary sex differences. And she knew that she didn't want to do this. But there was the cat—a small stray from a neighboring house, gray and slightly mottled like Virginia, the cat at her dad's house, the one animal that had survived our departure from the farm when we left her dad. The cat needed to be saved; too much had already been lost. When she came home, she was restless, unsettled, distraught.

"Are you all right? Did anyone touch you or hurt you?"

And now I go blank. I cannot remember her answer, no matter how hard I try. What I do remember is a flood of relief: she is all right; she has told me, knowing I am on her side, trusting that I will know what to do.

But I also remember a burning anxiety: I *didn't* know what to do.

I began with a conversation with Scott's mother, checking what Scott had experienced, how he felt, what we could do. Then, together at my makeshift dining room table—an old door on two saw horses, for I had not yet invested in furniture—she and I talked with the parents of the "big boy" whom both Kara and Scott had identified. As I should have expected, these parents denied any possibility that their son could be involved. In their need to protect their own adolescent son, they were adamant. Speaking hostilely, they advised us to go ahead and contact the police.

And so we did, for we knew we needed to act to protect our children. The police came and sat with us at the makeshift table. But they did not provide protection in their response: if we went forward, Kara and Scott would have to testify, to bear courtroom witness. Could we do that to our five-year-old children—ask them to tell again this frightening episode, to be questioned and examined and challenged, to engrave it indelibly in their minds? Could we go through that ourselves with so little assurance from the police that anything could come of the testimony of two such young children? This was, after all, before anybody really talked about sexual molestation, and even now, despite all the rhetoric, who listens to the broken narratives of half-comprehending children?

Inside me, the turmoil erupted. What of the other children, the children who might next hear these threats? What of the safety of our own children in this very neighborhood? But then: What of the lingering taint and monstrous stress if Kara and Scott were put through the further trauma of court proceedings, almost certainly—as the police insisted—without success? What of the memory that could not then be expunged?

I paced and worried into the night. I cried and talked on the phone with my sister. I hovered over my sleeping children, not knowing, not knowing what to do, whispering "I love you" into their sleeping ears. When finally I slept, I was haunted by my own nightmare visions: looming penises, hanging cats, frightened children, towering courtroom judges. And when I awoke, I decided to do my best to move on, to talk it through with Kara and her friend Scott, and then to let it go.

In subsequent months, Kara and Scott gradually let the memory slip away. But for years to come each time Kara passed the house in which the ringleader boy lived, she would feel a vague queasiness, revulsion tinged with fear. At least, that's what she told me several years later when I once again asked her if she remembered the incident with the "big boys" and the cat and the coerced response. "No. I only remember that I hurried real quick when I walked past that house."

ALL THESE YEARS LATER my emotional response to that house mimes Kara's: vague queasiness. By now, neither of us is even certain what actually happened. Did she submit to the coercion? Did Scott? Eileen's memory—events I whispered into the telephone, late at night, after the children were asleep—suggests a story of sexual imposition. But Kara maintains that she withstood coercion. And it is her memory on which I rely, for it is hers that is most consequential.

Perhaps for Eileen and for me, our imaginings simply came very much to life as we tried to sort out the rights and the wrongs, the strategies for action. I cannot be certain, for I have no way to test conflicting memories. But even now—as I worry about the other children, those who may well have submitted to the coercions next proffered by these "big boys"—I cannot regret that Kara, at least, did not suffer the second scarring of legal cross-questioning, events branded into her memory.

SEVERAL YEARS LATER, in 1979, after midnight, I would be wakened by a ringing telephone and then a child's voice saying to me: "Have you seen my mom? I looked all over the house for her, and I can't find her. My dad's here, but he's asleep, and I can't wake him."

This was Kara's friend Scott, seven months after we had moved to our second home in Wooster, no longer next door to him. He had wakened to a house that echoed with his loneliness. I talked to him for fifteen minutes, trying to assuage his worries, but I could not leave my own sleeping children to attend to his needs. After I said good-night to him, I drifted toward sleep, recalling his and Kara's narrow escape from sexual molestation two and a half years earlier. I worried about Scott's middle-of-the-night fears, about where his mother might be and whether his father was seriously ill or had fallen into a drunken stupor or maybe just into a deep exhaustion with life.

In my waking response, I had to trust that Scott would respond to my counsel to call another family member or perhaps, with persistence, to waken his father. Maybe I should have done more, but I did not feel confident that the family would welcome my intervention—or, more likely, I was simply feeling my own deep exhaustion with life. In my sleep, I dreamed of Scott's family home exploding, flames leaping from the roof, children caught in the damages of adult inattention.

NOW, with my memory reopened to old dangers, I walk farther up the street toward the college and recall another incident, an additional two years later, in 1981. A girl from the neighborhood had been playing in the college parking lot at the end of the street, half a block from our home at the time, two blocks up the street from our first home. She had picked up what turned out to be a live grenade, brought to campus by an unthinking college student. As I cross the parking lot, I reimagine the incident: the grenade exploding in a young girl's hands, the rush to the hospital, the scarring injury to her face and arms, the eventual repeated bouts of painful reconstructive surgery. I recall the wife of a college official saying to me, "Well, really, where was her mother? Why was she playing that way unsupervised?" I winced then and wince again now. For this child lived just across the street from us—an occasional playmate of my daughters, who at ten and six regularly played on their own in the neighborhood.

FROM THE SLOUGH OF MEMORY arises one more terrifying incident, also too close to home: on July 11, 1982, Krista Lea Harrison was abducted from the park across the street from her home in a small town in Wayne County, not far from our own small town in the same county. She was eleven years old, as was Kara, who had just celebrated her birthday that month. Krista's body was found six days later.

I tried to hide my uneasiness every time Kara and Adriane went to play on the swings and slide and see-saws in Jaycee Park across the street from our house. Over the years, I have continued to ask myself just where parents should draw the line: What vigilance is required for our children's well-being, and when must we take the risk—knowing it is a risk—of granting them the freedom to explore? And how are we to balance their needs against our own yearnings?

DESPITE SUPPRESSED ANXIETIES, I held fast to my new freedoms, my childcare arrangements, my commitment to my work and my daughters, my new life in neighborhoods near the college and in Kauke Hall. I settled into routines, developing a new confidence in classrooms and committee meetings, working with students who engaged my attention and colleagues who challenged my thought. Each day I welcomed Pauline for morning childcare and headed off to campus to teach my classes; most afternoons I aimed to return home—to work there while Kara was in kindergarten and, when I was lucky, Adriane napped. Increasingly, I needed to spend longer and longer hours on campus, but Pauline was flexible, responsive to the vagaries of my irregular work hours. And mostly I felt that I was successfully balancing my work and my daughters.

STILL, that first autumn a small respite in my schedule would occasionally open in me a loneliness, even a sexual loneliness, that I had not yet felt in the aftermath of my divorce from Lawrence. I usually managed to push this ache aside by reaching for the phone to contact old friends or by piling the three of us into the car for an impromptu weekend visit with my sister's family. I subdued these unwelcome feelings and returned to work, but I knew that in this crevice of loneliness lay a latent hunger.

My senses, then, leapt to attention when a male colleague paused in my office door one day during December. The college was between quarters, my children still on their own schedules of school and childcare—a hiatus when I could turn my attention to the scholarly writing I needed to do but also could set my own pace. Because Michael was from a different department— someone I had met in the mailroom and heard speak at faculty meetings, not someone I saw regularly during the semester—he seemed to belong in this hiatus. Standing in the doorway of my office, casually suggesting a lunch one day the next week, he seemed a welcome and unthreatening diversion.

But because I can still see him standing there, I know that my senses marked this encounter: a welcome presence, whether threatening or not I could not yet say. The threat, in any case, seemed minor: a ripple in my care-fully balanced life of work and children. I did not then yet know that he was married and did not think it necessary to inquire. For a lunch together, I would not even need to know, though at that point I assumed his invitation was entirely open, unshadowed by any need for secrecy or covert response.

By January, when we made a dinner plan, I knew that he had a wife and children, but I still felt confident that he would not have been so open if his marriage was "real." Our conversation at dinner ranged comfortably over campus politics, ideas of structuralism, ways to study gender in college courses—with only small smatterings of personal reference. After dinner, he offered to take the babysitter home and then returned for a glass of wine and more conversation.

Sitting on the living room floor—I still had no furniture—we then talked, opening that well of loneliness inside me. Tentatively, we acknowledged untapped dreams, spinning threads of affinity as we spoke of alternative lives, bigger than the ones we were at that moment living. I remember telling him that I meant to leave the Midwest—an enclosure I had long sought to escape—to make a life somewhere near the ocean and to write. With my children safely asleep in their bedrooms above me, I sat on the bare living room floor in the new home I thought was temporary, hesitantly reaching to touch Michael's hand as I limned a fantasy life beyond this one: a life of larger vision, greater range, higher purpose. I looked out the large double-hung window, mesmerized by the climb of the nearly full moon across the night sky, dreaming of some future life.

Even then I must have known such a life was fantasy, but there was something energizing about sharing a fantasy in this zone of absolute privacy: the two of us, dreaming futures beyond Wooster, beyond current constraints. I caught my eye on the glint of the moon and felt the beat of the ocean inside me.

"SAYING 'FUCK,' MOMMY? Are you crying, Mommy? Are you sick, Mommy?"

Yes, Adriane, I thought. I am sick. Surely I am sick.

NOT QUITE A YEAR LATER, the facade of success, which had already begun to crack in that first October in Wooster and had cracked a little more when Michael dreamed with me on my living room floor a few months later, ruptured visibly. The exuberance of my arrival had been real—my sister's joy in our proximity, my brother's visit as we together erected a backyard fence for my children's safety, my unshakable confidence that it all would work out; everything had seemed possible, all difficulties surmountable, bee sting and all. Now, my work was under way: I had walked through the arch of Kauke Hall into an academic life that welcomed me and prodded me into a public life I had not previously thought myself capable of. And my home was made, my daughters cared for, never mind that I had no furniture, little money. But my tears now were also real; my obscenities were shouted out against a life I couldn't after all contain: a year and a half beyond my divorce and already my freedoms battered their wings against the dangers that crowded around me.

Yes, Adriane, I am sick. But not sick in a way I can describe to you, a mere two and a half years old. Not sick in a way I can take to a doctor or explain to anyone. I am not even sick as I used to be sick at age nineteen, crying and pacing in an empty house, home from college for break, having just read Camus's *Caligula* and not knowing where to turn for reason and purpose. Now I am sick with the emotional pacing inside me, the physical pacing of the floor, the draining of tears down my cheeks, the crying out against something I still don't know how to name. I am sick with fear, sick with weariness and loneliness, sick with uncertainty.

Yes, Adriane, I am saying "fuck," pacing in the dining room, unable to see reason in my life, to move beyond the tears and the pacing, to know how to nurture you and your sister and myself, unable to close my throat against the obscenity.

I know that I must close my throat, staunch the tears—but not yet. Behind the refrigerator there is a closet, not really a storage area, but a place where things can be put, behind the exposed backside of coils and electrical cord. Into this small open space, I take my pacing, still crying, still saying "fuck." Here is a place to close the door, to bang my fists against the resisting oak, to calm the tears and the obscenities away from the questioning child on the other side of the door.

DID I REALLY DO THAT? Did I really cry out loud, failing so visibly to repress my anguish? Did I really say "fuck" and share tears with a two-and-a-half-year-old child? "Sickness unto death" was the phrase from Kierkegaard, but mine wasn't a metaphysical illness. It was a sickness unto myself.

THAT AUTUMN AFTERNOON—a Sunday, I believe—I had paused in my relentless work schedule and set aside a few hours to be genuinely *with* Kara and Adriane, to do something explicitly for and with them, not just to juggle the work and the usual weekend survival activities. Together we had set off to a campus performance of *Cinderella,* ostensibly produced for the benefit of small children. Though outings were not really my strong suit, I was pleased at this one—the portrayal of a folk story that Kara and Adriane knew well, an excursion for the three of us as well as a bit of social life, which was sorely lacking in my single life with my daughters. Children were still seen as a hindrance to professional life, a shadow presence to be held in obscurity. Indeed, at that point, I was aware of no colleagues with children as young as mine, no women with whom to talk about this double commitment, though I later learned that there were a very few of them and that they, too, lived their own covert parental lives. And to that I had added the secret relationship with Michael, further confining me even as it nourished some other part of me.

At *Cinderella,* we settled in to enjoy the performance and the community. Kara, already a very grown-up first grader, watched and listened attentively, taking in the familiar story. Adriane sat beside me, watching too, but needing to question: "Are those the bad guys, Mom? Cinderella's the good guy, right?" Using the easy division of good guys and bad guys, she negotiated her way through the play's caricatured stepmother and stepsisters and toward a comfortable division of the world. But, familiar as the story was, she kept wanting to confirm her understanding—"Those are the bad guys, right?"—until finally the woman next to her hissed sharply at me: "Could you please shut her up? Some of us are trying to hear the play."

The woman was no doubt well within her rights as an audience member. Perhaps others in the audience were glad for her admonishing presence. But I couldn't think beyond my own broken yearning toward community, my own fear that I had slipped into the social role of "bad guy." Fighting back tears, I quieted the beating inside me and merely tried to contain Adriane's words and my unreasonable anger until the end of the performance.

"MOMMY, ARE YOU CRYING? Saying 'fuck,' Mommy? Are you sick, Mommy?"

HOME FROM THE PLAY, we regrouped for the afternoon. Kara went out to play in the neighborhood. Adriane and I settled into the dining room qua playroom to try to distract ourselves. But now that we were home, I could no longer close out the Furies that pursued me. How was I making my life? What were the damages of the choices I had made? Where might I find some sense of commonality or possible community?

The tears I had fought back for the sake of public decorum now crowded to the surface, but with them came much more than an unknown audience member's remark. With them came all the rushing thoughts of the life I was trying to construct—the pressures of a job that would soon become a passion as well, the loneliness of raising children on my own, the worry about not only my own children, but also all the other children. And tangled into those concerns was the complicated relationship with Michael that had by now developed its own depth, well beyond the zone of safety within which we had first shared our larger dreams. All of these thoughts rushed at me, buzzing around me, tormenting me as I strove to keep my place in the weltered uncertainty that was my life.

Where was I to find safety? How was I to construct a secure world for my daughters? How was I to live a life large enough to encompass all of my dreams and hungers? I could no longer tell if what I wanted was premised on safety or openness to adventure. I could not tell in what ways my own needs and hungers were congruent with my children's needs and hungers.

Even now I cannot be certain of the choices that I made in those early years as a single mother. Like Tillie Olsen's single-mother narrator, I keep "dredging the past," weighed down by the mother memory of how a child grows and suffers; like her, I risk becoming "engulfed with all I did or did not do, with what should have been and what cannot be helped." I, too, feel the pressure of wisdom that may sometimes come "too late." I ask my own recurrent questions—about my life, about my daughters' lives, about other children's lives and other mothers' lives, about the knots and hazards that arise when lives pull against one another.

"SAYING 'FUCK,' MOMMY? Are you crying, Mommy?"

EMERGING FROM BEHIND THE CLOSET DOOR, I tried to calm myself. I stopped saying anything and simply sat on the floor. Still crying, I sat cross-legged next to Adriane in the dining room that had no table, only a door on two sawhorses, the dining room that was a playroom, virtually unchanged from the previous October when the orchard and I still seemed innocent, though so much else had changed in this one year in Wooster. Still crying, I sat there helplessly and stared at the litter of blocks and Legos and Lite Brites, at the Fisher-Price barn with all its tranquil animals, at the Fisher-Price castle with its trap door and its dungeon and its smiling little cylinder people.

I was still staring blankly when Adriane crawled onto my lap, patted my face, and wiped away my tears.

"Don't worry, Mommy. I'll keep the monsters away."

15

Why Are You Doing That?

S ummer has ended, and I have returned to campus. My time to write this book is gone, but I have barely begun to sort through my memories of those early years in Wooster. People ask me what I am writing about. They try to be supportive, but they wonder: What's the plot? Where's the conflict? Who would be interested in the story of an ordinary mother? I look for models that will help me, and I find a growing abundance of mother stories: humor columns in daily newspapers, problem-solving narratives of mothers with ill or difficult children, tragic stories of loss, and joyful stories of love affirmed. But as for plot, the same tired choice seems to prevail: my children or my work, my family or my "selfish" desires. In these agonistic plots, the battle is intense, but the resolution is clear from the outset: children and family must win; selfish desires must be beaten back.

And still I cannot begin to address all the questions when I keep hearing echoes of the reproach: What kind of mother centers a story on herself rather than on her children? Only a few rare narratives take the risk of Jane Lazarre's groundbreaking work *The Mother Knot:* to probe a mother's own experience in its distinctive complexity. And always that word: *selfish*. A selfish mother is monstrous, not really a mother at all.

THAT FALL IN 1977 I was again looking for work: my contract with the College of Wooster would expire the following spring, and I had as yet no option on a future contract. I half-heartedly sent out applications, knowing that my survival and my daughters' required a job. At the same time, I was absorbed by the job I held, the people I was getting to know. I looked beyond Wooster toward some dim future I could not see, though the roots of my life and my daughters' lives were already growing into the soil here.

156

At Thanksgiving, my parents came for a visit. I had never seen them openly argue, but now, as they settled into partial retirement, they were increasingly short with each other. Even here in my home for a brief visit, they allowed disputes about money and household chores to surface. My father was critical of my mother's impulse to "run around so much"—engaged in a wide range of community activities that took her away from home. I rallied silently in her support, appalled that anyone would want to restrain her active involvement and lively curiosity. But I was unwilling to choose between my parents, one against the other. The most I could say: "Leave me out of it—though you know where I stand: I could never encourage anyone to be solely a housewife." And yet I honored the commitment at the core of their nearly forty years of marriage.

During their visit, I took walks in the snow with my mother, even went on a shopping excursion for clothing—never my first choice of recreation. Though common enough for most mothers and daughters, shopping was for us just a way of being alone together at this difficult time. We talked carefully about her tensions with my father, as well as about the problems that both of my parents had in understanding my relationship with Michael. Because Michael was by then a central part of my life, I had taken the risk of sharing with them his importance to me; I had also been clear that my time together with him was necessarily shrouded in secrecy. Despite the threat of judgment, I could not withhold from my fundamentally caring and supportive parents this important dimension of my first year in Wooster.

My father said, "I don't understand how he can betray a marriage like that—or how you can live such a lie."

My mother said, "I can't imagine any other life richer, more meaningful than the life that we have lived as a family."

I tried to talk with them about the falseness that pervades so many marriages, that seemed to me to lie at the heart of Michael's marriage. I shared my criticisms of marriage as an institution, even as I reaffirmed with them the joy of my own childhood, my own growing up in a family shaped, at least in part, by the norms of the time and the gender expectations that lay behind them. The conversation was unsettling for them, painful for me, nonetheless necessary to the fabric of trust among us, a trust I needed to sustain.

During their visit, I also went car shopping with my father. It was time for me to purchase a car I could rely on, wherever I ended up moving on to, whatever decisions about work and love, about my children and my freedom, might yet lie ahead of me. Based on my father's advice, I did buy a car shortly after Thanksgiving. Having decided that the Ford Fiesta was the most reliable car within my budget—two values that were central to my father's worldview and of immediate interest to me—I purchased the only one available in my shopping area: insistently bright orange, not at all the color that either my father or I would have chosen, neither of us liking to call attention to ourselves. Kara and Adriane and I dubbed it "Marigold" to make its color more palatable to us; after that, we always called her "Goldie" and grew to love her, knowing that she was female like the rest of us.

THAT CHRISTMAS Goldie took her first real road trip, carrying Kara and Adriane to meet their father for the holiday. The trip was initially delayed by snow, brilliantly glistening snow, that caused Lawrence to postpone our plan to meet somewhere along I-70; we had not yet developed our routine of meeting at family restaurants and pancake houses at clearly designated locations. Several days running he phoned to inform us of the delay; we remained in the warmth of our home, waiting for the directive he would issue. Enclosed by the snow, needing my own space desperately, apprehensive about their visit to their dad, I lashed out at Kara and Adriane as they struggled with their uncertain disappointment. And then I hugged and held them intensely, almost compulsively: "I'm sorry I got so angry. I love you." Adriane, apparently unthreatened by my angers, was caught in her own worries: "I won't cry when I'm at Daddy's. I'll say, 'Where's Mommy? I miss Mommy. Is Mommy at home?' But I won't cry when I'm at Daddy's."

When Lawrence finally phoned to say he was ready, we set out for the planned meeting place, identified only by a hypothetical exit number, "Exit 1," which, it turned out, did not exist. We searched frantically up and down the freeway, seeking other exits and rest stops. Finding no sign of Lawrence, I phoned the highway patrol, asking about possible accidents; I phoned my parents, asking them to be alert to any possible message from Lawrence. Leaving messages, hoping for messages, we were desperate for some information as to where he might be, how we might find him.

Finally, the three of us settled at the first truck stop we had tried, though it was now closed due to power failure. We waited there anyway, developing

with the staff a sort of emergency camaraderie. When we could no longer repress our restlessness, I decided to drive on to Bloomington myself, leaving a note for Lawrence with the cashier in case he did eventually show up, though it was already three hours past the expected time. As the children and I headed toward the door in defeat, I looked up and straight at Lawrence two feet in front of us.

My relief overrode any possible anger, and his greeting astutely pushed me into a defensive posture: "We never should have done it today—I couldn't get my car started; the roads were terrible." He was so cleverly aggressive in this comment that I was on my way home before I realized that he could have forestalled all of this trouble by careful planning and a timely departure. We organized the children's gear—amid his usual grumblings about how much "stuff" they had brought—said our good-byes, and departed in opposite directions. I waved to them as they left, conflicted by the sense of liberation I felt, a freedom threaded through by exhaustion and loss.

On the return drive, I reflected on my life, especially my need to free some emotional time and energy specifically for Kara and Adriane despite the tensions and uncertainties I was experiencing. I reviewed the previous fall, noting its barrenness as I had worked to balance competing needs and wishes.

When I arrived home, the phone was ringing. I was greeted by the reassuring voice of my mother, who needed reassurance herself, having been worried ever since my earlier call. After we said good-bye, I turned toward self-nurturing: a simple meal of leftovers, accompanied by a glass of wine and a book to read.

By the time Michael came over the following afternoon, I had partially restored my equilibrium and was grateful to share time and conversation and touch. As we lay together in bed after lunch, I asked him what he was thinking. My journal records his response: "I'm thinking I spend a lot of time lately wondering what you're thinking."

And mine: "I spent the whole fall inhibiting my urges to say what I was thinking, and now it's hard to talk, to express those thoughts."

"We still have to talk," he said in the loaded language of relationships in distress.

"Yes, we do still have to talk."

But we couldn't really talk in the way that I needed, for his marriage remained the bedrock of a life with his children that held me in shadow. And my children remained my own bedrock.

AS CHRISTMAS BREAK NEARED ITS END, I turned my attention to that other central commitment and headed out to Chicago for the Modern Language Association convention, where I was interviewing for jobs in light of my two-year terminal contract. The interviews were markedly unsatisfactory. Though I remember few details, I recall one interview with the male representatives of a large department, gathered in a small hotel room, lounging on the beds, sitting on the floor, asking me questions that didn't even interest me much. Sensing condescension, I grew flippant, probably unprofessional. As I closed the door behind me, I nursed my loyalty to the job I then held, trying to ignore the fact that it was about to expire and that I had no other prospects.

Discouraged, I drove to my parents' home, where they had been taking care of Kara and Adriane while Lawrence also went on to the convention. In South Bend, I hugged my children hard as they strained to accommodate this next transition. We exchanged belated Christmas gifts with their grandparents, striving toward a holiday spirit.

The next day, after I had put the children to bed, my mother and I went to the grocery store for a few items, then sat in the car and talked. Enclosed in Goldie on the driveway outside my parents' home where my children slept and my father waited, we opened subjects we could hardly approach in unguarded spaces. She spoke to me of times when she felt she had failed me, painful experiences of her own motherhood and of my growing up, though I could not recall ever feeling neglected as a child. And we moved from those disclosures to her ongoing need to talk about my relationship with Michael.

She asked, "How is all of this affecting Kara and Adriane?"

I responded, "I'm not *just* a mother. I'm a person as well."

"Yes, but you *are* a mother. You wanted those girls very badly."

Even my mother could only barely begin to grasp why I might be part of such a relationship. What's worse, she seemed to judge me as a faulty mother. My father, she told me, was completely unable to understand. With an absolutist morality, allowing no mitigating circumstances, no emotional complexities, he found me guilty of adultery. And as I reflect back on that period of my life, I, too, shudder in self-judgment. I do not find myself guilty of adultery—I was not the one who was married, not the one breaking a pledge of fidelity—but I struggle now to understand the ease with which I took on the secrecy, subjecting my children to the disruptive effects of untruths at the core of my life.

Even so, I did my best not to lie to them. And somehow that bond of trust remained an essential part of our lives together. Early on in the relationship, Michael had occasionally come by when the children were around, and a five-and-a-half-year-old Kara had later asked, "Why don't we invite Michael over to play? Remember Michael—he did Lite Brites with me." Two-year-old Adriane had at least once wakened from a nap and come down the stairs to find me sitting in the living room talking with him. When he left, she asked: "Where does he sleep?" And then, "Where did that man go?" My response, "He went home," did not satisfy her: "No, he went to the store. He said he was going to the store."

Always I answered them as honestly as I thought possible; always I walked a line between the need to be open and the need to protect Michael from public disclosure. It was mostly easier to see him in private, after they were in deep sleep or during times when they were with their father. Even then I knew that the secrecy would become increasingly impossible as the children grew older and developed public lives of their own.

My response to my mother was accurate: I *wasn't* just a mother, and my needs as a person also surged within me. But whatever those needs, I certainly was pledged as well to attend to my children's needs. I had wanted those girls very badly; I did need to ensure their well-being. Could I do that and still hold myself together as the complex adult I knew myself to be—resisting the threat of fragmentation?

WHEN KARA, ADRIANE, AND I left my parents' home the next day, I felt excoriated, newly alone. We left a day earlier than planned, ostensibly because of a predicted snowstorm, but also because I had no more emotional resources: the job interviews in Chicago had not gone well; my parents sat in judgment upon me; my children needed a quiet space to be alone with their mother.

On the drive home, taking relatively untraveled roads, moving through the dark toward Wooster, I settled into the comfort of the car, a safe space to be with my daughters, away from the vertiginous pulls around us. But on these untraveled roads, there were few gas stations, fewer still that bothered to be open on a Saturday night during a gas shortage. My daughters and I moved through the night, pulled toward the safety of our home, threatened by the impending empty fuel tank.

Goldie was still new, so I had no sense of how far beyond the empty mark I could push. But I seemed to have no choice except to push on: there were no available gas stations. As I drove, with Kara sleeping in the back seat, Adriane in her car seat next to me talked without ceasing for five hours. Her refrain for the last part of our journey echoed the smallest but the most immediate of my own worries: "Where have all the gas stations gone? The witches and ghostes have taken all of the gas stations. Which way did they go? Did they go this way? Did they go that way?"

AS WINTER PLODDED DREARILY ON, I sought respite from the incessant balancing act by enlisting my sister and brother-in-law to look after Kara and Adriane while I went off for a weekend with Michael. Eileen and Jim did not approve of this relationship, but they supported me and knew I needed time to sort out my own life, so they were willing to add Kara and Adriane to their own three children to give me this adult time.

When the weekend came to an end—much of it enclosed by a literal fog that would not lift—I got into Goldie with rain falling around me as Michael set off in his own direction. By the time I arrived at my sister's house and retrieved my children, the fog was more emotional than literal, but the rain was turning to ice. The weather-prompted adrenaline probably would have kept me going, even without the coffee I had downed as a precaution against fatigue: early on the roads were frightening.

But the worst was ahead. Pulling onto I-271, I joined the flow of traffic, moderated to fifty miles per hour in consideration of the weather. Kara dozed in the back seat, but Adriane persisted in lively talk, even climbing in and out of her car seat—the kind you would not find in stores anymore, though it was then considered the safest model for toddlers and was even recommended for use in the front seat. In her exuberance, she regularly bumped against me. When one of those bumps pushed us onto a ridge of ice, I strove frantically to keep on course as we veered from right to left, first

verging toward the rail and steep gulf on one side of the highway and then toward the slightly less steep incline into the median. Behind me followed a group of cars, also going fifty miles per hour, exerting that pressure to maintain speed while regaining my course.

Throughout this wild ride, Adriane persisted in conversation: "Why are you doing that, Mommy?"

Finally, I began to slow as, helpless, I allowed the car to aim toward the grass median, turn a full 180 degrees, and halt, unscarred, facing the traffic. I watched the other cars pass, unable to tell whether the drivers were smiling or leering as they drove on by.

I took a deep breath, turned the ignition key, waited for a clear highway and pulled back into traffic, chastened and still panicked, grazed by death—not only my own, but my children's.

"WHY ARE YOU DOING THAT?" the voices chattered around me. The self-fracturing that had threatened me now exerted pressure in all directions: internal and external. But every direction in which I tried to move felt wrong. Though my children thrived, I do not know what the consequences were to them of my having deliberately chosen to live outside the norm in that period of their lives, hoping to make of my many facets a crystal that could sustain both them and me.

16

Shards of Freedom

It has already been a year since I returned to Wooster from my New York sabbatical. Teaching commitments have prevailed, though I try to resurrect the writing now that the academic year has come to an end. On these summer days, I often waken with the sun. I think about writing, but I'm not yet ready. I retrieve the newspaper from the front porch; I pour my first mug of coffee. Before I sit down to the daily ritual of coffee and newspaper, I walk into the small front sunroom beside the porch. Looking out across the street at the trees and the still nearly empty college parking lot, I find the angle of the early light as it reaches over Kauke Hall and through the leafy branches of the large black walnut tree across the street. Most mornings I greet the sun by placing my crystal in its rays, deliberately splitting the light into multiple rainbows, radiant in their full spectra of colors.

The summer ends—still no progress. I sigh deeply and return to the classroom, to my other work life in Kauke Hall, where I plunge into yet another academic year, watching the seasons go by.

The year proceeds; the earth continues to turn. In winter, the sun often cannot penetrate the leaden clouds that shroud it. When it is visible, it rises late, stays low on the horizon, and angles through the side windows to the south for much of the day. After the winter solstice, it shifts almost indiscernibly toward the north, and by midsummer on clear days it again rises over the tower of Kauke Hall, shines through the walnut tree, and finds its way into the front windows, just past dawn. I continue to watch the sun, to marvel at the light, to split it into radiant colors by positioning the crystal in first one window and then another, finding even more locations that draw colors from the setting sun as well. I renew my sense of wonder at the crystal's many facets, its heft and depth—my sense of wonder at the angle of

the sun and the complexity of light itself. I indulge in the secret pleasures of metaphor.

But still I am slow to write. The story remains resistant; I grow tired of saying "I," of trying to understand the rifts within me. Month gives way to month, season to season; time passes. We enter a new millennium: 2000.

ONE MORNING IN THE WINTER, I waken unusually early, even before the sun has risen, before I really need to be up in order to finish preparing for my morning class. The house seems strangely lit, and when I walk into the kitchen at the back of the house, I am greeted by a penetrating white light: a full moon hanging among the bare branches of the maple tree in back casts its eerie whiteness into a path across the floor. I recall Jane Eyre in her throes of agony after Rochester has shown her his mad wife in the attic: it is to a moon mother that she turns for advice. "My daughter, flee temptation," the moon says. But I do not live in the nineteenth century; I do not so easily lock madness away in the attic, confined in someone else. Nor do I espouse a moral code that defines for me what counts as a temptation that one must flee.

Let me then return to my first years in Wooster. I had no moon mother to direct me in that tumultuous time, and I still have no path toward certainty: the old models yield little guidance. But I need to keep groping for clarity.

I THINK AGAIN of Adriane's comment as she crawled onto my lap and patted my tear-streaked face, offering comfort: "Don't worry, Mommy. I'll keep the monsters away." I know that I did rely on my daughters' comfort, their reassurance. Already at age two and a half, Adriane had the capacity to love and protect, as did Kara at age six. But what if the monster is a version of oneself, the madness a simple extension of the ordinary? Who can provide protection then?

I rarely considered myself monstrous during those early years when I worked hard to affirm my freedom, even as I worked to give care to my two daughters and relied on their care for me. I often drew upon my sister, Eileen, to mirror my life back to me, to help me interpret and understand my experiences, even as she herself lived within the family norms I was resisting. As my mirror, she confirmed my sense of liberation when she accompanied me to sell my wedding ring and gold-and-pearl engagement pin to an itinerant gold merchant. I needed the money; I needed to be rid of these marks of marital obligation. She rejoiced with me in this symbolic unshackling even as she held back her own possible judgments of the life I was making.

My friend Elizabeth provided a different sort of mirroring: a rare shared reality beyond family. Feeling isolated as a single mother, I had been grateful when she—the only other single mother I knew at the time—sought me out and asked if she could come by my house to talk one afternoon in my early weeks in Wooster. Her circumstances differed from mine—she had only one child, older than Kara, and she already had roots in the community. But we rapidly developed an intimacy based largely on our feelings of mutual marginality and our pursuit of independent lives.

That first afternoon we sat on the floor in my unfurnished living room drinking coffee, talking.

"Do you call yourself a feminist?" she asked.

I nodded hesitantly, lacking the certainty that has since become insistent. And so we talked about what being a feminist might mean to us in the lives we were then living. Not yet divorced, she was on a short-term appointment at the college, recently separated from her husband, and trying to decide what came next.

As the months went by, each of us became a touchstone for the other, a gauge for the emotional minefields we were negotiating. Both of us newly freed from the constraints of difficult marriages, we struggled with basic survival but also celebrated our new independence and potential for sexual expression. This was the period when we also entered into relationships with men who were married—considering ourselves, in this as in other ways, "free women," defining our lives for ourselves.

THE PHRASE returned with a twist one evening the following spring. It was 1977; I must again circle back, turning the lens a little differently on this strand of the story. I had gone to Elizabeth's house for social respite, a rare moment away from both work and children. While I was there, her soon-to-be exhusband, Allen, forced his way into the house after she had refused to let him in. Furious over her counterproposal for property settlement as they negotiated their divorce agreement, he stood over her, leaning forward, hands on hips, glowering. She sat taut, a line of pure tension, holding herself together.

When he turned to me, he accused me of luring her into the life of the free woman. "You *independent* women," he sneered. "I know you. You married an older man because you were a child and you wanted someone to take care of you. Now you think you want to grow up. And you influence *my wife*."

He kept calling Elizabeth "weak"—"a weak woman who let three men fuck you." He insisted that he had given her "everything," waving his hands expansively at the house. He then turned to me, pointing an accusing finger: "This is *my* house. Get out of *my* house."

Tangled in the web of marriage, property, motherhood, and sex, I merely asserted friendship: "I am here visiting my friend Elizabeth in her house, and I'm not leaving." I tried to speak calmly, but I was shaking with fear and rage and complicity.

When I did go home to my own house, my own children, I did not elude that web. Although I had left behind the claims of wifehood and nuclear family, I could not so easily be a "free woman."

The question haunted me: How am I to be free? What is the meaning of "independent woman," especially for a mother? Allen had spat the words at me as an insult, but I was not to be insulted that way. Even my unashamed embrace of a married lover did not taint my pride in self-definition. Indeed, I sometimes took nourishment from that choice. After all, I was not the one with marital vows at stake; I was "free," and I certainly had no wish to marry again. Such a thought made me shiver with apprehension. I had my work and my daughters and no wish whatsoever for a husband.

But I did have sexual desire and desire for companionship. At first, Michael had seemed the perfect answer: enmeshed in a marriage he could not leave because of his children, he was both available and unavailable, open to a relationship that could not, would not, threaten to become entangled with property, possession, control. My children and I would remain in my own control.

That's how things had seemed at first: I would be "free," an independent woman with two daughters, a job, and a lover on the side—though you already know that this view was a distortion, even then.

ALL ALONG I recognized some irony in the phrase *free woman*. I had, after all, adopted it in part from *The Golden Notebook,* where Doris Lessing uses it with a keen sense of irony. She is fully conscious that Anna Wulf and her friend Molly cannot be genuinely free, are instead constrained: as women, as sexual beings, as material beings, as prisoners of their own culture. I saw this irony, but I also yearned toward the kind of bond they seem to share in their lives as "free women," constructing their own lives apart from men, acting on their sexual desires, and caring for children alone. I rejoiced in the novel's central attention to a woman's point of view—the validity of what Lessing calls "that filter which is a woman's way of looking at life." And yet I really could see that the section titled "Free Women" is bound by its conventional narrative form as well as by the constraints on its characters' lives.

In my own efforts to understand my life as a woman, I turned often to *The Golden Notebook,* with its themes of motherhood, friendship between women, sexual freedom, fragmentation, madness. Perhaps, like Anna Wulf, I saw myself and my friend Elizabeth "living the kind of life women never lived before," or perhaps I was simply continuing my lifelong pattern of testing my life against literary texts. In any case, the question persisted: What does "freedom" mean for a woman, for a mother—for me?

I REGULARLY EXPLORED these questions in my journal, a form I had returned to with new vigor in my attempts to understand my newly wrought life as a single mother. In this, I was also like Anna, obsessively writing things down to try to control the chaos of this period of my life. Deliberately imitating her, I bought a blue notebook, filling page after page with my personal experiences, and a yellow notebook as a place to record ideas for writing. Unlike Anna, I let the yellow notebook languish. But I stuck with the blue notebook, following the first one with numerous others—all spiral, all blue—that gradually stacked up in the corner of my bedroom.

I felt like a shriveled counterfeit of Anna, who tries to render the complexity of the world around her, including politics and international events. These larger concerns were too much for me: my writing life was mired in my personal life. But I adopted Anna's strategy of deliberate fragmentation as a way to control my chaos. In my journal, I periodically assessed the different parts of my life by category: "professional," "maternal," "sexual," "social." I checked off successes and failures, trying to contain the conflicting demands on me.

This strategy worked in its way. I could see concrete evidence that I actually was living a full life, rich in rewards and even scattered with a few successes. My teaching was going well; my daughters were bright, articulate, and pleasant to be around; my colleagues were respectful; my life was defined by my goals even as it was also enmeshed in the lives of others around me. In an early professional review, the vice president of the college spoke highly of my effective teaching and my willingness to take on extra duties. Above all, he emphasized my "eminent reasonableness," citing numerous stories in support of this quality in my professional behavior. My public persona was apparently succeeding: an independent woman.

BUT MY CLAIMS ON FREEDOM, independence, and reason were fragile. Beneath the surface, my emotions roiled, and my rational strategies ruptured: my strategic fragmentation began to look like a ruse. My journal periodically records voracious eating, as if I am filling a bottomless hunger: "greedily, mindlessly—watching myself and thinking—'so, you're *not* ready to stop yet—how interesting.'" Popcorn, toast with butter, bagels with cream cheese—as soon as I have put the children to bed, I try to fill my emptiness and numb my anxieties with carbohydrates.

In endless pages, my journal shows me as besotted and sex obsessed, hardly suggesting that free choice of sexual expression of which I was so proud. When Michael was in my bed, I explicitly enacted my fragmentation by locking my bedroom door, always prepared to grab my flannel nightgown and leap to respond when a wakeful child came looking for her usual maternal comfort—keeping the parts of my life separate from each other.

I took on more and more tasks at work. I floundered among too many goals and obligations, repressing the judgments made by my parents, by the culture around me. My recurrent refrain, "I am so tired," was joined by another refrain, "I am so lonely." In short, despite my "eminent reasonableness," I was lonely, disoriented, fragmented—not by strategy, but by necessity. In one journal entry, I concluded that single parenthood was the loneliest experience I could think of.

IT IS PAINFUL to me now to reread my journal from those years, to see there yet again the image of the madwoman so familiar from literature. The pages become an endless emotional vortex, drawing me into that self-absorption, showing me what others might see as monstrous irresponsibility in my mothering, in my sucking neediness. As I read, I sometimes lose track of which year I am reading about, which time period in the unceasing pattern of breaking up and coming together with Michael, of brutal fatigue and overwhelming responsibilities. I grieve at the relative absence of my daughters in my obsessive narrating of my experience; I catch only glimpses of the professional person I know I was becoming; I cannot find the mythic self who was strong on behalf of her daughters and her freedom. What I thought were independent choices fall instead into the hazardous patterns of Cinderella or Sleeping Beauty—waiting to be rescued.

I sometimes confronted that risk directly—"No, I am no Snow White, no Cinderella. Defiantly, I look at my life: I am living a full and self-reliant life. I am doing, alone, what most of the world seems to assume requires the inevitable effort of two people. Defiantly, I shake my fist at the world and at that vulnerable, sad, insecure self lurking inside me, the self who is waiting." Goading myself with unacceptable fairy-tale models, I would then decide to break up with Michael and focus exclusively on my daughters and my work. That relationship, after all, was bound by secrecy anyway and thus impossible to integrate into the rest of my life. It was the one fragment that I might break off from the whole.

IN ONE OF THE MORE POTENT BREAKUPS—January 1978, one year after we had our first dinner together—Michael and I have met at a friend's apartment, away from my home, my children, our other commitments. It is a third-floor apartment in an older house: we can look out over neighboring rooftops, through snow-laden branches. Icicles hang from the eaves, dripping and glistening in the sun as they magically grow ever longer, ice spears constructed by melting and freezing. We watch them as we lie together on the couch, silent, wrenched in anguish, unable to speak. We cry together, holding each other as we heave forth our sobs. The world outside lies still and beautiful, the snow clean, deep, pure.

He says, "This is probably the most beautiful day of the winter." I ask him to read my recent journal entries, trying to make him see my pain. He sees judgment there and pleads, "Don't think those things you've written about me in your journal are true." Touching his face, I respond: "One thing: you *are* worthy of love. I wouldn't do this if I could see any other way." Abruptly, I say good-bye and leave.

BUT THAT WAS NOT OUR LAST BREAKUP. We had yet many more comings together and splittings apart before we finally did come to the end of the affair. In that first breakup, I had again turned to *The Golden Notebook* as a reference point: "Anna Wulf says there are some kinds of pain one never gets over—I think *this* will be such a pain."

That's how it felt: one of those moments at which time stops, freezing the emotional intensity into permanence. That's how it felt: there was something unique and central about this love in which I felt for the first time in my life simultaneously treasured in body, honored for intelligence, loved for who I saw myself to be. The irony is obvious—that I felt whole in this relationship premised on the necessity of fragmentation—but the feeling was real enough.

As months went by, I retained those feelings even as I came to understand that the breakups finally did need to be permanent: my freedom was deeply compromised, as was his life. Like most affairs, this one was no doubt electrified by the currents of secrecy, the extra adrenaline charge that comes from existing apart from the rest of life, intensified by seclusion. Like most affairs, this one no doubt went on much longer than could possibly have been healthy for either of us. Like most people involved in affairs, we thought we were different from all of the others.

In that era, as in this, advice columns regularly ran responses to letters from suffering "other women": get out of that situation, they said; what he does to his wife is what he will eventually do to you. My sister, again my confidante, warned me that any relationship that existed in isolation from other parts of one's life could not truly be tested. My parents referred me to a "Dear Abby" column citing "Mistresses, Anonymous" for women who couldn't break free of an obsessive affair.

And it's true that I suppressed many warning signals, including a comment that Michael would make to me: "I couldn't live with you because I couldn't live with your daughters." On those rare occasions when he saw them—risking small breaches in our secrecy and seclusion—they did not know how to behave around him; they were not used to my attention being split between them and a man, and they immediately acted out. I knew that I should heed such warnings and especially that there was something dangerous about being told that the problem was my daughters. But I needed intimacy and may well have been able to develop it only in that protected enclave: perhaps I, too, could not endure a split in my attention.

My daughters and my freedom—and sexual intimacy, too? Was it remotely possible to have them all? And if not, what would I have to sacrifice?

AFTER MICHAEL AND I finally did break up, I made rare but instructive forays into a dating life. One evening, for instance, my date and I kissed passionately at the door as we said good night. But then he pulled back: "I don't want to become intimate with you—you're too independent. Even though you are all the things I value—intelligent, independent, attractive— I've decided it's better to avoid feminists. Relationships with women are safer if merely sexual." At least that's the distillation I wrote in my journal. And the conversation certainly reinforced a perception of most men that I had long since formulated. Another case in point: after going out with me for a few months, a different man finally told me of another woman he was seeing in Colorado. He told me he "admired" me, but that I lacked the mystery and unpredictability of this other woman: I was too much what I seemed to be.

Even though I was not particularly interested in long-term relationships with either of these men, both left me feeling rejected. Both reinforced my sense that for most men, independent self-definition was antithetical to sexual attractiveness in a woman. Children did not belong in either model. The pieces could not be assembled into a single whole.

BUT I HAD CHOSEN to make a life of these conflicting pieces, even a life outside the structures of marriage, resistant to the dynamics of ownership that I saw there. I disliked the proprietary sense that both men and women invested in their marriages. I tried not to resent the casual conversations in grocery stores, at school potlucks, on lawns as children played: the conversations in which wives claimed as their own the multiple accomplishments of their husbands and made clear that I could not possibly be doing as good a professional job as their husbands or as good a mothering job as they themselves were doing.

These wives were right to see my life as a possible challenge to choices they had made. I was right to notice how little cultural support any of us women had for the lives we were trying to make. And all of us were right to wonder what children require of their parents in order to thrive. What would it take for my own children to thrive?

I WORRIED INCESSANTLY over this question. I had had this debate with Michael many times. I had even accused him of joining the forces of the wives that I saw ranged around me in hostility. They were the chorus of the culture, and I felt a pariah. The judgment that I was "selfish" rang harshly in my ears, though no one really spoke it aloud. My silent internal response often was, "Guilty as charged," and yet I continued to resist that guilt, always struggling to assemble myself from what seemed to be broken shards.

I would continue to struggle with these questions well after Michael and I ended our relationship, though I was moving on in halting steps. I would soon be in the midst of my fourth year at the college—employment eked out one year at a time once the first two-year contract had ended. I would also lose my friendship with Elizabeth. Encumbered with choices of her own, she decided we could no longer be friends. That mirror was broken. Eileen would remain, as would my parents and brother.

But even then, Michael continued to be a kind of internal gauge for my thinking, and when *Newsweek* published a cover story in February 1980 titled "Children of Divorce," I was prompted to try again to explain to him my views on marriage and divorce, despite the long silence since we had broken up. I still have a copy of a letter I wrote to him. I began by quoting something he had said to me insistently: "I do not believe in divorce." I was still angry at the moral absolutism, but even more at the implicit judgment of my own decision. And so I went on to argue that my decision to divorce had been "full of moral complexity, but both moral and essential—the first major decision that I made as an autonomous adult" and central to "who I am, how I can and must live."

I was arguing with Michael, but I was also arguing with the views I saw at the core of the *Newsweek* article as it decried the loss of a stable society and seemed to forecast inevitable disaster for children of divorce. Though it offered, buried in the penultimate paragraph, the standard admission that it is probably worse for children to live in an "embattled household," I felt the weight of the article join the weight of Michael's opinion: divorce is bad. And again I felt judged.

But my growing feminist awareness also led me to see that the increase in divorces—a pattern I had participated in—suggested what I called "a period of cultural ferment," some of which was urgently necessary. Apparently still trying to convince Michael, I wrote: "You once told me that one of the main things I had given you was a fuller understanding of feminist issues. And I remember thinking: is that all? . . . But now I see what a profound gift that is—or could have been: the felt knowledge of how so many social structures devalue women—encase both men and women—and the need for fundamental revaluation of human relationships and lived experience."

When I read this letter now, I hear echoes of the work I had begun to do in women's studies as well as the pain I still felt at Michael's departure from my life. But most of all I hear a poignant need to make someone *hear* my thoughts about my life choices. I concluded the letter: "To me there are no ideal circumstances for raising children in our current society—all we can do is try to live our own lives as best we can and hope to share something of value with them, offering them love and support. But I guess that's really what you're trying to do, too, isn't it?"

IN COMING YEARS, I would continue to maneuver among my multiple commitments, testing out what might come next. What I didn't notice as I dodged through the halls of Kauke in those early years, meeting my obligations despite my hidden life, was that Wooster had become my home—the place my daughters might grow, the place where I had work that mattered, whatever my dreams of elsewhere and other things might have been. Perhaps

I could assemble the shards of my freedom anew. At the center, I would place my work and my daughters, the forces that drew together what remained. But I still did not know if all the pieces *could* coalesce: a profession, children, and a mother who lives her life fully without jeopardizing her children, a free mother, a whole person. Was such a life possible?

17

Not Demeter

September 2001. Among my courses this semester, I am teaching "Seminar in Women's Studies," a small group of students meeting Tuesday and Thursday mornings. We are currently investigating feminism in other cultures, focusing this week on the complexities of women's activism in Egypt among the entanglements of Islam, nationalism, and shifting historical emphases. But our intense discussion Tuesday morning is bizarrely interrupted by the dean of the faculty, who comes unannounced into our classroom as he moves from room to room, saying: "The Twin Towers have fallen; the Pentagon is on fire. We think it is inappropriate to continue with classes under the circumstances."

The students and I look at each other in stunned disbelief, murmuring our mutual incomprehension before quietly gathering books and papers and straggling out into different parts of the campus to seek information, comfort, the possibility of comprehension. Finding no one to clarify events, I seek a television from which to get more concrete information. But instead of insight all I get is a picture of the mayor of Cleveland, announcing that the city has been shut down because of a likely threat on the airport there.

Still uncomprehending, denied phone access to New York and Cleveland and now frantic about the safety of loved ones—Kara and Adriane, both living in New York, and Ron, working in Cleveland—I decide to go home, where I can gather news while I wait to hear from these disparate family members. Seeking clarity but not wanting actually to see events as they unfold, I tune every radio in the house to NPR. Up and down the stairs from basement to third floor I pace—up and down, again and again—willing the phone to ring, to be reassured that my loved ones are safe, even as I grieve the fallen towers, the lost lives, the terror intruding from unknown sources.

Hours of uncertainty pass before I am able to make contact with all of my loved ones. I finally hear that Kara and Adriane are safe, though they were uncomfortably close to the site of the horrifying images that play repeatedly across television screens. Ron, too, is safe—as it turns out, there never was a real threat on Cleveland. None of us share in the immediate tragedy, but, like most Americans, we are a bit more fragile in our return to daily life, our security ruptured. My maternal anxiety surges anew: such concern does not end with children's departures into adult lives of their own.

I RETURN to classrooms and committee meetings, carrying forward from day to day. But I am finding it increasingly difficult to focus on my past life while the outside world clamors around me. Already bruised by the divisive presidential election last November, I am more and more debilitated in thoughts of political change.

And once again we are a nation at war. Since childhood, I have held to my pacifist convictions even as I have tried to develop a more complex understanding of the role of violence in history. Following these terrorist attacks, I try anew to comprehend a rationale for war. But the "enemy" in Afghanistan remains blurry, and I abhor the thought of sending young American men and women to die and to kill. Is this another senseless war?

Again I set this writing aside until I can find more uninterrupted time and clearer thinking: the end of the academic year.

SUMMER 2002. On my daily walks through Wooster, I decide to take a new direction, seeking out different paths from the outworn ones, trying to free my thinking. Now I walk out away from the college, down into and then up through Christmas Run Park—a municipal park built against a bluff above the small creek that runs through it; at its base is the playground; opposite the bluff is one of the city swimming pools. I walk through the park early enough that the heat and humidity are still bearable; I feel the warmth of the sun gather on my back as I walk west and then on my face as I return. I watch the changing vegetation as June moves into July: the wild roses no longer bloom; the blackberries glisten darkly among their thorns.

This morning I find seven ripe berries—left behind by the birds—black and lustrous, earthy, tart. I pause, savoring, as I listen to the mourning dove on the wire above me. Listening, I focus not on the final *whoo, hoo, whoo*—the mournful sound by which the bird is christened—but rather on the second of its five syllables. First comes the almost inaudible initial intake of breath, a grace note, and then the second, more profound intake, a rising plaintive call to prepare for the mourning. This second intake, for me, holds the real sound of pain in the bird's call.

Each day as I walk and watch, listen and taste, I also muse, recalling and constructing. In the background, I hear the plaintive call, leaving behind its initial alto, questioning as it rises higher.

I TRY TO REMEMBER how it really was: the repeated separations thrust upon my daughters, children of divorce—thrust, too, upon their mother and their father. For most of my daughters' growing years, we lived through these seasonal divisions, one after another, unnatural but tied to the rhythms of both nature and culture: school years with me; Christmas break, an occasional spring break, and much of the summer with their father. As the seasons blossomed and faded, Kara and Adriane made their journeys back and forth between their mother's world and their father's.

Lawrence and I would usually meet midway at some nondescript family restaurant, neutral territory, our daughters moving from one car to the other and taking with them the myriad belongings by which they tried to transfer a feeling of home: stuffed animals, special toys, books. They worked hard to establish themselves in both places; I worked hard to maintain my own place in the rhythm of the seasons. Like Demeter's mythical world when Persephone was stolen from her, my world blossomed when my daughters were with me and faded when they and their aura of belonging were gone. But it is also true that sometimes I needed the fallow time of their absence, time to myself.

NOW, in my need to remember, I intentionally and self-consciously spend four days in pure solitude, reading through old journals, again asking myself: What sort of life have I made? What were the consequences for Kara and Adriane of making our lives, so deliberately, apart from their father but also connected to him? Divorcing their father was surely the catapult into the life that they and I then went on to make together.

As I read through those old journals, I am overcome by grief for my daughters: how unattended they must have often felt, how lonely on the earth of their childhood, especially during those summers when we were apart. Indeed, among the journals, I find a few of the letters they wrote to me during those summers: careful in their expressions of hurt and loneliness, the pain they felt at their father's denials and outbursts, and the love they nonetheless nourished for him and for me in our separation.

I think of the life I left in 1975 as well as of the life I went on to make. Leaving the farm life that we had shared, I relinquished not only my position within a nuclear family, but also my tenuous links to the natural world, the rhythms of growth and harvest. But even when I lived that life—watching for sun and rain and frost, feeding the animals, planting and hoeing and weeding in the garden—I never had any of that power that resides so vividly in Demeter, who could make the earth bloom or not according to whether Persephone was with her.

Though Lawrence regularly and seasonally pulled Kara and Adriane away from me to a different place, he was not Hades, their kidnapper, prince of the underworld. He was their father. And I was no Demeter; I could not control the seasons or my daughters' happiness—I had few ways even to influence their father's choices as to summer or winter visits, joy or gloom. But I did make choices with the resources that were available to me. I mostly drew upon more ordinary human resources: the honesty, the trust, the respect, and the laughter, too, that reside at the core of my love for my daughters.

IRONICALLY, I was the one who had initially enforced what I came to see as my daughters' recurrent journeys into an underworld. I had known full well that I needed this divorce, but I also knew that my daughters should not be severed from their father. It was I who first insisted, against Kara's protests, that she must go with her father. Adriane, still breastfeeding, would remain with her mother for this first visit to the father, though it would not be long until she would follow her sister in this pattern.

The memory is painful: that first spring of our outlaw existence, while we were still in Bloomington, I bodily carried a kicking and screaming Kara from our apartment to her father's car; I was the physical instrument that enforced this division of her self. Needing to give comfort, I murmured to Kara, providing an undercurrent for her screams, that she needed this time with her father, that he, too, needed time with her. Needing comfort myself, I added the silent reassurance that this visit was essential to the life we needed to make. Almost wordlessly I strapped her into the seat belt, there in the gravel parking space behind our poverty-marked apartment. I carried her, a flailing four-and-a-half-year-old, to her father's forest green Datsun station wagon and clipped the belt into place, constraining her into this new life that she had not chosen. She would go with her father for our own good, like it or not.

GRADUALLY we settled into our rhythms, though the undercurrent of tension persisted. During our first spring in Wooster in 1977, we reiterated and confirmed the pattern. This time there was no kicking or screaming, only a small node of stress. As we anticipated Lawrence's coming to retrieve Kara and Adriane from their maternal home—a rare time when he picked them up rather than our meeting midway—Kara was dilatory in getting ready for bed, as children often are. I called out a directive, as a parent often does: "Speed it, Kara." She responded, again as children often do, from her own apprehension. Her words, though voiced as angry outburst, nonetheless conveyed wisdom beyond her years: "Don't you know I'm only a *child*?"

She *was* only a child, not yet six years old. And I was the mother, required by self-definition and by cultural assumption to give priority to her care, to exert my power on her behalf. But as her mother, I often felt that I had little available power of my own—or little energy: I relied very heavily on her to care for herself and often for her sister, too.

I have come to see this highly developed sense of responsibility as a common characteristic among oldest children—surely my own older sister, parented in a traditional nuclear family, exemplifies this quality—but there is more to it than that. It is not incidental that Kara's outburst took place at a time of anticipating a visit to her father's house. Beginning with that first visit to the farm from our apartment in town, the moments of transition were always difficult. Still, I cannot dispute the perception that in many ways I did require both of my daughters to take on responsibility at very young ages; I gave them very little time to be "only a *child*." How were they, then, to choose the nature, the seasons, of their own world? They could not choose to be with their father or their mother. They could only choose to make their own lives split between two quite different worlds.

THE RETURN DRIVE was almost always easier: all three of us would rejoice in our reunion after we had said good-bye to their father. In the early years, Goldie would fill with Adriane's jubilant talk and gleeful laughter as Kara read quietly, with focused concentration; when Adriane fell asleep, Kara would join me in deeper talk, sharing experiences, probing for insight into their life with their father or their life with me.

Even in those early years, Kara observed emotions very carefully, and Adriane soon joined in. "Mommy, why do Daddy's feelings get hurt more easily than yours?" Kara would ask. "I can say things to you that I can't say to him." Or she would tell me of her anger and her stubborn resistance to her father's rules—choosing to go to her room to read and forfeit dinner rather than comply with his demand that she work with him on the jigsaw puzzle in order to "earn" her meal. Or she might again ask that loaded question: "Why did you have Adriane when you were going to get divorced so soon?" And a few years later Adriane might chime in, with near pride, "I'm almost illegitimate"—figuring out that she was loved for herself, not for her place in a "normal" family. Talking through their observations, we would mend the tears in our bonds and find again our ways of being together. Sometimes, too, we would join together in silly songs or rhyming games. Nearly always, in relieved alliance, we would share feelings and thoughts, silliness and sadness and joy, the three of us moving through the miles toward home.

BUT ONCE WE ARRIVED HOME, the mood of joy and easy trust could not persist indefinitely. I think of our reentry in March 1978. Kara and Adriane—like most children returning to their home turf—ran outside in pursuit of neighborhood friends. Recovering my household identity, I swung into action. I started to cook supper, put milk on to boil to make yogurt, fiddled with a fickle light bulb in the kitchen—and blew an electrical fuse, leaving me in panicked darkness. While I was in the basement, changing the fuse, the milk on the stove boiled over. No doubt I, too, boiled over. Hollering out for help amidst all this chaos, I sent Kara into genuine grief: "You don't want me home. I thought you wanted me home—but you don't."

I *did* want them home, *did* need them home. I needed the seriousness of Kara's voice when we engaged in grown-up conversations; I needed the softness of her newly washed hair and the gentleness of her smile; I needed her strength of will, her emergent wisdom, the edge of her self-assertion. I needed, too, the glimmer in Adriane's eye as she teased me—her verbal quickness and the curved flesh of her bottom as I carried her to bed. I needed the sensory pleasures of bathing both of them—their play with bubbles and dripping hair; I needed the cuddling at bedtime as I read "Rumpelstiltskin" or *Little House on the Prairie*. I *did* want them home, but the transitions from solitude to family for me, from one life to the other for all of us, were often turbulent.

LIKE MY DAUGHTERS' LIVES, my own life was constructed on this split, Lawrence's world and mine. But I also lived on my own rift between freedom and loss, love and responsibility. On the drive home after I delivered Kara and Adriane to their father, that rift would be my emotional dynamic: freedom and loss. Though it is sometimes tempting to see this duality as my own maternal inadequacy, I also see that it is what parents often feel when their children are otherwise occupied. Indeed, it is in some sense at the core of parenting: the children reside at the heart of all matters, but they also deplete emotional resources. Surely every parent needs occasional reprieve? Perhaps even Demeter, roaming the barren earth, mourning Persephone's absence, secretly rejoiced in the temporary release from responsibility.

ON ONE OF THOSE EARLY JOURNEYS between worlds—on July 31, 1977, when Kara was six and Adriane was two—I took them the full distance, delivering them to their father in Indiana and then immediately turning around for the return drive: 680 miles total. The girls had been particularly difficult in the car on the way, whining and complaining. I surmised that this was because I was delivering them to their father or perhaps because I was myself on edge as I anticipated the long drive, the encounter with Lawrence, the direct confrontation with the split in our lives. When we arrived at his house, I was edgy, nervous, pacing as if caged, unable to sit still for the lunch he had prepared or to listen to his observations on my parenting. Finally, I kissed the girls good-bye, told Lawrence that he would have to apply the impetigo medicine that they both needed, and drove off alone, already missing the girls yet needing space desperately.

As I set off, I felt free but without ballast. Aching with fatigue, I pushed on. Partway into Ohio, I paused for coffee and a bite to eat—slipping, while eating, into total absorption in the Alice Munro stories I had brought along for company. I think it was *Dance of the Happy Shades,* an early book, when Munro was coming into her extraordinary gift of portraying the relational life of families unsettled by undercurrents of rupture and peril. Perhaps through the alchemy of these stories with their many layers of reality—or perhaps it was more simply because of food and caffeine—something changed during that stop. When I returned to the car, I was no longer fatigued or ungrounded. My nerve endings sprang to the surface, alert, open to sensation. I drove on into the gathering dusk with an altered sentience, open to the world through which I drove, repressing any underlying peril in my own family life.

Heading east on I-70, through farm land, toward the increasing traffic around Columbus, I followed my thoughts with this heightened alertness even as I followed the highway east, relishing my freedom, both grieving over and rejoicing in my daughters' absence. In the distance, I saw a gathering of patrol cars—three or four of them—lined up beside the road ahead, blue and red lights flashing. As I approached, slowing with the traffic, the scene redefined itself: a heifer came into vision just ahead of the patrol cars, moving parallel to the road, facing into the traffic. She loped along easily, not seeming conscious of either the cars passing her or the officers behind her: fawn colored, doe-eyed, a Jersey. Thinking of my daughters and remembering our lost life on the farm, I smiled nostalgically as I looked over at her, momentarily opposite my passenger-side window: I've always liked Jerseys, their look of gentleness, deerlike, and the rich cream you can skim off the top of their raw milk. I kept on moving with the traffic, my mind split between past and present, still sentient, alert.

Had it been a deer, I would have known, I think, to sense a threat—deer leap unpredictably into the highway, leaving radiators smashed, drivers pinioned, and flesh rotting beside the road. But this was a loping heifer, nearly old enough to mate, soon ready to give birth, to give milk—not likely to leap unpredictably into the slowing traffic. So I didn't see the danger. I just drove along with the traffic, absorbed in my own thoughts—loss and freedom—bracketing my concern for how my daughters felt in their father's volatile household.

The heifer was already behind me when I saw the officer, legs apart, solid on his feet, reach into his holster, pull out his gun and take careful aim, his right arm steadied at the wrist with his left hand. I saw the tension in the man's body build and then jerk in release. As I kept on driving, I heard the gun fire eight or ten times, methodically, repeatedly. And then I was past as the last shot hung in the air.

That was all. Moving with the traffic, I saw no more. I only imagined the falling body, the young heifer bleeding beside the road, head thrown back, eyes wide open in shock. In my rearview mirror, I saw only the slowed traffic, now clotting, the blue and red lights still flashing. I saw no resolution to the scene that had been set. But I held in mind that image of the healthy, casual animal and forced myself to imagine as well the corpse that now lay behind me on the shoulder of the highway as other cars drove on by, taking in this instantaneous impression of death—the Jersey heifer, deerlike, lying lifeless beside the road—as I had the previous moment taken in the vision of life. I still couldn't decide just where the danger lay: With the heifer who might drift into traffic? With the officers and the guns? Or simply with some collision of bodies, of events apparently beyond anyone's control?

Farther on, as evening approached, the clouds nearly overpowered the declining sun; then the sun reemerged and etched pictures in the sky. In my state of receptive sentience, I felt all the images playing along my nerves. First, I saw a huge mound, billowy yet solid, a majestic throne from which lines of light rayed upward—recalling some painting I had seen in a museum or perhaps a stained-glass window in a church years earlier: a deity emerging from the clouds, reaching into the heavens. I watched this configuration over the miles as I drove onward, thinking wryly, "This is the sign that a friend had suggested I seek in my troubled life." But how was I, an unbeliever, to interpret this "sign from God"—with all of my nerve endings exposed, my grief for my daughters' lives with their father unarticulated, and my worries about their lives with me repressed?

I continued to watch as the rays of light dissipated. The mound itself broke apart and the cloud next to the "throne of God" became a giant open mouth, ready to devour stray fragments. Finally, the mouth itself dissipated, and the sky became gray, rain laden, imageless, except for one small pure white peak that caught the sunlight from behind while all the rest remained heavy and dark. The small white peak, still catching the light, became a statuesque head, shone sharply against the sky, and then lost its radiant whiteness. I was left with formless clouds in a sky fading toward night, without a hint of significance.

I turned my attention from sky to landscape, and the ordinary farmlands became imbued with power: the rolling green meadows, the randomly scattered grazing cows, the occasional red barn, a white farmhouse—the fertile heartland, set off by the heightened ethereal light of the setting sun, its rays extending from below the dark clouds. This was the landscape of the life I had failed to live fully, the life that both Lawrence and I had left behind. This was the image of the life that we had chased in fleeting moments but had never captured. It was not a life I yearned for or could have lived.

And then came the night: the finish of my journey, enclosed and sheltered in my own world, my alternative life. Now the darkness enveloped me beneficently. Few cars now, the road nearly empty, mine, no threats in sight, my daughters beyond my purview. I was alone, without responsibility: free but ungrounded, as ephemeral as a passing cloud or a puff of dandelion on the wind.

A FEW DAYS LATER, when I phoned Kara and Adriane at their father's house, I asked them how their visit was going. Kara responded: "The time is going so fast! It seems like we just got here yesterday!" Adriane responded: "Daddy loves me, too." This visit apparently was a good one for them, one that they would have chosen for themselves. And they did love their father, as he loved them. Perhaps it wasn't a dark underworld to them. Perhaps the contrast was really my own. Perhaps we could all experience these new versions of our lives as beneficent.

THAT VISIT now opens onto a pattern for my daughters' movements back and forth: sometimes happy, usually tension ridden, rarely as halcyon as their first summer visit had seemed. Over the years, as these visits stacked up in repeated formations, Kara and Adriane would complain of loneliness, yearning for home. They would send me letters shrouded in tension and uncertainty—letters in which I read grief and loneliness between the lines. I would send them stamps so that their communications would not be limited by their father's provision of postage. They would phone with muted voices, their father not allowing them to express real yearnings to their absent mother. Lawrence would storm in the background, angry at them for wanting to be with me, angry at me for providing the place that they considered home. Their voices reached through the phone lines, speaking our enduring bond.

I also heard, from what sometimes seemed like a sunless underworld, their father's raging somehow shot through with the power of his love. Rarely did I say to them, "All right, then, come home right now." Rather, I tended to say, "Work it out, try to know how to be with your father, who loves you." Sometimes he would say, "Okay, go home," but they knew that if they actually did so, they would be severing something too important to them. Always, they worked hard to maintain this vexed love for their father.

INDEED, Kara had learned a painful lesson from observing her father's alienation from *his* father. On her own initiative, when she was ten or so, she reached out to Harry, her paternal grandfather, himself out of communication with his son. She wrote affectionate letters to him, received affectionate responses, nurtured this family relationship out of the sense that it would enrich her own life and ease pain in the life of this grandfather she could hardly remember even meeting. She saw the consequences in her father's life of not maintaining kinship across generations; she developed the relationship with her distant grandfather; she recognized and persisted in the fraught relationship with her own father.

AND THIS WAS NOT EASY, for any of us. There were times during those years when I felt myself to be Lawrence's only friend—when he *told* me he had no one else to turn to in a particular phase of depression. There were times in those years when I even considered him my friend, when I knew him to be the only person in my life who shared my most important core: a full personal interest in Kara and Adriane. There were times in those years when he was my worst enemy: when, unable to work out plans to his satisfaction, he shouted hostilities over the phone not just at me, but at Kara or Adriane, and then hung up on whichever daughter he was talking to. (The three of us would sit together, arms around each other, tears streaming down our cheeks.) There were times in those years when he challenged what he saw as the inadequate care I was giving them—"How much time *do* you spend with the kids? Are they being given sufficient intellectual stimulation?"— and then, grimly, "There are steps I can take."

But there was more. At particularly troubled moments in his life—when I may well have been his primary friend—he would phone, sometimes late at night, and speak bitterly of his unhappiness. He would tell me, sub rosa, what his debts were and which oriental rugs he particularly wanted Kara and Adriane to have—and me to hold for them until they were grown—"if something should happen." In these calls, his voice would be full of tears, his speech slurred. I would keep him on the phone, telling him that his daughters loved him, his daughters needed him. These calls were the worst if Kara and Adriane were at his house with him; I was terrified of what the consequences of his depression would be for them. Should I swoop down and rescue them, snatching them from him? But I had already done that when I left the marriage. Should I allow them to become in some sense his primary human connection? But they already were that—or, by contrast, that was exactly what I had already denied to him when I took them away, into the life we had made together in Wooster, distant from him, though punctuated by these difficult visits.

When he would call in this bleak mood and the girls were with me, I would sometimes put them on the phone, carefully choosing the best possible moment for them to offer words of love and assurance. On one such occasion—this was when Kara was eight—Kara returned the call the following night, gaining reassurance, giving reassurance, and then coming to me: "Daddy's feeling a little better. He's still sad, but not quite so sad."

I do not mean to misrepresent. Such calls were infrequent, paced out across the years of our separate lives. Nor was Lawrence the only one wrestling with grief in private darkness. In 1983, when Adriane was very ill and I did not know what steps to take, I was terrified that my usual choice to wait it out—hovering over her, fevered, asleep for now—would be the wrong one, that, lacking the coparent that children deserve, I would fail to see that this illness might be something that really required attention, as when her cousin had spinal meningitis. With two parents, Travis had been safely taken into medical care. What if the decisions that I made as one parent, alone, would miss something so life threatening? I felt incessantly the strain of hovering and holding back and rushing forward, of making all these decisions—large and small, about Kara and Adriane and about their father—alone.

So I did sometimes rejoice in my freedom when they were off with their father: the responsibility was not mine then. And I usually ignored the gnawing thought that these visits might not be best for them. But as soon as they were gone, I would discover the conversations I wanted to be having with them, the joys I wished to share with them. Then I would go on to absorb myself in my life apart from them, pushing forward with my work, my freedoms. But a few days before they would return home, I reopened the urgent need to be with them, to feel them as ballast in my life. Held off during their absence, the love now surged.

NOW, too, the love surges, as does the sorrow. Now I ask myself: Did I know what those summers were like for them? Did I know how unattended they felt when they were with me and how much more so when they were with their father? Did I begin to know the undercurrents of violence that might have threatened them?

As I pull from them the stories of their childhood visits that they held in confidence, protecting their father, protecting me, I grieve anew. I could not have made the life I made, for myself or for them, had I known—had I let myself know—how alone they felt in their summer months. I could not have made this life had I known what potential for violence may have lurked in their summer home: that there were guns in the closet, bullets in the filing cabinet. But I know that I must have known. And in any case I *did* know the kind of verbal and emotional violence that had been part of my life with their father and that I had witnessed them experiencing in telephone exchanges.

In the early years of my separation from Lawrence, I followed the advice of the divorce books—to refrain from criticizing the absent parent. But then the time came when I recognized that this dogma left my daughters without any external gauge of their view of reality. Gradually, I did begin to tell them that their perceptions were astute, that their father *was* volatile, sometimes mean, sometimes charismatic, sometimes empathetic—often judgmental and alienating to other people, but always loving his daughters. I tried to do this honestly while also honoring their love for him, their need to love him, their need not to lose him. I tried to do this as I nourished their complex sense of who they are—each herself and both bound to father as to mother. I tried to do this as I guarded my own love for them alongside my need for respite, for sometime solitude.

IN NOVEMBER 1994, I drove west on Interstate 70 across Ohio, toward Indiana, repeating the trip I had taken uncountable times during my daughters' childhood. But this time was different. Kara and Adriane were grown and living their own lives elsewhere. I was alone, driving the entire distance, heading toward the town in which Lawrence had lived, the town in which he and I had first made our lives together—the town in which he had killed himself the previous July. There I would attend his memorial service at the university—alone there, too—representing his family in this mix of his colleagues and students. Kara and Adriane, having shared in an earlier memorial with Lawrence's family, would not be there.

Inevitably, I would find myself not only examining Lawrence's life but also examining the life I had chosen, as much as possible, apart from him. As I followed the known road, approaching the Dayton exit where Lawrence and I had so often met for the exchange of daughters, the alternative radio station was playing a song I had never heard before and have not heard since. It was a song suited to my self-examination: "Demeter's Daughter."

Though the song did not really mirror our lives, its reminder of the grief of absence, the seasonal transitions, and the complications of love did refract some of the experiences of our ruptured family. As I drove and listened, my thoughts followed the music, tracing the movement between two worlds that our divorce had enforced upon our daughters. The song reminded me of the power of their father's charisma and brooding sensibility; it reminded me of mysteriously tangled webs of emotion.

NEITHER THE SONG NOR THE MYTH can tell our particular story. Though a dark underworld was surely part of my daughters' growing years, the seasons of their lives were not bound by it. Not Hades or Zeus either, not a god at all, their father gave them a heritage rich in human complexity: his bitter melancholy and his harsh criticisms, but also his vibrant curiosity, his wry wit, his keen intellect, his love of books, his love for his daughters.

As for me, I did not have the power to make their lives ideal or to control their seasons of blossoming. But does anyone? Lacking Demeter's powers, lacking, too, her resolute and singular response to a daughter absence, I embraced both my freedom and my loss. I was a mother on my own terms, giving nurture to the best of my ability. Like their father, I, too, must have given them much. How else could they now be so full of life, so mindful of others, so luminous and strong? Only human, all four of us did our best to live and grow through our seasons, together and apart, the shifting patterns of our imperfect lives, our encumbered honesty, our knotted and abiding love.

18

That Crazy Carousel

This narrative has no sequence, no clear cause and effect. I try to nudge the story forward, but instead keep circling over the past, caught in the whorl of life dilemmas, apparent contradictions. Now, at least, I again have a greater gift of time, a breather from classroom responsibilities: it is late in the summer of 2002, and I am about to begin another research leave. This one is already assigned to new projects, a return to analytical work, so I must, as before, snatch this writing from the grasping hands of other commitments. But the summer is still mine for remembering.

When weather permits, Ron and I continue to sit on the porch in the early evening: the end of our workdays, our time to share. Since my work these days is this project—memory work, writing work—that is what I share in our conversations. I tell him of my efforts to make sense of the exchanges with Lawrence, of the stresses of parenting alone, of my loneliness and worries and sexual frustrations. Ron reminds me not to focus so much on the sorrows, to recall instead the happy times, for I have often told him of my pleasure and pride in our single-parent family. So I tell him, too, of the thoughts I have come to on recent morning walks, of my summer days with Kara and Adriane, of sitting on the porch with them as I now sit on the porch with him. And I tell him of the other sound I have only recently noticed on my walks: the twittering that mourning doves emit as they rise from the ground to the branches above, adding a happy chatter to the mournful questioning.

As we talk, we also watch the squirrels at play—calling to mind the squirrels I used to watch swing down from the bars of the jungle gym in the backyard of our first Wooster home. We are amused this evening by their games on the knoll across the street, chasing each other up the trees, leaping

191

from trunk to fragile twig with no apparent care. We wonder at the squirrels' preternatural balance, precarious as it seems to the onlooker, their unshakable confidence in graceful motion. We watch with awe the agile movement of one coming across the street on the wire extended from the college campus toward our home.

This one, small and black, carries in its mouth a vividly green ball that is so big I first think it's a tennis ball. But it's not, for when the squirrel uncharacteristically drops it into the street below, we can see that it is an unusually large walnut, still wearing its green coat over the black shell that protects the meaty nut inside. This squirrel was apparently at work rather than at play.

With the walnut lying in the street, I worry that the squirrel will risk its life to retrieve it—running carelessly onto the pavement, oblivious of oncoming traffic. Deciding to participate in this drama rather than merely watch it, I pull the walnut into a safer zone in the grass. When the squirrel climbs down the tree onto which it has leapt from the wire above, it runs into the street, knowing exactly where it has dropped the nut. It looks around, puzzled, blind to an approaching car. I yell at it, to startle it out of danger; it looks up at me and chatters angrily. But it does move, eventually finding the lost walnut.

As I return to my writing, I am dizzy with the effort to bring my life into focus, to move beyond old stories and look closely at the hazards I had tried to ignore, the personal failings I had bleached away in memory. *A monster mother, a sexual mother, a mad mother, a neglectful mother, a selfish mother*—labels leer out at me from the past. *A hard-working mother, a listening mother, an attentive mother, a loving mother*—other labels rise up in self-defense. *A playful mother? A laughing mother?*

I TURN AGAIN to *The Golden Notebook*, to one of the diaries where Anna Wulf describes an emotional dynamic I recognize. Janet voices a familiar plea, "Come and play, mummy." But Anna cannot respond at first, and when she does, her reaction is robotic: "I couldn't move. I forced myself up out of the chair after a while and sat on the floor beside the little girl. I looked at her, and thought: 'That's my child, my flesh and blood.' But I couldn't feel it. She said again: 'Play, mummy.' I moved wooden bricks for a house, but like a machine. Making myself perform every movement." Unlike Anna, I don't think that I ever lost sight of the flesh-and-blood relation to my daughters. But I am certain that I was very much like Anna in one sense: I often felt robotic, unable to play, unable to laugh, acting out the role of "mummy" under coercion.

I HAVE OCCASIONALLY BEEN TOLD—usually critically by colleagues or lovers—that I am a serious person, too serious, and that I don't know how to play. And yet I have also been told, by my students, by my daughters, and more recently by Ron, that they like to laugh with me, even that they find me funny or fun to be with. And I think that all of these perceptions are accurate. I *am* a serious person; I often do not know how to play. Indeed, both my marriage to Lawrence and my Mennonite background had encouraged me to see play as frivolous. But I do like to laugh.

I recall my father's parents, filled with serious purpose, dedicated to education and social service. And I recall my mother's stories of her own mother's insistent solemnity, forbidding her daughter to dance or play cards or even to cut her hair. But my mother always said how much she had yearned to dance, despite these prohibitions. And during my own growing years, she would often laugh and sometimes join my brother in an impromptu dance at lunchtime. Even my serious father had taken from his parents the rituals of Saturday night family games and popcorn and the sound of the piano playing in the living room and music all around.

I knew that I, too, needed to break out of the harsher judgments, as I had seen my parents begin to do. More than that, I knew that children, especially, need to play. And I think I did learn, with my daughters and with my students, to adopt a more playful attitude, though I was always best able to laugh and to play when it was not a question of being commanded—"Come and play, mummy"—but rather a feeling of mutual pleasure that would arrive unheralded.

When Ron first visited us in February 1988 in our self-constituted home of three females, I felt as if he brought with him a new dimension of playfulness. Almost immediately he and Adriane and I initiated our family feeling by playing "Monkey in the Middle" in the driveway—throwing the basketball over each other's heads, getting to know each other as we laughed in glee at the sheer foolishness of it. But he now tells me, "I didn't play like that until I met you guys." Perhaps, after all, we did know something about play.

AFTER SCHOOL WAS OUT, when Kara and Adriane were still quite young and not yet spending most of their summer weeks with their father, I continued to go to the office part days, but I usually kept afternoons free. In those leisurely hours, we would sometimes sit together in the backyard, chatting and cuddling and making clover coronets, talking of the big circus ring my siblings and friends and I had made by tying the clover flowers together when I was a child. Watching the squirrels at play, we would blend my childhood with theirs, telling stories of circuses and kings and queens with coronets on their heads.

Another day I'd come home after a summer half-day at the office, wash my hair, and sit on the porch with a towel on my head, one child on each knee, just talking, the three of us alert to each other and to the passing world. Or yet another day we'd sit on the porch, watching a thunderstorm, rain pouring down in torrents, the heat finally breaking. Then they would play in the lighter rain, splashing in the newly wrought river-street. I sat on the porch and watched, assuring myself, when fears surfaced, that I would surely notice any passing cars in time, slowed as they would be by the depths of the water.

I loved sitting on the porch with them—perhaps it reminded me of sitting on the porch at the farm, or perhaps it simply brought me to a level of ease that was otherwise so hard to reach. We would sit and talk and dawdle, their friends drifting through. We would make popcorn and watch the rain and read stories to each other. Lawrence's repeated challenge that I was spending insufficient time with them would sometimes come directly on the heels of such a dawdling afternoon. And how could I say that this time together constituted the intellectual stimulation that he was convinced I was failing to give them? Or the concentrated time and attention—the "quality time"—that the parenting books insisted upon?

Anyway, such times were not always "pure," as when I disrupted the leisure by shouting out after a wayward Kara who had raced off too quickly and too far down the street to check out the fire engines' destination. Or when I failed to be calm because of an infuriated half-hour search for my shoes, which Adriane had put in a suitcase, packing for her own imaginary adventures. Or when—in a rush to retrieve Kara's glasses left behind at the swimming pool—I pulled Goldie into the path of an oncoming motorcycle that I had failed to see, leaving our "new car" permanently misaligned as we kept working to align ourselves. Though such situations had no dire consequences, they regularly reminded me that our fragilely constructed lives could go awry. And yet from these threads of the everyday, I first wove the affirmation of the life I loved as a single mother, the identity I hold centrally even now.

DURING OUR EARLY WOOSTER YEARS, I often gauged these ordinary events against "normal" family expectations, testing whether my daughters were suffering in our single-parent family. I sometimes even tried to match these phantom models myself, as when I planned a picnic with my sister and her family in July 1977. We were to meet Eileen, Jim, and their three sons— the Burry cousins—at a lake midway between our houses. This picnic would give the children time with their cousins and me the adult companionship I so craved. It might even make us feel like a "normal family."

Preparations did, however, need to be made, and I hoped to do so in the quiet of the morning. But it was a July day in Ohio. The heat and humidity had made it impossible for any of us to sleep well the night before, and we wakened hot, tired, grumpy. Trying to fade away for a few minutes of peace and a cup of coffee, I turned on *Captain Kangaroo*. When the TV wouldn't come on, I jiggled the cord—as was our habit with this old hand-me-down television—and the cord promptly burst into flames. I should have recognized the portent in all of this; instead, I merely unplugged the television and pushed it away from the draperies. Captain Kangaroo would have to carry on in his own liminal space; we would pack our picnic and set off for the beach.

But even this simple outing was not to be so easy. Fifteen miles out of town, entering another small town in too much of a hurry, having just passed a truck, I failed to notice the officer lying in wait for me in the new speed zone: flashing lights pulled me to the side of the road. The officer was very polite but intransigent: "I'm only doing this for the sake of those lovely children. It's my job to protect you and your lovely children." Chastened, ticket in hand, and with a commitment to show up on a designated date for the mayor's court, I drove off for the day at the beach.

A fun day, playing in the sand, splashing in the water, talking as we walked along the beach and shared food among the trees above the sand— our two families together. But the hovering dangers cast clouds over this sunny day: fire, my own driving, officers around blind corners, a later diagnosis of possible hepatitis for one of my nephews suggesting a contaminated lake. Still, despite the surrounding perils, we had had our picnic.

A YEAR LATER—1978—I was looking forward to drawing the cousins together under my own roof. Doug and Matt and Steve would spend five days with us during a portion of their parents' trip to Europe. I had offered this contribution to their childcare needs: I owed Eileen and Jim some reciprocity for the times they had taken care of Kara and Adriane, but, more than that, I anticipated with pleasure sharing in the summer fun of these five children.

Recall with me this particularly fraught period when I was struggling on so many levels: still trying to figure out my relationship with Michael, unclear about my job future, unable to see how to piece this life together. This was the summer when my two-year contract at the college had come to an end; I had only a one-year additional contract at present and no option on a job beyond that. And my lease on our first home had run out. Before the summer was up, I would need to decide where Kara and Adriane and I would next make our home, and I had decided to buy a house if necessary, however foolish that was in the midst of so many unknowns. But I still take pleasure in my memory of that summer when we all did enjoy each other.

I HAVE PHOTOS of the five cousins on the front porch of the house we would soon leave behind. Doug, the oldest cousin, holds Adriane, the youngest, in his arms; the others are lined up in age and size order, from Doug to Matt, Steve, and Kara. The picture doesn't show Steve's homesickness or Doug's heightened feelings of nurturance and responsibility or Matt's uncertainty in his middle-child role, nor does it show any fear of displacement that Kara and Adriane may have been feeling. Indeed, I don't really know what feelings any of them had, though I do recall that Steve felt sad at bedtime and that Doug was especially attentive to his small cousin Adriane. I also remember a fair amount of good-natured teasing, even an attempt by the older boys to trick Adriane into peeing in her cousin Steve's shoe.

I know I felt some disquiet about trying to meet all of these children's needs, assuaging possible homesickness, moderating the teasing, giving full attention to Kara's seventh birthday, which fell during that week, dealing with children's summer energies and activities, with Fourth of July and fireworks, Adriane's first. But when I read my journal entries from that week, I am struck by how much I was enjoying myself. And I seemed oddly pleased to have taken on a "housewife" role—not split between work and children. I celebrated this role as a relief: surely no one could fault me for giving each day over to supervising five children, preparing food, organizing trips to the swimming pool and library.

When I ask the Burry boys—now grown, with families of their own—about that summer, I am bemused by their uncanny recall of the layout of our house, affectionate thoughts of teasing their youngest cousin, and childish frustration with the strangeness of the food they were offered: eggplant one evening, followed the next evening by their dashed hopes when the pizza I served turned out to be homemade with a whole-wheat crust. But we shared those meals, laughing and talking. And still we laugh in recollection.

BY A QUIRK OF TIMING, a house that had caught my eye came onto the market during the week I was single-parenting five children: same neighborhood—two blocks up the street—three bedrooms, a usable basement, a finished third floor, oak moldings in the living room and up the stairs, a pocket door near the entry, and again a front porch. Once the five children had been moved on into other people's care—Doug and Matt and Steve to my parents, their grandparents; Kara and Adriane to their father—I returned home to the obsessive concern with obtaining this house. I had already made an initial offer of $34,000 and received an immediate counteroffer of $37,000. (Remember: this was 1978 in a small midwestern town.) But the bidding had stalled, and my pleasure in the children's company gradually drained away into what seemed like endless waiting and a tepid attempt at additional searching as I still focused on the house I had identified as our next home.

Finally, on the Friday morning after the children's Sunday departures, I received news that my last desperate bid of $36,650 had been accepted. The house would be mine, though only in serious partnership with the bank. And suddenly I felt not freed from worry, but shackled to this new possession. With no assurance of a job beyond the coming year, I had committed myself to a monthly mortgage payment I was not at all confident I could sustain.

I spent my days trying to write the article that was my summer project, an analysis of Woolf's *The Voyage Out,* carved from the old, nearly sterile dissertation work. I paced this intellectual effort by seeking out the few material goods with which I would supplement my current collection of hand-me-down furniture: a mattress to put on the floor—it would be years before I would actually have a bed to sleep in—also a refrigerator (used), a used table for the breakfast nook, and fabric with which to sew the curtains I couldn't afford to buy. I spent my nights in yearning loneliness and occasional exchange of time with Michael. Nothing seemed quite right. The children were gone; I was spending uncharacteristic time shopping; and Michael was so absorbed in his own life that I felt doubly on my own with all of these new responsibilities.

I had never learned the gender roles that were supposed to have come easily to me as a woman: consumer and maker of a home. I had no male partner to balance the cultural equation. I was taking on a new set of financial responsibilities—dealing with banks and lawyers and insurance agents, tasks that were still usually assigned to men; indeed, in some locations during that era, banks unabashedly refused to give mortgages to women alone. My work was faltering for lack of clearly defined goals, though I knew that I needed to publish quickly if I expected to remain an academic when this job ran out. And my daughters were not there to anchor me.

Nonetheless, when Kara and Adriane returned from their summer weeks with their dad, they returned to a new home, complete with cat. I had managed, with the help of two male friends, to move my minimal furniture from one house to another in a rented trailer, being sure to do my share even with the labor of getting the washer and dryer down the stairs to the basement, though one of my friends reminded me, "You don't really have to prove how macho you are." I had positioned the additional newly purchased furniture in appropriate rooms; I had made plans to strip the football-player wallpaper from my own bedroom and paint the walls a nondescript off-white. And I had accepted, as a housewarming gift from Michael, a Siamese kitten.

The house only needed the stamp of my daughters' presence and their participation in naming this small fuzzy white creature with ears, nose, and paws tipped in black: we decided to call him "Chang" after the younger brother in the children's story *Tikki Tikki Tembo*. In a photo of him as a kitten, still snowy white, Kara holds him up gently for the camera as she sits on the edge of the sandbox made from a tractor tire. After that, he became an indoor cat, confined to the house we were making our new home. Though only weeks earlier the house had felt all wrong as I talked with realtors and bankers, signed papers, and sought out furniture, it now suddenly felt again just right: Kara and Adriane and Chang were there.

And so we continued to mark this place as our home: hanging out in the kitchen, eating casually at the picnic table in the backyard, playing games at the dining room table or jacks on the kitchen floor. I still had my limits, could not tolerate a game of *Candyland* or *Sorry* or even join in ordinary doll play. For these activities, my daughters would have to find playmates. But I liked the challenge of *Yahtzee*, trying to best my own best score. And I would sometimes join in building projects with the wooden blocks I had purchased—the expensive set, plain polished wood, beyond my budget. Lured by the joys of spatial relationships, of symmetry and fragile asymmetry, I was glad to help make something, even if I remained, like Anna, a bit robotic. I might also be cajoled into Lego projects and Lite Brites, again taking pleasure in design. I even might—in rare moments—make a place in my frazzled schedule to sit side by side with a child for a coloring or clay-formation project. And we still had a porch, an invitation to dawdle together, laughing and talking.

We further christened the house as ours when Eileen, Jim, Doug, Matt, and Steve came for a weekend family visit that fall. Now here were my sister and family; now here were my three nephews in our home again, but this time with parents of their own. We shared experiences—talk of my summer difficulties, of Eileen and Jim's trip to Europe, of the visible well-being of these five children. Never mind that my sister is allergic to cats and had to fight off sneezing and congestion; never mind that we also needed again to talk of Eileen's difficulty in understanding my relationship with Michael; never mind that my stresses remained: job insecurity, professional dissatisfaction, fraught love life. I tugged on the threads of identity—mother, sister, aunt, householder, lover, professor, seeker of meanings, resister of cultural certainties—feeling them begin to settle within me.

GROUNDED NOW in this second Wooster home, I gradually became bolder, ready to take outings without other adults. One September Sunday in 1979, Kara, Adriane, and I set off for a hike, exploring ravines and woods that so much reminded me of the farm we had left behind in Indiana. We were joined by Kara's good friend Sarah—daughter of Jim Turner, a friend and colleague in the Women's Studies Program at the College of Wooster—as we often were in those years. It was a gorgeous fall day, full of promise and sunshine. I remember the sense of duty: I must make this outing happen. But my mood wasn't completely mechanical. I remember, too, a feeling of respite and pleasure: we will explore together the outdoor world in which we can all revel.

And we did. We hiked up the bluff and over the ridge and down toward the bottom of the ravine, where we would cross the creek. This was a familiar hike for us and one that I loved. When we got to the bottom of the ravine, we all felt that perhaps it was *too* familiar: Why not try something more adventurous? So we headed up off into new terrain, less clearly marked, exploring as we went: the outer trail. We felt bold and energetic—until the trail seemed to disappear, the markings erased by time and weather. The bluffs and ravines cast their own shadows, and it was hard to see just which way the sun was moving. How, then, were we to find the parking lot?

For three hours we wandered up and down the hills, trying to relocate the trail. Responsible, I nonetheless chided the children forward. They were worried that we would be late in meeting Sarah's father to see the Muppet movie. I silenced my own worry that we would wander endlessly among trees and ravines that always seemed to point toward a way out but repeatedly obscured the orientation of the sun. Never mind the Muppet movie: What if night came upon us before we found our way out—myself and three children, turning and turning in confusion, all my responsibility?

In those days—indeed, even now—I had difficulty distinguishing real risks from false ones. I allowed the children a great deal of autonomy and independence, the opportunity to roam on their own, to explore the world for themselves. I rarely spoke my real concerns—all of the "what ifs" that haunt any parenting commitment. Indeed, most of the time I didn't even articulate those concerns to myself. Now, on this outing, I felt the convergence of regular daily responsibility: it was up to me to make sure that my daughters and Sarah were returned safely to their homes. That feeling rose more vividly to the surface on such outings; I usually just assumed that our lives would go forward without crisis.

And this time, too, we had no crisis. Late, but safe, we poked our way out of the woods into a new subdivision on the edge of the park. We had surely lost our trail but had at last found the sun in its proper orientation in the sky. It seemed surreal to be suddenly among new split-level houses and cul-de-sacs, but we walked on by, out onto the county road and back toward the parking lot at the edge of the nature preserve: slightly stressed, but exhilarated by our safe arrival. When—only marginally late for the next planned outing—we met Sarah's father, all of us set off happily toward a more relaxing remainder of our Sunday afternoon. It felt good to sit quietly in the theater, comfortable in this companionable group. We watched Miss Piggy and Kermit the frog and the other Muppets. I laughed with the others, buttressed now by the presence of another adult and a distracting movie.

Emboldened by this success, I tried another Sunday outing a month later, this time alone with Adriane—Kara had plans of her own, and I wanted some relaxed time with Adriane, to focus on her and renew my own participation in the natural world. In Goldie's embrace, the two of us headed toward a different wilderness area, one I had first visited with Michael. I liked the idea that I could be fully with Adriane and at the same time privately muse on other parts of my life—pointing out to her the pond in which I had seen a blue heron on a different visit to this preserve, recalling adult conversations as I now carried on with a mother–daughter conversation, following the nature trails through the wilderness.

Secluded in Goldie as we made the forty-five minute drive, I was patient and attendant; Adriane rejoiced in this outing, a rare time alone with her mother, not even her sister with us. Her way in this period of her life was to speak incessantly, desperate to share. Not so long before, when her aunt Eileen and I—trying to have an adult conversation of our own—had suggested that she try to moderate her constant stream of words, she had responded: "How will I know what I think if I don't say it?" And for most of her very young life—I sometimes joked that she was born talking—that was her way of knowing the world and touching the people around her.

Now on this drive, committed to patience, I listened calmly to her chattering commentary and constant questions. Her mind was in ceaseless activity. She loved words, she loved to speculate, and she needed to figure things out. I loved these qualities in her and wanted to encourage them, but I also needed a bit of respite from the ceaseless flow of language. This time I didn't say anything, but I did breathe out a little sigh, very quietly, before I carried on with our mother–daughter exchange.

Adriane, having just a moment earlier been given over to her own rush of words, came instantly to attention: "I know I ask a lot of questions, but I'm just a little child, and I don't know very much." She was four years old; her sister was eight. Between them, they were always teaching me—things I didn't know, things I needed to know, for their well-being and for my own.

I HAVE LATELY been listening repeatedly to music I associate with the early days in our second Wooster home: *Jacques Brel Is Alive and Well and Living in Paris.* I try to use the aural to take me back in time, to return to the worn living room with homemade curtains and sagging couch, with new kitten and pocket doors tucked mysteriously into the wall behind the couch. The stereo was positioned on low bookshelves in front of the large window looking out on the porch. Sometimes we gathered in the living room to listen together to music, though we didn't easily share musical tastes during their childhood years: they liked whatever was popular among their peers; I preferred Bach and Mozart and Beethoven. In self-protection, I usually kept the radio in the living room tuned to the regional NPR station for news and classical music.

But we all did enjoy *Jacques Brel*, an album Michael had given me that I played often. In the early years, it was a way to listen to music in which all three of us took pleasure; it was also a way to have Michael present in my life with my daughters, although he was kept carefully separate from that life. Then the music gradually became not his, but ours—Kara's and Adriane's and mine—even the songs that were clearly not appropriate for young children, songs of drug addiction and sexual obsessions into which we were drawn by the irony and wit and rhythm. We mostly ignored those songs, though, and listened for what drew us together: "Carousel."

The song began slowly, lazily, speaking of cotton candy and calliopes. At first it was possible to sit still, soaking up its alliterations and seductive rhythms. But as it gathered momentum, with carnival rides in frenzied motion, we would spontaneously get up and begin to turn ourselves, picking up speed with the music until we were whirling wildly, in dizziness and joy, around and around, as the music sped on. By the end, the words were coming so fast they nearly turned to gibberish, the summary phrase—"the crazy carousel"—barely distinguishable before the abrupt finale, "la la la la *la*," at which we fell to the ground in mutual, pleasurable exhaustion.

Spinning around, never certain whether we would end up or down, but always again around, I don't know why I couldn't simply accept the complexity, the warp and weft of ordinary joys and hazards by which most of us must make our way. I'm certain that I saw so much more of that complexity as deriving from single parenthood than actually did: Which life, however "normal," forms a clear narrative trajectory, without resistances and difficulties? Yet I also want to celebrate the particulars of my own life as a single mother.

EVEN AS MY ATTENTION seemed to be turned elsewhere, I was gradually learning to laugh, to shrug off most suggestions of rupture in our lives: we were, after all, on a carousel. When a six-year-old Adriane said to me, "I want a divorce," I first responded, "That's not possible. You can't divorce your mother." Ever quick with words, she parried: "Then I want an 'orvorce.'" I rallied: "And I want a reverse."

How could we do other than dissolve in laughter, turning the language of rupture, of fractured lives—separations and reversals, play and sorrow, rising and falling—into its own dizzying bond? How could we do other than continue to ride this crazy carousel, this wild merry-go-round, life reeling around us?

19

Professor-Mother

March 2003. Ron and I have just returned from New York—a visit to both Kara and Adriane in their ongoing lives there, but also a purposeful trip to help Kara pack up her East Village apartment, store away pieces of her life, so that she can take her next journey: to London to join her partner Andrzej. There she will focus on her writing, having relinquished the office job that has paid her bills until now.

The four of us worked together on this enormous task, both emotional and physical: preparation for Kara's departure across the ocean into a different life. As we sorted the material artifacts of her nearly thirty-two years, I recalled that other time the four of us sorted through life effects together in the aftermath of their father's death, both times weighing what to save and what to leave behind. This time, too, the process is tinged by grief as we anticipate Kara's absence. But it is also decidedly different: the dominant emotion now is joy, a celebration of her happiness as she moves on into a new life. Still, I cannot help being aware that the added distance extends the sphere of my maternal anxiety: no more easy phone calls or quickly booked flights for short visits.

And the world itself seems increasingly dangerous now that we are again a nation newly at war: the US invasion of Iraq this month a further reminder of instabilities and dangers. My own resistance to war rises up against this particular war, for which there seems to be no reason at all. I fear the carnage that lies ahead, and I cringe at the war-mongering politics. The political atmosphere reminds me of Virginia Woolf's critique of war and nationalism, competition and capitalism, and patriarchy in *Three Guineas,* a book that draws together my feminism and my hatred of war, a book I have regularly shared with students in the course "Seminar in Women's Studies."

Ron's and my return home to Wooster, framed by these reminders of changing lives, sends me back to this memory work, though I have not come close to finishing my research project for this year: analysis of how a woman's life and thought as a mother might affect her ways of writing. My current year of leave nears its end, but I again must take some time away from the research project to squeeze in a few more weeks of this other kind of writing. Family life and work life converge and overlap, threaten each other, sometimes even refuse to differentiate.

THIS HABIT OF CONVERGENCE is deeply ingrained, prompted by the many years I lived as both English professor and single mother. During the academic year early on in my time at Wooster, I would sit in my chair in the living room—furniture purchased from someone's basement—reading, thinking, preparing classes, grading papers on my clipboard. Or I would claim the occasional lounge in bed, accompanied by coffee, books, and papers. In subsequent years, in the midst of a major project, I would stake out long-term residency at the dining room table—adopted from a friend's attic—with books and note cards and xeroxed pages stacked up or strewn around in front of me. But that came later and usually happened only when my daughters were with their father. In the very early years, I didn't even have a dining room table or the capacity to take on major projects. When my daughters were home with me, I would work in our mutual living space, in my chair, with them and sometimes not really with them, but always in the midst of their lives.

Even now, years after my daughters have moved through our shared home, on to college, and then into lives of their own, I retain these ingrained habits. I can often be found sitting in my current chair in the living room or at the dining room table with course materials spread in front of me or trying to eke out a few hours for this manuscript or for a current research project, working in the midst of the living space. I roam the house, leaving piles of papers and books in nearly every room, covering all available surfaces with printed matter, making no real distinction between my living space and my work space. When the semester is under way, I add student papers to this mix, cultivating the many intersections of thought and scattered pieces of paper. This practice is not so easy for Ron, who nonetheless accepts the intransigence of my long-established patterns and asks only that I relinquish that other habit of spreading books and papers in arcs around me on the bed.

SO IT WAS WHEN KARA AND ADRIANE WERE YOUNG. When I was home, they had only to look around them in order to find me at my work, on the bed, at the table, in my chair: reading, thinking, writing in the midst of things, never behind a closed door. Adriane, age four, would sidle up to me: "Do you still love me when you're doing that work?" Or, more confronta-tionally, at age seven: "Which do you love more—me or your work?" I've been told that I was seriously remiss in my answer to the latter. But I had made a pledge of honesty to my daughters from the very beginning, and so I would say, "You can't make me choose. I have to do my work, not just for money, but for me. But I have to be with you, too. I love you, and I love my work." My answer is deeply etched in memory by the surrounding cultural guilt that told me that there was only one right answer: "I love you most of all, my darling." But I was obdurate in my pledge to be honest. I truly loved my work, even as my daughters were at the core of my being.

I DID ALWAYS LOVE MY DAUGHTERS, though I was often angry with them and pushed to the limit by the strains of single parenthood. But, at first, I didn't love my work, not with a real passion. When I took the job at Wooster, I had only been able to see it as a temporary stopping place, my good luck to make a living doing what I had always done: reading books. I certainly needed the income, and I thought I knew something about teaching and about research. Reading had always been a passion. The rest was really just a way to make a living for myself, for my daughters.

In my first year or two in Wooster, I had often paced the floor in lonely tears, counted my quarters and dollars as I approached the checkout in the grocery store, fretted over child care and child freedom. I did not feel like a professor, and though I was developing a confidence that was unfamiliar to me, I kept asking myself whether I had any professional goals. The obvious first choice would be to carry on from my dissertation on Virginia Woolf, but I hadn't figured out how to go beyond the stale thinking I had already done or how to escape the deeply ingrained practice of close reading, which felt sterile. Having loved grappling with ideas in my own undergraduate education and having grown up in a family of teachers, I knew something about teaching: the value of learning was woven into my worldview. But who was I as a professor? And how did that fit into my relationship with my daughters, my life as a mother?

REMEMBER: when I was first offered the job at Wooster, I had laughed at the idea that I might want to stay longer than the initial two-year contract. How could I make the life I meant to make—a life that expanded into the future—there in a small town in Ohio? But by the time I was offered another interim contract, certainly nothing tenure track or secure, I yearned to make this place my home. Any prospect of an expansive future had succumbed to my knotty personal life and my effort to keep my daughters safe. I still thought in the short term, and I could hardly have imagined that this would be the rest of my life, but I was grateful for some continuity in the life I was struggling to make, year by year, patching together terminal contracts.

Making my life and making my living could not so easily be seen as distinct projects. When I sat in my living room chair, I was not working in some separate space of my own, as Woolf so aptly suggested women need. But neither was I working under cover, as in the myth about Jane Austen, discreetly slipping pages under a blotter when a guest or family member entered the drawing room. What I had gradually learned to aim for was a new balancing act: to do my work—openly and passionately—in the midst of our family life. When Kara and Adriane drifted in and out of the room, they knew that they would usually find me there at the heartbeat of the house, in the armchair with its matching hassock: books on my lap, papers on the floor around me and on the hassock, dodging my feet. Olive green, threadbare, with naked foam peering through, the armchair became a kind of alternative hearth. Here, work and family might come together, frayed threads crisscrossing irreconcilable needs and competing demands.

I recall one morning after we were well settled in our second house: I sat in my worn chair, desperate to make last-minute class preparations for a twentieth-century literature course. Kara had left for school; Pauline had not yet arrived. When Adriane, age four, came whining to my side, I scooped her onto my lap and read aloud to her from the book I held: Faulkner's *Absalom, Absalom!* With its arcane diction, endless sentences, and obscure meanings, it was hardly a child's book. But Adriane already loved the rhythms of language and didn't seem to care so much that she didn't get the meanings. At least on that morning, she nestled into the sound of my voice, the flow of words, and the attention I gave her, however rifted.

That same morning in class, when my students complained about the arcane language and obscure meanings, I suggested that they follow the example of my four-year-old daughter: listen to the language—actually hear it—and immerse themselves in the flow of words. Colleagues had advised me that I should keep my personal life out of the classroom, but I was not so sure that they understood either the hazards or the value of breaching this prohibition. This time I took the desperate measure of bringing my mother life into the classroom; my work life was, after all, a constant presence in my home life. My students, though puzzled, seemed unfazed by this brief glimpse of my life beyond the classroom.

BUT I WAS ALSO BEGINNING TO LEARN more crucial lessons from my daughters, most particularly about the way in which gender operated in our lives. Inchoate understandings hovered just beneath the surface of my consciousness as I grappled with the questions that were core to both my personal and my academic life. How fully could I bring my experiential knowledge into my writing and into the classroom? To what extent could that knowledge be articulated within academic spaces? And more: How could I draw upon my growing feminist understanding to help me nourish my daughters even as I learned from them?

This was a central parenting question as well as one that was arising in feminist scholarship. How could we raise children to survive in the culture we had while still trying to challenge that culture, especially its definitions of what it means to be a "girl" or a "boy"? I did not want my children to become instruments of my political convictions, but neither did I want to sacrifice them to the status quo. In this, as in much else, I had to learn with them and through our lives.

WHEN I SAT ON THE PORCH WITH MY DAUGHTERS, I pulled one or the other onto my lap, reaching out and touching. When I sometimes imaged them as boys, I felt less able to do that, inhibited by some restriction I hadn't even named to myself. When I urged them into the world, wanting them to know their own strengths and capacities, I wanted also to guard them against the derision that girls with aspirations were likely to encounter as well as against the more palpable dangers.

We listened together to *Free to Be . . . You and Me*, the feminist children's recording of the era. We laughed at "Ladies First" and its joke on the girl who insists on feminine privilege and then gets eaten by a tiger. We celebrated William's right to want a doll and everybody's right to cry. We laughed especially heartily at the gender confusion of the new babies who try to use cultural codes to decide who is a boy and who is a girl. And we rejoiced at Atalanta's victory in the race to decide her own future.

BEFORE I BECAME ENGROSSED IN WOMEN'S STUDIES, I was already being drawn into a full campus life: teaching, conferring with students, attending meetings. Early on, during my third year at the college, my schedule became particularly full since I had not only departmental obligations, but also service on the collegewide Educational Policy Committee. Participation in this committee was unusual for a person so new to the faculty, and I knew I had been elected in part because faculty members had recently recognized a need for greater representation of women. I felt a particular responsibility to be reliable in my attendance and in my representation of women's concerns. Sometimes I had to stretch my time away from home much more than I would have wished. In these times, it was crucial that we had Pauline in our lives, still in our home daily, caring for Kara and Adriane in my absence.

That was the case when on a Wednesday afternoon in October 1978 the president of the college called an emergency meeting that would take us well into the evening: I felt obligated to scramble quickly to alter my usual Wednesday release of Pauline at six o'clock. Taking advantage of a brief break in the meeting, I went into the president's office to use his phone and call home. I put my request to Pauline, pledging that such late work nights would not become a pattern. I was grateful when she agreed.

But she added another twist before I hurried back to the meeting: "Adriane's friend Christopher cut Adriane's hair this afternoon. I took her to my hairdresser to even it out, but it's really short. I wanted to warn you before you come home." Unshaken, I assured her that this was fine, that I was grateful she had dealt with the problem, and I thanked her profusely for being willing to work late this one night.

I got home at 10:30, exhausted from an unusually long day on campus and worried that I had taken advantage of Pauline's ready agreement. I was not worried about the haircut. But after I had released Pauline until the next morning, I went to check on my sleeping children, to whisper my usual "Good night, I love you" into their sleeping ears.

I found Kara flung across her bed, her record player still on, though her usual bedtime recording had already concluded: Judy Collins's *Bread and Roses*. I turned off the record player, straightened her covers, stroked her hair aside so that I could whisper into her ear.

In Adriane's room, I found the light still on—as was her habit—and her covers thrown completely off. But when I went to whisper in her ear, I faltered at the sight of her hair, cut by Pauline's hairdresser to a close-cropped crew cut. I ran my hand over the stubble and felt a surge of tenderness at the vulnerability of the nearly naked head—like a newborn's or like the lightly feathered skull of a freshly hatched bird. Into her exposed ear, I whispered, "Good night, I love you."

IN THE WEEKS THAT FOLLOWED, I found this vulnerability reframing itself. An exposed skull was not all that was at stake.

When I took Adriane with me to the office to pick up my mail one late afternoon, we were met by a colleague from another department, who greeted us: "Is this big boy your son?"

"No, this is my daughter, Adriane."

Without missing a beat, he shifted his body, flipped his wrist, rejoined: "And what a pretty little thing she is."

And now that she looked like a "boy," when I took her to the grocery store with me—as I had often done—she was offered new opportunities that had never been available to her as a girl. The young man bagging groceries, who had never noticed her before, now turned to her/him, made direct eye contact, and said: "You look like a big strong boy. Would you like to carry the pumpkin to the car?"

In her nursery school photo from that fall, Adriane stands proudly in front of a backdrop of autumn leaves, her hair still closely cropped. By chance, she is wearing gold and red plaid pants (hand-me-downs of unknown origin) and a burnt gold cotton knit shirt, a "girl's" shirt that I had actually purchased specifically for her. She looks beautifully natural among the leaves of gold and red and brown.

On Halloween, we carved faces in several pumpkins. We weren't sure which ones were girls and which ones were boys. They all had open mouths and ears and eyes, alert to the world around them.

WHEN I LATER became fully involved in women's studies, I would learn to use this incident of apparent gender transformation as an example of cultural pressures that we don't often recognize. But at first I simply stored it away as an amusing anecdote about raising my daughters; I hadn't yet found the academic home for feminist awareness that would enable me to articulate these insights. It wasn't until much later—in 1986—that I would begin teaching a course that I have repeated at irregular intervals in the years since: "Feminist Perspectives on Motherhood." In this course, I would draw primarily on the writings that were emerging in the 1970s and 1980s. I would also surreptitiously draw upon my own life with my daughters, even though it was not until they were considerably older that I would be able to really plait these understandings together.

Nonetheless, beneath the frayed surface of my life, connections were beginning to tighten. I did not know how to make a professional life, but I knew that my academic pursuits were beginning to brush against my life with my daughters, even if I couldn't yet name the insights. During my first year at Wooster, I had proposed a course called "Fiction by Women"; the visible focus on women led to my appointment to the Committee on the Status of Women. In 1976–77, this chain of association, tenuous as it was, pulled me into interdisciplinary work that was developing across the nation and toward an emerging discipline: women's studies. Through random circumstances and a dearth of women faculty members, I was pulled toward ideas to which I couldn't yet give form. But I was entering a vortex of intellectual and social currents that had been circling me for years.

Appointed chair of the Committee on the Status of Women during my second year at the college, I received a directive: develop and propose a minor in women's studies. Still unseasoned and ill prepared for campus politics, I nonetheless understood duty. And so I worked with colleagues on the committee—most notably Sarah's dad, Jim Turner, a generous and supportive colleague from the history department—and drew up a rudimentary proposal: a smattering of "women in" courses, an experimental introductory course that was already on the books, and a new course called "Seminar in Women's Studies."

When our proposal won the nearly unanimous support of the faculty in February 1978, I rejoiced in a triumph that was both personal and collective. In the spirit of triumph and responsibility, Jim Turner and I selected ourselves to team teach the new course, as an overload, to a handful of eager students. In the dogma of the time, experiential insights from women's lives were central. Together we met with the students over lunch in the campus dining hall, spring of 1979, probing those insights, placing women's diaries and narratives in conversation with feminist theory. We argued out the ideas and repercussions of the rich but scarce texts of the era—*The Second Sex, Of Woman Born, Working It Out, Revelations.* We would later add such texts as *But Some of Us Are Brave, The Woman Warrior,* and *Making Face, Making Soul,* but at first we had to supplement with xeroxed materials, news items, and personal experiences. As we drew upon our own lives, I allowed a new breach in my public facade, reforming my nascent professional identity.

Jim's daughter, Sarah, eventually became Kara's closest childhood friend, and his wife was also an academic and friend. Jim's and my shared experiences, differentiated by gender, helped us to probe our emerging feminist thinking; the Turner family became a vital part of my community in those early years. And my teaching in women's studies reinvigorated my love for talking about language and literature: I was partly finding and partly making an alternative home in academic life.

Still I suffered: Who was I, as a professor, as a mother? How could I be both? I vividly recall a conversation at the home of other friends—John and Rena Hondros—whose dinner table became the nerve center of my adult social world throughout my life in Wooster. The discussion, late at night after numerous glasses of wine, turned on the question of what it means to be human. At what moment does a child become "a person"? Are reason and hence choice the sole defining human characteristics?

At one point, another friend and colleague whom I held in highest esteem asserted: "Really, a six-month-old baby is no different from a dog." This claim struck me as manifestly false and unresponsive to the real question: How do we assess human selfhood on some continuum between responding organism and pure freedom of intellectual choice? And when does a child in fact achieve sufficient reason to be held responsible for his or her own choices? How does a child move from being the responding organism—which a new infant seems to be—to becoming the responsible adult each of us claims to be? I called my friend's comment "stupid" but then fell into a paroxysm of silence: I couldn't speak the evidentiary base for my real thoughts.

Grappling with the loneliness of my life, I knew that my own parenting experiences were relevant to how I understood these questions, and I wanted to be able to draw upon them as part of my knowledge base. I felt that I *knew* some things because of what I had lived with my daughters, but I also felt that my colleagues would see these things as ordinary life, not knowledge. And even though I'd felt supported by the experience in "Seminar in Women's Studies," I hadn't yet developed the tools for professing this kind of knowledge and integrating it into my book knowledge. Despite my emergent campus successes and affiliations, I felt split, vulnerable, still alone.

WITH KARA OFF IN GRADE SCHOOL and Adriane off in preschool, I sometimes sat alone in my frayed chair at the heart of the house and simply settled into my solitude, resisting loneliness, guarding against interruption. In September 1979, during my first research leave—a ten-week period in which I was working on an article on Virginia Woolf's *Mrs. Dalloway*—I sat in that chair and wrote in my journal: "here I can enjoy the movement of leaf shadows on the rug, wavering in the sunlight as the breeze nudges the leaves outside. Chang sits on the stereo looking out the window; the sunlight shimmers silver in his hair. With Mozart on the stereo, a cup of coffee beside me, I will savor. I will taste the available pleasures in this space of mine. Why wait for future, unavailable pleasures?" The Woolf article was languishing, though I would complete it and even publish it, again dutifully. My personal life was intractable, and my professional identity was held hostage by the demands of textual analysis and professorial distance. I turned to the transient pleasures of language and sensory experience: light, the cat, music, taste. And when my daughters later wandered through the living room, I turned again to Adriane's lively squirming body and ready questions or Kara's quieter presence and probing thought as each in turn took her place beside my chair.

AT THE SAME TIME, another alchemy was at work. In my journal, my private self faltered, sounding forlorn and inadequate, falling short of phantom standards for both professor and mother. Yet during those same years, I took on not only the campus role of proposing and leading the early Women's Studies Program, but also a series of public lectures: marking my progress toward a new confluence of my personal life and my professional life.

The first lecture—as with much that I undertook in those early years— was in response to an external request in 1979: that I participate in a symposium on critics and criticism titled "Mimesis and Meaning." At least I chose my own title: "Female Realities in Fictional Structures." I spoke from notes for sixty uninterrupted minutes—not something I ever did in the classroom, where I always felt the need to interact with students' ideas. But here I spoke and even gained confidence in my own knowledge in this interdisciplinary forum, buoyed by a new pleasure in public performance. Besides, I was beginning to discern a different relationship between "reality" and "fictional structure" and to seek ways to tell women's experiences beyond the confinements of traditional narrative forms.

Chafing at the limits of this old straitjacket, I soon took on another public lecture in the fall of 1980: "Feminist Literary Criticism: Two Frames of Reference or One?" As I recall, the audience here was exclusively faculty, some invited from other institutions as well. Here, too, I spoke from notes, poking through the fissures in the dense walls of my previous thought: in speaking, I could blur my categories, probe for new insights without yet confronting the possible contradictions directly. I remember citing the metaphor of Scylla and Charybdis as a frequent favorite among feminist critics: I, too, was trying to slip through the impossible framing of our choices. I was exhilarated by the audience response but still tormented by all of the impossible choices that lined the cliffs of my emotional and professional life. I regularly averted my eyes from the choice that I would not make: my daughters or my work.

The women's studies vortex that I had been drawn into seemed to have become a maze I was trying to slip through with cagey intellect. At the same time, I was also facing an endless series of performance reviews and interim contracts. The college did not yet have a tenure-track system, so my survival depended on proving myself irreplaceable: since my appointment, every year or two had brought another evaluation of my teaching and my professional work—an opportunity to prove my value, but also the possibility of being found inadequate. Almost before I acknowledged the very real consequences, I had agreed to yet another public lecture: January 1981, under the judging eyes of review committees and tenure procedures. This year had been designated the one in which my possibility for continued employment would be finally decided.

My lecture this time was open to the entire campus: "Women: Living Stories, Telling Lives." Moving in on a paradox to which I thought I could give form, not just a conflict with which I must live, I wagered my professional future on talking about ideas I had not yet settled in my own mind. I drew on strands of thought from dinner table conversations, from small lectures, from committee meetings and classrooms, and from my own private musings; I laid out the core of the argument I had been trying to make for years: What is the relationship between the stories we are told and the way we understand our lives? How might women tell our own experiences, resisting the limits that old stories and expectations have placed on our lives? What are the consequences when women speak—claiming an "I"—and aim for an honest rendering of our own experiences?

I had many sources of knowledge for the questions I was asking: first and always, writers who had nourished my life when I had felt little other nourishment—Virginia Woolf, Doris Lessing, Adrienne Rich, Tillie Olsen, Margaret Drabble, Alice Munro, Toni Morrison; but also feminist analysis, narrative theory, psychology, sociology, scholarly inquiry into the nature of selfhood. For me, all these strands of inquiry were not separate, but part of the same whole. Beneath the surface of the life I thought I could not contain, I had returned to my insatiable hunger to figure out the central questions about how human beings make their lives. Exhilarated by my boldness in this lecture, nourished by my life with my daughters, propelled through a successful tenure review, I nonetheless still held off the other question: What does my own experience as a mother have to do with it all? At that point, I could only claim snippets of parental understanding—mostly in the women's studies classroom. I could not yet affirm as scholarly knowledge what I felt to be so potent as personal knowledge.

ADRIANE'S TWO QUESTIONS about love and work are suggestive of questions that children regularly pose about parental love, present and absent. By the time she posed the second question—"Which do you love more?"— she had already succumbed to the imposed either/or choice. But her earlier question—"Do you still love me when you're doing that work?"—is the more complex expression of a child's ongoing anxiety, and it is the question to which I responded with a resounding "yes" even as I continued with my work.

As I recall, she posed the either/or question while I was working on yet another lecture—this one to be delivered at the invitation of a former lover (still friend) at a sibling institution, about an author who would actually be in the audience: Tillie Olsen. This was yet another situation designed to induce anxiety. My writing about Olsen had taken the form of textual analysis, but it had been driven by personal circumstances. Olsen's short story "I Stand Here Ironing" had focused questions that I myself had asked as a single parent: What *is* the power of circumstances? How does a mother begin to understand "all that compounds a human being"? How can a child overcome the hazards of her own era—or a mother determine how best to live her own life, with and apart from her children? Having written and published on this story, I was an "authority" to be invited to Kenyon College during a visit by Tillie Olsen herself. Having lived my own experience as a single mother, I nonetheless felt a need to be discreet about personal history.

As I was trying to finish this lecture, desperate for the time and focus that it required, Kara fell ill. I rushed her to the doctor but continued desperately to work. Adriane hovered nearby—"Which do you love more, me or your work?"—needing attention too. Olsen's narrator begins, "I stand here ironing and what you asked me moves tormented back and forth with the iron." Sitting in the doctor's office, I did understand Olsen's narrator, tormented. And I understood, a bit, what it had taken for Olsen to have written this classic story, composing it as she rode the bus to work or at night as she moved her own iron back and forth to the rhythms of language. My lecture was titled "Rereading Women's Lives: Tillie Olsen's Generic Female." It was decidedly born of my own experiences as a woman, as a mother.

When my former lover—the one who had rejected me for the more mysterious woman in Colorado—phoned the next week, congratulating me on my success, I spoke of the sheer exhilaration of productive solitude, an overwhelming need to *claim* that solitude as real and positive. But my assertion was disingenuous: I was not alone—I had Kara and Adriane—and what I needed to claim was my life as well as within that life my solitude *and* my commitment to my daughters. When Tillie Olsen had spoken of "the college of motherhood" in her own lecture during the visit to Kenyon College, I had attended to that great paradox of parenthood: knowing my daughters, loving them, sharing my life with them had enriched my understanding far beyond what it would otherwise be, and yet that understanding had to struggle continually to find expression, struggle against so many cultural assumptions about motherhood—struggle, too, against all the odds that responsibility for children and interruption by children inevitably set up.

I knew that I sometimes yelled at my own children, bemoaned their intrusions, wished them out of the room—occasionally even pounded the mattresses of their beds in sheer frustration. But not for a moment did I wish them undone. The incredible core of human caring, the mystery of human development, the particularity of their individual existences—these things they brought to me, these things I would never wish away.

20

Chang and the Girls

A sunny September weekend in London, still 2003. We are here for Kara's wedding, a day to celebrate publicly: thirty friends and family members will gather in simple celebrations as Kara officially joins her life with Andrzej's. But I begin this September 1 by reflecting privately on my love for my daughters, setting my course by their presence as I have so often done in their growing years. On this wedding day, they will be together in the brief morning hours before the larger gatherings. En route to them, I undertake my first task of the day, for I told Kara I would buy some flowers myself.

Alone but suffused with family feeling, I open the door of the Brompton Hotel, smiling as I descend the steps in front and enter the sunny morning of late summer in London. I wait while cabs whiz past and pedestrians gather impatiently. When the light changes, I step off the curb across from the South Kensington tube station and move toward the triangular traffic island, nearly filled by flowers arranged in bunches. My eyes seek among the blooms, large and small, still being put out, for the day is early. In the morning bustle, the island dazzles with color—vivid magenta, pale pink, yellow, purple, blue, red. I pick out what Kara has requested: bunches of ivory roses and purple delphiniums to add to the red roses and more elaborate arrangements she has already purchased.

With my arms full of flowers, I look toward a day bursting with joyful celebrants. For now, I savor my own happiness, alone, as I walk on toward the apartment in which Kara prepares for her wedding, attended by her sister. Behind me in the hotel, others are rousing themselves and beginning to dress, stirred from jet lag into wakeful anticipation. Ron will put on his new suit— a father-of-the-bride suit that I helped him purchase a month ago. Other wedding guests, few in number, intimates of Kara and Andrzej, will later converge on their Fulham Road apartment and then head off together to the Chelsea Town Hall. But first Adriane and I will have these quiet moments with Kara in her bedroom, providing extra hands as she arranges delicate beaded pins in her hair, fastens her floor-length ivory satin and lace dress, gets ready for this momentous occasion—the three of us in joyous preparation.

HAVING SNATCHED FOUR DAYS from the first weeks of this semester by carefully arranging syllabi and student assignments so as not to neglect my academic responsibilities, I managed to be fully present at the wedding. Now I have returned to a schedule crammed with campus commitments. But I carry within me the joy of that celebration. The power of this recent memory jostles against the power of more distant memories of times when we three worked so hard to collaborate as a single-parent family.

I pause to rejoice in Kara's happiness with Andrzej as I picture her there in her new life in London while the rest of us resettle in our distant homes: Adriane in New York, where she misses her sister but thrives in her own life among friends and her current work in children's publishing; Ron and I here in Wooster, the home that all of us still have in common, now inhabited only by the two of us, not even a cat to share our daily rhythms. These are the changes of our lives: sending daughters forth into independent choices and new commitments, reassembling hearts and selves at home.

The house to which Ron and I have returned is not the house in which Kara, Adriane, and I lived most of our lives as a single-parent family, though it is the same one into which we moved in 1988 as we approached the end of those years. I had met Ron the previous winter; we would marry a year later. But for the preceding thirteen years, my daughters and I relied upon each other, together making our family of three. As we survived our early years in Wooster, I gradually accepted that this was our life, not some temporary stopping place on the way to something else, though I also knew that the eventual goal was for each of my daughters to go on to make a life of her own. And I knew that such lives would take them elsewhere.

FALL BREAK, OCTOBER 2003: the earth continues to turn. Trees burst into fiery colors, burnt colors, shining with the light that falls on them, casting deep shadows as evening comes on a little earlier each day. I am trying to use these few days of pause in the semester to return again to our lives as a family of three, when Kara and Adriane and I were still forging our single-parent family. Now, full of the knowledge of their distance, their rapidly changing lives, I must work all the harder to reenter that time.

ONCE I HAD BEEN GRANTED TENURE in the spring of 1981, we began to see our lives in Wooster as more rooted, more clearly ours to make, at least for these growing years. And those lives required a concerted effort for all three of us, particularly that next fall when Adriane was in school full-time, and Pauline, needing a job that would provide her with more hours and income, no longer worked for us. This shift was unsettling for all of us as we jointly decided that Kara and Adriane would have mutual responsibility for themselves every day after school on days when I could not get home from campus by 3:30. My office was only three blocks away, and I could almost always be reached by telephone during the after-school hours. Nonetheless, Kara, age ten, would inevitably take on the extra burden of responsibility, though it was my hope that they would provide mutual support for each other. All three of us were increasingly working together on making our lives.

We were by then a proud household of females—that is, unless you include Chang, our Siamese cat, who had joined us midstream in 1978. But he was neutered and, after all, only a cat. Still, he never thought he was only a cat, and he never accepted that he was neutered. He usually acted as if he was in charge: imperiously guarding us from outside intruders, even from people we wanted to welcome. He would sit on the post at the bottom of the stairs, watching for arrivals, glaring at the front door immediately before him.

I sometimes joked that we had allowed him in our household only because he was neutered. After all, that's the way many people saw feminists in those days: "ball breakers" was the common label. Why not adopt it humorously? I usually blushed with shame even as I made my joke: my ideas about gender were so much more complicated than that. But it is true that Kara and Adriane and I resisted most notions of authority as well as any idea that we needed a male presence in order to be a family.

THAT IS MY RECOLLECTION, at least, but I do not wish to rely on my own singular perspective. And so I rummage through the papers I have gathered around me to locate an associative essay that Kara wrote during her senior year of college in a course on women's writing. Writing her memories in a stream of consciousness, she described our second house in Wooster—her primary childhood home. She sent a copy to me. As I read the essay now, I see this house anew: it is as I recall it, and yet it is angled through a child's eyes, a young adult's memories; it is shaped by her own worries and angers and observations and strengths.

The TV room was upstairs. The front door was heavy. And solid. But it was fragile because there was a big glass pane centered in the dark wood (was it oak?). There was a white gauzy curtain tautly covering the glass—but you could peek through it to see who was on the porch. Once [Julie] slammed the screen door hard. The glass broke. She could have hurt someone. I was Angry. I was scared. I wanted to cry, but she made me too angry. She shouldn't have done that; and I knew it.

When you came through the front door the stairs were right in front of you. The cat sat at the pillar at the bottom. The pillar was dark oak; varnished and old. The cat was Siamese. He was new. But he knew that only certain people went upstairs. He protected us; he swatted his paws at strangers; he hissed; sometimes he bit people. I loved him. He was cautious and certain, angry and strong. He knew when I was upset. He loved me.

The TV room was upstairs. There was a mirror at the top of the stairs. Square and high. It had dark oak borders like the stairs. Glossy and polished; and dusty. I could see my face in it. The TV room was straight left, right there at that end of the hall. It was usually messy; that was my fault, but sometimes my sister's fault too. I remember when there were lite-brite pegs all over the floor. And legos. And a sleeping bag for lying on. And books too—lots of them. . . . I liked Scooby Doo. You could watch him at 4 o'clock when mom wasn't home from work and you were supposed to be doing something else.

IT IS NO SURPRISE that Kara's description of our family home highlights not only her love for our cat—feisty and original and certain of his role in our family—as well as her interest in television and toys, but also her own feeling of responsibility, for this feeling was very real. My children were "latch-key kids"—as the press liked to call them in that era—and I drew heavily upon the independence I had cultivated in them throughout their lives. They came home from school to an empty house; they negotiated their own conflicts with playmates in the neighborhood—witness the slammed door, with broken glass, or witness Adriane's story of a winter encounter with a neighborhood friend. That same Julie who figures in Kara's memory tormented Adriane on a snowy hill, frightening her into a mad dash home, arriving at our front door—oak, with a large glass window pane—with wet socks, cold feet, and a missing boot.

NOT SO LONG AGO, years after both Kara and Adriane had moved on into their adult lives, I encountered Julie-of-the-broken-glass, now a young adult, busy with her own life. We chatted a bit, and she recalled a story of the day when Adriane and she had obtained the key to the xerox machine at the college library—assuming it was free and using my name as authorization—and then rampantly xeroxed hands and elbows and various parts of their own bodies before returning the key. She reminded me that when I had discovered this transgression—knowing that my professional credibility had been tarnished—I had briefly lost my temper at them before telling them that it would be their responsibility to repay the cost of the nickel-a-page xeroxing they had done on the good-faith response of the student at the library desk who had given them the key. Reminiscing, Julie said to me all these years later, still puzzled by my response, "But you were Ms. Freedom."

Even in these ways, I was trying to balance my freedoms against my responsibilities, my daughters' freedom against their need for nurture. But so, too, were Kara and Adriane: all three of us needed constantly to renegotiate how to live this balance. How else were they to grow into the independent and capable young women they needed to be?

When Adriane, in response to the sexism of a grade-school gym teacher, decided to march on the sidewalk carrying a sign, "Girls are people, too," I rejoiced in her self-affirmation. But I knew that relying on simple slogans would not be sufficient as we worked out our own ways in a resistant culture. "Ms. Freedom" needed always to be conscious of the hazards of the world around us.

I had not, of course, forgotten the apple orchard, site of Kara's early sexual molestation, nor could I simply dismiss the risks I had taken in my own behavior as a "free woman." How, then, to nurture their independence as growing girls without subjecting them to the worst hazards of freedom?

I RECALL NOW something that Kara said to me earlier as she prepared to enter third grade: "Mom, I don't know how a third-grader is supposed to act." The comment had amused me, for I had had no idea that a third-grader would be conscious of acting any differently than a second-grader. But Kara was experiencing a jolt up the ladder of maturity and sensed that she would be called to different behavior: no longer a small child.

But she wasn't grown up either. When she refused to allow me to comb all of the tangles out of her hair, I gave her an ultimatum: comb it out yourself, or we'll need to get your hair cut. I can't remember exactly how these events transpired, but I do recall at least one day on which I allowed her to go to school with an ugly nest of tangles in the back of her hair, following her own assumption of responsibility for the hair she would not have cut. Did I allow that to happen more than once? Did I allow it to happen even once? I must have done so, in keeping with my pledge to give her choices as well as to avoid a conflict I had come to hate.

But the image of the nest of tangles, barely covered by a surface of combed hair haunts me: How is the mother of a third-grader supposed to act? How is the mother of daughters supposed to act? How was I to prepare them for the responsibilities I would hand to them with increasing regularity in the coming years? Could I be a responsible parent when I relied so heavily on them to care for themselves?

I NEVER WAS THE KIND OF MOTHER WHO HOVERED, who made her daughters' growth into femininity a central concern, whether by demands or by careful attention. In her memoir of growing up as Margaret Mead's daughter, Catherine Bateson recalls lovingly the attention that her mother had always given to Catherine's hair, grooming and nurturing in close attendance upon her daughter. I have also read the affirmations of many African American daughters who treasure the memories of their mothers' close attention to their hair, carefully segmenting and combing and oiling. I read longingly of these daughters' memories. But then I think of my own mother's problem with her mother's conservative expectation that she retain her coiled braid of uncut hair, not breaking that code until after her mother's death.

For good or ill, I was not like any of these other mothers: I did not want to be a hair monitor. After a certain age, I expected my daughters to take care of their own hair, and even before they reached that age, I had little patience for grooming activities. My initial reaction to news of Adriane's peer haircut was pretty typical: I was not particularly invested in cultivating any kind of explicit "girlness." But my experience of the aftermath of Adriane's haircut drew me into a more complicated response: I did not like subjecting my daughters to the gender expectations of the world around them, and yet it remained my job as their mother to help them survive within that world.

THE FIRST YEAR we no longer had Pauline in our lives, Adriane, in first grade, decided to refuse to wear socks. Seeing no harm in this refusal, I allowed her to go to school with bare feet inside her shoes. But her teacher objected and insisted that Adriane be denied recess—"so you won't get blisters." Other children taunted her, too, calling her "stinky feet" and asking her why she never wore skirts to school: "Don't you have any dresses? Are you some kind of boy?" I asked her if she wanted to have dresses and to wear socks, but she continued to prefer what she preferred: bare feet and the freedom of pants on the playground. At least I had the sense to challenge the teacher's denial of recess: I saw no logic in that. Neither Adriane nor I ever received an apology, but at my insistence her independent choice at last prevailed.

For Kara, feeling overweight and awkward during her late grade-school years, clothes were a different issue: no outward apparel seemed to match her sense of self, the kernel of self-possession now nearly lost to self-doubt. With her friend Sarah and Sarah's mother, she even joined Weight Watchers for a while in fifth grade. Hating diets and also hating her diminished self-esteem, I wasn't sure how to respond as she wrestled with her changing body—the preteen, excited to have her first period, phoning me from Sarah's house in glee and racing home on her bike for an affirming hug, was also awkwardly aware of her own flesh.

But in her claim on this new body, she became attentive to clothing and began to develop a new sense of style. This was something I had little experience with, no reservoir of feminine skill in apparel to draw upon: I felt my Mennonite heritage as a disadvantage. But she knew her own wishes, and I was learning to honor that. I later gave her a clothing allowance through junior high and high school, gradually building up responsibility for purchases and for the money I provided: the money was hers to allocate, and the clothing mistakes that everybody makes were hers to make. She increasingly developed confidence in those decisions. But much later, when she was fifteen and we were driving home from a trip to the mall, she commented on the choice of a blouse (both frilly and expensive) she had decided to purchase: "I know you think I'm immoral, Mom, but I really wanted that blouse even if it did cost so much."

Over time, we learned each other's differences, fought to accept them. We worked together, sometimes bumping against each other uneasily, sometimes mirroring each other's moods and perceptions. And each of my daughters grew in self-definition as we persisted in our household of shared responsibility, resisting imposed authority. We would converge on the kitchen to collaborate on dinner preparation and hang out, eating our fake-it meals, sometimes just sitting on the floor together. We would talk through our respective days and needs, with no one in particular in charge.

We spent those years together developing mutual respect and trust, even as I relied so heavily on Kara and Adriane to care for themselves, taking risks with their independence and doubting whether the nurturing I did provide was enough. But I eventually trusted Kara's observation at fifteen or so, as we walked together to a neighborhood home at which she would be babysitting: "You're the best mother I know—we have the best relationship of mothers and daughters I know." And yet I know that the heavy burden of early responsibility took its toll.

IN THE MORE THAN TWO DECADES since I last talked with Pauline, I have thought of her often, honoring her contributions to Kara's, Adriane's, and my own early life in Wooster. So I was gratified as well as amazed when I received a phone call just this past August, shortly before Kara's wedding. An unfamiliar voice inquired, "Are you the Joanne Frye who used to teach at the College of Wooster?" When I said yes, she responded, "My mother used to take care of your children. We were just sitting around and trying to remember the name of your Siamese cat."

"That was Chang," I said, still stunned by this voice from the past. When Pauline herself came on the phone, she reminisced briefly about an incident that has often been on my mind: the time when Christopher and the cat gave Adriane a haircut. I never knew that Chang was involved in the haircut, but when Pauline told me that I could write a book about those experiences, I was thrown again into my reflective reality: I *could* write a book about those experiences; indeed, I *was*, I *am* writing a book about those experiences, about Pauline and Chang, about socks and haircuts, about each of my daughters growing into herself, despite our misshapen world.

KARA AND ADRIANE: they were girls, each in her own way, and people, each in her own way. The second year after we began forging ahead without Pauline, one of Adriane's grade-school teachers said, "I really love that little girl. She has such sparkle and energy and intelligence. And she is learning, too, to be still." And Kara's sixth-grade teacher said, "She's really complex. There's so much there: her astute perceptions, her deep insights. I love her quiet intelligence and growing self-confidence."

As for me, I loved their differences, loved their individual presences. I did not want them to have to be "girls," cut to an unyielding mold, but I needed them to grow into strong women, able to make their own lives. I am grateful that over the years Chang and Pauline and I—as well as the men and women around us—did our best to encourage their distinctiveness, to guard their humanity, even as we noted the hazards of the surrounding culture. And I am grateful to Kara and Adriane for all the ways in which they took on the responsibilities I handed to them.

When I look at them now—in wonder and awe—I see as well the many selves each contains. These selves are not like Russian dolls, all identical, tidily tucked one inside the other, in ever-shrinking mimicry. They are instead the shape-shifting realities of each one's unique individuality.

Eerily—as I look back—Kara forms and reforms before my eyes: the radiant bride and dedicated writer dissolves into the eager college student and gifted linguist, then into the determined teenager seeking a larger world, the awkward and anxious preteen who nonetheless knew her own competence, the quiet grade-schooler with a book in her hands, the self-possessed two-year-old. So, too, with Adriane: the confident New York editor, writer, and lover of young children transforms in my memory into the honors college student turned inward, the proud distance runner, the nervous ninth-grader en route to a new high school in California, the constant questioner, the lithe and lively child full of words and stories, the mischievous toddler and climber of monkey bars. And I look forward, knowing that these metamorphoses will continue, challenging my thought anew as each daughter illuminates her own distinctive ways of being. Though they have moved on from our shared home of three, each has also woven into her being the threads of the life that we made together, resisting imposed ideas of authority as we collaborated with each other, even if we sometimes let Chang think that he was the one in charge.

21

Rumors of Crickets

Wilbur burst into tears. 'I don't *want* to die,' he moaned. 'I want to stay alive, right here in my comfortable manure pile with all my friends. I want to breathe the beautiful air and lie in the beautiful sun.'" I have found this passage in our musty copy of *Charlotte's Web*, stored in a third-floor closet with other children's books, stuffed animals, and games from my daughters' childhood.

I pause in the pressures of this academic year, needing to revisit an earlier winter season during this current winter break. Though I rarely have time for my walks—and the crickets and mourning doves have long since fallen into silence—I will find the time to return to a fragile period in the early 1980s, a time of grief and uncertainty that ruptured our growing confidence as a single-parent family.

ADRIANE AND I were snuggled together on the couch in the living room for some early evening reading time when the telephone interrupted. She waited impatiently as I answered it, spoke briefly, and then returned to my spot next to her. Seeing tears in my eyes, she reassured me: "Don't worry, Mom. They won't kill Wilbur. Remember?"

Wilbur would serve as an excuse a six-year-old could understand, but my tears sprang from a different well of grief. The phone call had delivered the news that Michael had made the definitive decision to leave town, to move on into a different life. Though he and I had long since ceased hoping to make a life together, the news of his departure touched an emptiness in my life: a persistent loneliness, a yearning for adult companionship.

But there was more to come from this well, now tapped by a random phone call. It had already been a year and a half since my father's diagnosis with prostate cancer. He would be dead in less than a year. I did not yet know the timing of his death, but I had begun to recognize its imminence. At that moment, I felt surrounded by loss and the threat of loss. I snuggled closer to Adriane as we continued reading, waiting for the glorious miracle that would save the life of Wilbur the pig: words spun from the entrails of a self-sacrificing spider.

THE SUMMER after my father's diagnosis, when we thought he was in remission, he and I had spent extended time together remodeling the bathroom in the house I had moved into two years previously. The girls and I could no longer be satisfied with a bathtub; we needed a shower, too. Working with my father, I was reminded of the long hours he and I had spent in my waning days on the farm, working in the garage to build the bookshelves I would leave behind as a monument to a failed marriage. On this bathroom project, we again shared manual labor and talk, developing a closeness that came most easily for him with constructive physical effort. In that earlier time, I had learned by inference that my marriage with Lawrence could not be repaired. Now we shared in other ways: probing our differences about religion, about family, about work.

In the process, we not only had agreed to accept our differences but had also come to a new understanding of a commonality between our work lives that gave me secret pleasure. His work as an engineer and a remodeler required the effort of wrestling with space, imagining objects in interrelationship. As we worked, I realized that I experienced my work as a literary critic in remarkably similar terms, wrestling ideas into a new spatial arrangement, developing a new intricacy of interrelationship. During our work on the bathroom—tracking down a small radiator that would fit the available space, planning a hidden panel that would give access to the pipes for the shower, sawing boards to precise measurement on sawhorses on the porch, cutting plasterboard to fit the odd spaces in the ceiling—he and I talked of this new recognition of commonality. As we worked together I sensed that he was ready to stop judging me for life decisions he could not understand.

A YEAR LATER, 1981, the remission was not so certain. Earlier that fall, just before school had resumed, Kara, Adriane, and I had visited my parents in South Bend. We had gone to the zoo, played games, canoed on the St. Joseph River in front of their home. Three generations of family: we had laughed and walked and talked together. But my father had not been feeling well. As we had played, we had watched the ripple of pain that crossed his face. We had been silent when he retreated to lie down. He had not talked much about his illness, but on one of our walks he had told me that he was particularly worried about me: he could not see who would be there to take care of me when he died.

On the drive home, Kara and Adriane and I had talked of their grandfather's illness, of mortality, of the uncertainty with which we all watched him suffer. I kept silent about his fear that I would be abandoned—without male protection—if he died. I was warmed by my father's concern, but I did not want my daughters to think that we needed male protection. Still, I felt my loneliness in my own way and also knew that this loneliness was part of what was on my father's mind.

THAT FALL AND WINTER I carried on with my life, trying to renew my claim on my freedom and my daughters as I trudged from one day to the next, feeling the burden of need around me. This was our first year without Pauline, so I was relying more and more on Kara to be in charge after school, but this increased reliance also meant that I worried much more, felt a greater need to be available, to come home as soon as possible, to bridge the stresses of home and work without any buffer.

In my waking nightmares, I sometimes saw myself standing very still as multiple hands reached out and grabbed at me, removing my flesh in great chunks until I stood naked and skeletal and alone, used up. Knowing that I needed the pieces of my flesh for my own sustenance, I resisted the reaching hands of others who might simply grab them from me. And yet I also knew that the needs of my father, my mother, my daughters were urgent, not to be denied.

In December, I wrote in my journal: "I see myself leaping off a high peak, caught mid-air, alone, high up, suspended momentarily with the knowledge that the fall is inevitable." I don't know what I was leaping toward or if I could have done other than fall. Finally, I said out loud what I had been thinking all along: "I think my father is dying." I said this to Michael in our farewell conversation, trying to absorb just how alone I felt.

THAT JANUARY I decided quite peremptorily to undergo a tubal ligation, an outpatient procedure I could schedule between terms and while the children were in school. When my mind—absorbed by responsibilities, by bodies, by mortality and loss, by sexual desire and maternal nurture—tossed up this idea, I simply acted upon it. Regardless of future prospects, I understood that I could not risk being stretched further, could not risk some hypothetical future plea that I have another child—even should I ever again wish to join my life with a man.

THE FOLLOWING MARCH, with my father's condition deteriorating rapidly, my parents suffered the further crisis of a flood from the river overflowing its banks, creeping its way into their home. As the pump in the basement worked overtime, something malfunctioned, and even my strong mother fell ill with carbon monoxide poisoning. Where was I supposed to be? In the classroom with my students, doing the job I was paid to do? At home with my daughters, who needed parental guidance, lacking even a paid childcare giver? At my parents' side as they suffered a new physical and emotional assault?

I relied on my sister to rush to my parents' aid; she, too, had many commitments of her own, but at least she also had a husband to keep things going at home. In this sense, my father had been right: I was unprotected. Kara and Adriane and I would later find a weekend to visit. But I never could do enough. I grieved now for my mother as well as for my father: How could she sustain this caregiving without respite? She, too, was unprotected.

When the girls and I visited for another weekend in May, my father was in hospice care at home. We arrived to find him skeletal in maroon pajamas in a hospital bed in the living room with an IV tube delivering basic sustenance. His flesh seemed to fall from him as he lay there, pale and weak. His face contorted with pain; his tongue grew thick with medication; his eyes blurred with tears. But he smiled when we walked in.

Adriane, at age seven still uninhibited by social convention, went directly to her grandfather's side: "How are you, Grandpa?" she asked. "Mommy thought you would die three weeks ago." Kara, nearly eleven, could not speak the words but sat quietly by his side, intermittently holding his hand.

We spent much of that visit gathered around the hospital bed, maps in hand, planning the trip that Kara, Adriane, and I would take to California that summer. It was important to my father that we not cancel this planned trip just because we all knew he was dying. Over the years, he had taken his young family on many such trips to visit his own brother and my mother's brother, both of whom lived in California with their families. He wanted us to do the same: camp our way across the country, visit my brother in California, make sure that we nourished these family bonds.

IT HAD NOT BEEN EASY to convince Lawrence to yield this particular portion of Kara and Adriane's summer to my vacation needs. Although he had kept our daughters with him for only several weeks at a stretch in their youngest years, he was by now invoking as his right the literal timetable indicated in our divorce agreement: "If the Husband's residence is more than 75 miles from the Wife's residence, the Husband shall be entitled to visit with the children up to thirteen (13) weeks per year at mutually agreeable times; said thirteen week limitation would include extended summer vacation which shall not exceed thirteen weeks."

Once we were living our separate lives, with Kara and Adriane in school and spring breaks almost never coinciding conveniently, the thirteen weeks had come to mean two weeks at Christmas break and a full eleven weeks of the summer—literally their entire summer vacation. In drafting the language of the agreement, we had necessarily been speaking hypothetically: we had had no idea where I would be living, what sort of schedule Kara and Adriane would have, what sort of wishes any of us would develop in the meantime. But in making actual arrangements, Lawrence, unless he had other wishes for his own summer, held tightly to his sense of entitlement.

The previous summer it had suited his schedule for Kara, Adriane, and me to take a one-week camping trip at the end of the summer. Perhaps he had had other plans of his own, or perhaps he had approved the people and places we had visited: we had stopped to see his brother, Richard, in New York, spent time in Boston with friends, and then left Kara for an additional one-week visit at Cape Cod with her friend Sarah and the Turner family before the return for school. But this summer he had no reason to want to put off the beginning of his visit with them, nor did he approve a travel plan that included a women's studies conference and a visit to my brother. So it had taken much cajoling to stem his rage and eke out this three and a half weeks from what he felt was his time.

HAVING WON the right to this vacation, we loaded into Goldie the tent and camp stove, the cooler and sleeping bags and clothing and set off toward California with the excitement of a rare adventure together. Our plan was to camp our way across country, attend the women's studies conference being held that June at Humboldt State University in Arcata, California, and then extend this work trip into a vacation with visits to my father's brother in the San Francisco Bay Area and my own brother in Sacramento. En route, we stopped in South Bend one more time to rehearse our plans, to say good-bye, not knowing if my father would survive the three and a half weeks of our trip.

When we left South Bend, we took with us, along with all of our gear, a change purse full of coins that my mother provided: this was before cell phones, and all of us knew we would need to be in touch regularly. At campgrounds in Iowa, Nebraska, Utah, Nevada, we sought out phone booths, dropped in our quarters and nickels and dimes at the operator's command, and waited anxiously for my mother to answer and reassure us that both she and my father were still holding steady.

At these campgrounds in Iowa, Nebraska, Utah, Nevada, we also pitched our tent, took walks through fields and woods, built fires, cooked our makeshift meals, listened in the night to trucks shifting gears on mountain highways. Kara and Adriane helped to cut vegetables and watch simmering pots, took turns washing and drying dishes—snapping wet dish towels at each other playfully. They worked with me each evening to pitch the tent and each morning to break camp. The drive was grueling—in a tin box of a car without air conditioning and only one driver—but the spirit in the car resisted the grief we carried with us. We were exploring the country on our second vacation together, and we were committed to enjoying the rare opportunity to be with one another, away from the usual stresses of our lives.

When I look at the photographs of that trip, I marvel at the joy we were able to make our own—tent sites by rivers and among mountains; crashing waves of the Pacific Ocean and obscure caves as backdrop to two girls poking in the sand for sea shells; one or the other of them wandering along the paths at Humboldt State, among huge redwoods and women's studies scholars; wildflowers on the cliffs high above the shore along Highway 1 down the California coast, two girls grinning happily; four cousins dripping chlorine from the swimming pool or playing with the Schnauzer in the backyard of my brother's home in Orangevale.

Among these joys, I recall as well the sorrows. The latter were especially activated when I attended a showing of a film made from Tillie Olsen's *Tell Me a Riddle*. Though I resisted the distortions of this adaptation, I wept in recognition as I watched Eva of the film, dying of cancer, scrabbling her fingers on the bedsheet just as my father was doing at home in Indiana. The sorrows: always knowing that death was at hand, that loss was integral to our travels.

I HAVE NO JOURNAL ENTRIES from that entire summer—nothing between June 7 and October 1. But I have memories. After the return trip—more phone booths, more pitching of the tent—we had one last family reunion, knowing that my father's death was imminent. A Fourth of July gathering: my parents; my brother Don and his wife and two sons; my sister Eileen and her husband and three sons; Kara and Adriane and I—all gathered from our disparate lives. We have a photo in which we are ranged together across the generations, centered on my mother and father, he gaunt in his maroon pajamas, barely able to sit. But we are laughing, for my dying father, never in the least off color, has just gotten his own inadvertent joke: "Did you remember to flash the cock?" he said as my brother-in-law hurried to join us in the picture after setting the automatic response. We all laughed together, though Adriane turned to me and asked: "What's funny?"

AFTER THAT, Kara and Adriane went to Bloomington to be with their father. I returned to South Bend to be with my own father during his last days and with my mother in her caregiving. This opportunity was again rare: for once, my own schedule was the most flexible. I had acted on my professional commitments by attending the women's studies conference; my daughters were safely ensconced with their father. I would meet my other obligations later. For once, my only obligation was to be with my parents.

I joined my mother's vigil, knowing that we did not have long. It was almost as if my father had been controlling his dying, waiting for us to return from our visit to my brother, his son; waiting for that final gathering of the entire family; waiting, again, for my sister's arrival at his deathbed and then his final good-bye to my mother, his wife.

I DON'T KNOW WHEN I made them, but I have notes on a napkin, recalling my father's last days. These notes are peppered with names of nurses, references to oxygen, and the question "Is this it?" But they do not make chronological sense. When did I arrive? When did we call my sister? When did I definitively say good-bye?

The notes say that on Tuesday he is still breathing, having trouble swallowing, needing the oxygen, scrabbling at the covers. He murmurs, "Let me go," and gestures for some kind of release. We phone Eileen, knowing that she would want to be here. When she arrives, we take turns keeping vigil, but the hours remaining are very few. He wants to be free of this life. I say good-night, good-bye, I love you, knowing this time will be the last. Now it is Mom's vigil, for which Dad has waited.

When he dies, we are ready. It is deep in the night, July 28, 1982. Eileen says we should open all the windows and rejoice that he has finally stopped suffering. We open all the windows; we rejoice; we cry; we breathe the night air. On the hospital bed in the living room, my father's body looks stark white in the moonlight.

THE NEXT MORNING I call Kara and Adriane at their father's house to tell them that their grandfather has died. I have yet to negotiate whether Lawrence will allow them to come to the memorial service since it will take place on his time—during his entitled weeks. This death is Kara and Adriane's first in the family, and I want them to experience it among family. I want, too, to have them with me in my own need.

When I call, they do not know how to respond; it is all too new to them. But Lawrence is clear in his own response: "You already took them away from me at the beginning of the summer. Anyway, it's not convenient for me to travel with them now."

After much cajoling on my part, we reach a compromise. He will allow them to attend their grandfather's memorial service if I do all of the driving, picking them up from Bloomington the day before the service and returning them to him in Bloomington the day after.

Again in Goldie's embrace, my daughters and I find comfort in each other's company, talking of mortality, remembering canoe trips and board games and walks along the river on previous visits to South Bend. We try to speak of death as a natural part of life. But Adriane says later, "I don't want to grow up, Mom. Then you'll die, and other people will die. I like being a child."

THAT FALL I began to have the only recurring dream I have ever had. In it, I am talking with my father, who lies skeletal and pale in a hospital bed, but already dead, his flesh cold and hard. With the logic of dreams, I know that he is dead, though still dying, and I say to him: "It's not fair that you have to go through this twice. No one should have to go through this twice."

In my waking hours, I moved among people as if going about my normal business. But I would surreptitiously peer into their faces when they weren't looking, and I would wonder: How can they go on, how can any of us go on, once a loved one has been taken from us?

LOOKING AT *CHARLOTTE'S WEB* NOW, I am struck anew by its themes of motherhood and mortality, growing up and the power of language. As the county fair approaches, the crickets sing: "Summer is over and gone. Over and gone, over and gone. Summer is dying, dying." The narrator comments: "The crickets spread the rumor of sadness and change." Charlotte herself, facing death, says, "After all, what's a life, anyway? We're born, we live a little while, we die." And when she dies, she dies alone, reassured at least that her children are safe.

As for Fern, she outgrows her commitment to Wilbur, moves through the fair and into her adolescence. Wilbur lives on happily in the barn among other animals, finding satisfaction in an ongoing conversation with Charlotte's offspring. The book's closing thoughts, however, return to Charlotte and play upon the results of her commitment to using words, spun magically into her web, to save Wilbur: "a true friend and a good writer." But no one really comments that she was a mother and a weaver of webs, a being with her own understanding of the world, her own problems in life.

22

Vertigo

The gaunt limbs of El Greco's St. Sebastian held me captive. I stared at the sinewy muscles, yearning with my body, grieving with my body. How was it that these elongated thighs of a religious martyr could suggest both sex and death, grief and desire?

In Washington, DC, August 1982, to serve on a panel evaluating NEH grant applications, I had taken a few hours for myself to visit the special El Greco exhibit at the National Gallery. Not being religious, I do not know why this particular image had halted me, but as I stared into the V of the thighs, I began to sway, needing to sit down. *This is what the Victorian novelists meant when they spoke of swooning*, I thought as the room spun around me.

MY WORLD WAS SPINNING during those years. Though I had been granted tenure in the spring of 1981, the process had kept me under such continual scrutiny over the entire period of my teaching life that its successful completion had brought me more uncertainty than relief: Was this how I meant to be making my life? And now: my father was dead, his gaunt limbs having become cold and hard. And now: Michael was permanently gone not just from my life, but from the town where I continued to make my home in his absence. And now: I was again alone, hungry for something more, gaunt in my own way but still needing to give nourishment to my daughters. Staring at St. Sebastian's limbs, I was dizzy with the losses, dizzy, too, with memory and desire, the ground unstable beneath my feet.

MICHAEL PASSED THROUGH TOWN THAT FALL, visiting his old haunts, his old acquaintances. As an old acquaintance, I, too, was visited. We sat upright, stilted, on the living room couch that matched my chair—frayed olive green threads over foam rubber—barely touching, barely knowing each other. Kara and Adriane drifted through the living room, saying hello, wondering why this strange, stiff man was visiting their mother.

YEARS EARLIER, during the peak of our time together, Michael and I had lain together in bed one afternoon, each of us reading. He was reading a law text. I was reading feminist essays. At first, I had felt exhilarated at a sense, even in my own private thinking, that I was part of a movement, participating in a cause: an independent woman, rejecting historical-traditional expectations that a woman is infinitely giving, always living for others. But as I lay in bed with my book propped on my naked rib cage and one leg thrown casually over Michael's, my thoughts turned against me, accusing me of selfishness, failure to attend to larger patterns at all, failure to attend to other people, to my own daughters, to anyone else, as I indulged my own self-satisfactions.

I had turned from Michael, turned into myself, curling around a central vulnerability I could not protect. Shaking deeply inside, unable to cry or shout or even to speak, I had fallen into a chaos of meaninglessness. This was a new kind of madness for me: I had always before cried or shouted out and had sensed another part of myself watching the hysteria. But this time I was deep inside the experience of chaos. I could not cry, and I was not watching myself.

Michael, eventually realizing that I had turned away, had put down his book and asked, "Are you crying?"

"No, I can't cry."

He had held me for a long time during which I completely lost track of minutes or hours, words or ideas. I had lain there, inert, taken over by the whirling chaos. Michael had questioned me, saying, "I can't help thinking if I weren't here, you wouldn't feel this deep unhappiness."

At that point, I had argued with him, voicing my need for him. But I had also been convinced that my unhappiness was somehow due to him.

FIVE YEARS LATER, seated unsteadily before the El Greco painting, I recalled that moment and knew that it hadn't been only about Michael. It really had been about some deep hunger to participate in something larger than myself and still to love myself. I had rejected the old absolutes. What if in embracing skepticism I had lost my grounding?

IN THE INTERVENING YEARS, I had continued to seek new grounding. Feminist analysis was central to this effort, but it also kept undercutting the ground I stood on. In February 1978, as chair of the Committee on the Status of Women, I had brought to the faculty a successful proposal for a women's studies minor at the college. In collaboration with my friend and colleague, Jim Turner, I had taught our newly developed course "Seminar in Women's Studies." I had, following upon Jim Turner's early version, developed my own course "Introduction to Women's Studies." In teaching that course, I had encountered anew a deep discouragement at the patterns of discrimination that converged on women, on my own life, though I had also grasped fragilely at the compensatory vitality of women's creative energies and capacities for self-expression.

In each of these endeavors, I had continued to question old premises, to relinquish old certainties. I had developed what has ever since been a kind of teaching mantra for me: *always ask the next hard question.* Asking the next hard question, I had begun to publish, had survived my tenure review, had continued to nourish my daughters. But the next hard question left me unmoored: I needed this skepticism, but I did not want to fall into cynicism.

Alone, I had sat in my chair doing my work: grading papers on a clipboard, reading novels with pen in hand, wringing out my own words and ideas as I tried to write. Kara and Adriane had drifted through, wondering what their mother was up to.

WHAT *WAS* THEIR MOTHER UP TO? Trying always to ask the next hard question, I was also trying to make my life. Having rejected the notion that work and motherhood were oppositional, I still had not found a way to include my need for sexual expression or even for men in my life. With my father dead and Michael gone, I was adrift. As a feminist critic, I had devoted much energy to a critique of heterosexual romance. Though I seemed to be indelibly heterosexual in my own preferences, I had learned that I need not look for the love of a man, and I certainly should not count on finding it. Why not let what was to happen happen?

AND DURING THOSE YEARS, I did find the occasional lover, though I was never able simply to claim disengaged sexual activity. By most people's standards, I could hardly be called promiscuous. Indeed, one of those occasional lovers accused me of celibacy when he heard how little I had been sexually active during those years. And I did write in my journal: "sometimes I think I will go mad from unspent sexual energy, if nothing else." I was—as I had been my entire life—selective about choosing with whom I would spend my time, let alone with whom I would risk sexual intimacy. Nonetheless, unmoored in my choices, I continually risked cynicism.

MY CHILDREN, too, grappled with the larger issues, mirroring in their own way the concerns that they saw in their mother's life.

In December 1982, the year of my father's death, the year I had to confront inconceivable loss, Adriane chose one evening at the dinner table to announce: "I'm going to pray."

Prayer was not a regular activity in our household, but open communication was a value. So we bowed our heads, and she proceeded: "I want there to be a cure for cancer. And I want all my family to be happy."

She looked up at me in the middle of her prayer and said, "I'm not praying to God."

"You can pray to God if you want to," I responded.

"No, I can't. I don't believe in God."

"Then who were you praying to?"

"The devil? Naw . . . I was just praying."

I, TOO, WAS PRAYING. But not to any god. I was praying in my own way for a new grounding upon which to make my life. That grounding could not be old formulations of religious faith. It could not be sterile versions of literary criticism. It could not be worn out patterns of romantic love or maternal self-sacrifice. I needed to keep asking the next hard question, but I still needed some ground to stand on.

In my journal the following January, I confronted the emotional repercussions of my converging life choices: "Nihilism—the why not? What does it matter? Nihilism based on a central numbing, the wish not to *feel*. The sense of being totally alone and the wish to bridge that aloneness or to shelter myself from its full reality. And now? Can I overcome the self-hatred and confront the reality of my aloneness—and refuse the nihilism? That is what I must do. And I must convince myself that it's not too late to do that. Each moment is a moment of new choice, new claiming of strength in my aloneness."

Several months later I returned to these themes: "a dark cloud enveloping me for weeks now—maybe months." And then: "over and over again, the pull of conflicting needs, conflicting responsibilities. Always—no matter what choices I make—I am somehow making wrong ones."

AND YET I had more time in those months—both for reflecting and for addressing my conflicting responsibilities—than I had had for years. Following my 1981 convocation "Women: Living Stories, Telling Lives," I had applied for a special grant from the college to develop this germ of an idea into a book. The wonder of it was that I felt enough confidence to seek this opportunity. The wonder of it was that as I wrote the proposal, I began to believe: I *can* write this book. The additional wonder of it was that I was actually given this grant: time free from teaching responsibilities from January until June 1983 to pursue this new ambition.

THE BOOK did not come easily. But it did give me a renewed sense of purpose: to think as deeply and complexly as I could about how fiction might be a source of knowledge about women's lives, particularly about women's subjectivity—the "I" that is a woman's own. Most of my two quarters of time released from teaching responsibilities I invested in reading, trying to puzzle out how my own responses related to other thinkers' responses. I immersed myself in novels and literary theory but also expanded further into sociology and psychology and history and anthropology: What does it mean to say "I" as a woman? This book was not to be a proverbial first, wrought from the dissertation. It was to be wrought from reading that took me wherever my questions led, wrought from the materials of my life, the ongoing simmering thought process: How am I to make sense of my own life as a woman, as a human being? Beneath my surface reasoning, I struggled with the emotional nihilism that I confronted only in my journal. And I struggled alone to integrate my experiences as a mother into these questions.

THAT SPRING I went with Kara to her orientation for junior high school, which she would begin the following fall. There we received the news that she had been placed in both the advanced English and the advanced math classes—no surprise to me. I sat behind her in the orientation, watching her hungrily as she accepted without comment the affirmation of her academic gifts. I sat behind her, feeling my breath stolen from me as I took in her self-possession, her beauty, seeing her as so clearly a separate person, so nearly grown up.

I felt the parental pride, of course, but also the wrenching of her imminent growth away from me. This was the age at which I remembered myself beginning to recognize that I was a "self," separate and different from what others expected of me. I recalled, too, the two-year-old Kara: self-possessed among strangers as she stood in the middle of the living room at the farm. Though that self-possession had seemed to go underground during the awkward years of late grade school, I now saw it beginning to reemerge. I watched her, as from a distance, moving on into a life of her own.

ALSO THAT SPRING, Kara and Adriane and I took a further step into confirming our life together: buying our first-ever new furniture. In a mad forty-eight hours of uncharacteristic shopping, we purchased three items: a picnic table to put in the backyard; a sofa, both design and fabric chosen for our mutual preferences; and a leather armchair with a reclinable back and an ottoman for weary feet or random books and papers. The picnic table confirmed our ongoing pleasure in informal meals together. The other items would replace the olive green chair and sofa, purchased early on from someone's basement, now frayed beyond tolerance over the naked foam beneath. Indeed, the shopping trip had been provoked when the chair—in which I was spending many hours that spring of intensive reading—had collapsed beneath me. When delivered, the sofa would bear our own label under the center cushion: "Custom designed for Joanne, Kara, and Adriane." The chair and ottoman—burnt orange, reminiscent of Goldie—became my new alternative hearth.

THAT CHAIR IS, in fact, the very chair in which I now sit twenty-one years later, so worn that I am embarrassed whenever I become conscious of how it looks. But it still seems to foster some of my very best thinking, and I do not easily relinquish my physical places of comfort, even as I work to open my mind to difficult new thoughts, still trying to ask the next hard question. Here I sit: the leather on the seat, torn and ragged, exposes raw foam beneath me; my feet extend onto the ottoman nearly covered with books and papers; my laptop perches precariously on my thighs. With the screen glowing in front of me, I try to prod my thoughts still further into areas of grief and personal uncertainty as well as insight and accomplishment. In that earlier time, it was all I could do to respond to the next hard question by weaving together the many strands of my intellectual thought. But my goals then and now are not so dissimilar: to understand the ways in which lives are made, to participate in the efforts of human understanding and feminist insight, to search out the prospects for cultural change, even when certainties elude me.

DURING THAT PERIOD of release from campus responsibilities in 1983, I rejoiced in the luxury of time I could spend in my chair, reading, thinking, assembling ideas in the pressure chamber of my feminist thinking about language, books, life. I relished the immersion in work of my own and the daily presence I could be to my daughters. I nourished the hope that with time and focus I could find my way through ever-multiplying questions toward some new ground upon which to stand in confidence.

When the phone rang one afternoon that May, I rose from my chair with no sense of apprehension: I was managing the multiple pulls of my life, developing a pattern that would work for me and for my daughters. But when I returned to my chair, having hung up the phone, I could hardly stop crying at the thought of this new thread that had been pulled loose from my carefully woven pattern. The call had been from the mother of one of Adriane's friends, objecting to "a game" that the two of them had been playing together in recent days: a game called "rape." I could not stop crying, fearing an unknown sexual imposition in my daughter's life, fearing that my own sexual needs had somehow taken distorted form in my daughter's play, fearing that community judgment would fall upon me, fearing that I would not know what to do.

When I eventually stopped crying, I did what I always did with my daughters: talked with them, as openly as I knew how. As a result of my general openness, Adriane understood much more about sex than most children her age. Still, she was only eight years old. When I asked her about this game, she described fantasy play: she and her friend were so sexually attractive in the game that the fantasized men found them irresistible. Chilled, I tried to tell her of the horrors of rape, the importance of finding sexual expression that was mutual, the complexity of growing into adult sexual expression. I recalled the ways in which she had been the recipient of teasing by an adolescent male when she was a very young child: he called her "sexy" and teased her "for a kiss." I thought about her sensory alertness, her responsiveness to touch, and her pleasure in stroking—wonderful qualities but so susceptible to manipulation by abusive elders. I held to our open communication: Surely if she had some familiarity with sexual imposition, she would tell me?

I CONTINUED TO WORK, always thinking, always with a split mind. I had scarcely written a word, but I knew that I was writing a book, and I felt that it was a book that would matter, at least to me and to my own questions. When my daughters left to spend their summer break with their father, I knew that this time was my only chance. I had spent the winter and spring months deep in thought, but split, ever ready for Kara and Adriane to return from school, to come into the heart of the house where I worked, where we made our mutual lives. Now I was in the summer months: my only uninterrupted time.

Day after day, night after night, I now sat in my chair in the living room and at the dining room table: notes spread around me, books stacked in front of me, electric typewriter at my fingertips. This was my only moment: to distill these tumultuous thoughts into some form or to give it all up. Day after day, night after night, I rejected social invitations; I refused interruptions. I sat cross-legged at the dining room table, thoughts raging in my head.

I had six weeks that summer. My ideas, though framed impersonally, were fully from my life, from reading done in the midst of my life. But I could write only in pure solitude: the weeks when my daughters were with their father. And in those six weeks I wrote a draft: rough, awkward, driven by an attempt at insight. In those six weeks, I sat in the midst of the home I shared with my daughters, but alone, uninterrupted. By the time they returned at the end of August, by the time classes resumed at the college in early September, I had a three-hundred-page manuscript. Six weeks of unremitting writing, a lifetime of unremitting thought. In the fervor of completion, the keys on my electric typewriter had glowed purple deep into the night. The xerox machine had taken hold of me demonically. But I sent it off—a book far short of what I knew that I knew.

I sent it off, reentered the classroom, returned to my home with my daughters, pulling myself back from total absorption in my own thoughts: "Living Stories, Telling Lives: Women and the Novel in Contemporary Experience."

WHEN THIS FIRST DRAFT was rejected in December 1983, I cried with the weariness of those many months of thinking and questioning and writing; I cried with the pain of rejection and the loss of fragilely wrought confidence. But then Adriane said, "All that work for *nothing?!*" And Kara—adopting a new preteen vocabulary and what was to her a gender-neutral usage—said, "Those *bitches!*" And with these responses to support me, I rallied to do the work that yet needed to be done: all that work could not be for nothing.

That same winter Kara and Adriane continued with their own burgeoning questions, following out the filaments of their thoughts toward their own understandings. With me, they were learning to question cultural certainties. Apart from me, they were also developing questions of their own.

During this period, Adriane suggested a new way of ending prayers, eschewing the traditional "Amen" used by a visiting friend to conclude a mealtime grace. "Why not 'Ah-women' and 'Ah-children'?" she questioned.

ALL THAT YEAR Kara was reading ravenously, trying, I suppose, to find in books that extension of her life that was so hard to find within the constraints of a small town. She continued to nurture her passion for New York City: the sense that she belonged there rather than here, even though she had not yet even visited the city. But at this moment her reading focused on British authors, for her hunger to go places had picked up the scent of a possible year in London when I next had a research leave.

Voracious, she read through all of Charlotte Brontë's novels, having been hooked first by *Jane Eyre*. She read through much of Jane Austen, nibbling at the bait of romance. She read Rosamund Lehman—upon whom she had stumbled on her own—and Margaret Drabble, whose work was central to some of my own critical inquiries. Once she found an author who interested her, she almost always wanted more of that same worldview—like her mother in this, hoping to find in novelists an angle on the world she lived in.

When she came upon Marilyn French's *The Women's Room*—could I possibly have recommended it to a seventh grader, or did she find it on her own?—she pulled herself sharply from the romantic tentacles of Jane Austen and Charlotte Brontë and commented: "If I'm ever thinking of getting married, I want to read it again. It will make me think carefully about what I'm doing. After I finished reading it, I thought about all the marriages I know—and I couldn't think of a single equal marriage."

I did not, of course, remind Kara to reread Marilyn French when she and Andrzej phoned last summer to tell us of their planned marriage. But I had already witnessed the balancing strengths that these two young adults brought to each other, and I knew from a lifetime of intimacy with Kara that she understands her own strengths and capacities. From my own life experience, I had also learned that "equal relationships" can be wrought only from love and respect, mutual support and difficult struggle over conflicting needs: the old idea of a "contract" for equality no longer seems apt to me.

CHRISTMAS VACATION IN 1983, the three of us drove together to meet their father. In the car, we carried on from these observations, examining the lives we made together, the lives of others around us. They grieved over their sense that I worked too hard, never had enough time. But they said: "We *like* our family the way it is. We like being different from other families—picnics on the floor, holidays on the dates we choose for ourselves. We don't want to live in one of those 'regular' families with a man in charge."

As I drove back from the exchange of children, I again promised myself to spend more time with Kara and Adriane in the coming year. I promised myself to help them to reaffirm the value of our off-kilter family, the bond among the three of us, despite the judgments of the rest of the world.

On December 24, I had already returned from that excursion, my own holidays behind me. I spent Christmas Day alone, reading, appreciating solitude, yearning for all the parts of my life to make sense. Gradually, I reentered the world of work, even as the rest of the world was still on holiday, turning again to the rejected book manuscript and my commitment to find the words for my understandings.

WAS IT THE INTENSITY of that commitment that made the first months of 1984 so difficult? Was it my ongoing inability to find reasonable balance? Was it the sense—despite our open conversations, our sharing of experiences, our affirmation of our off-kilter life together—that my daughters had no clear foundation?

"Mom," Adriane would begin. "I don't know whether I love Dad more than you. I don't know whether I love Sherry's guinea pig more than you." Surely I could honor the first concern, laugh about the latter? But then, "Mom, I don't know if I love Kirstina [Lawrence's friend] more than you. I don't know if I even love you. I don't know if *you* love anyone." And "Mom, why didn't you put a dime in the March of Dimes? Why aren't you more giving?"

What is love? What is giving? What makes goodness?

At first, it was amusing, this game of "what is love" and "who do I love more." At first, it was the sort of open conversation we always had. But day after day, night after night, the questions persisted. The next hard question fell into a groove of negation: How can we know what love is? Why does anything matter? Day after day, night after night, Adriane would put the questions to which I had no answers. A bleakness fell over us every night at bedtime, knowing that we would cry together as she repeated her unanswerable questions. I sat on the side of her bed, waiting for the wisdom by which I could reassure her.

I would put her to bed, eyes wet with tears, hug her, reassure her that she had not, in her phrase, "ruined the family." I would talk as calmly as possible with Kara about whatever was on her mind at bedtime. Finally, I would go into my own room and welcome the release of real tears, allowing them to wash down my cheeks, over my fragilely made life. I would phone my sister, welcome her reassurance and her reasoned advice that I could tell Adriane she didn't have to voice every thought she had.

"Which do you love more—me or your work?" Adriane had asked only a year or two earlier. Had that question been the precursor to these new questions? Had my immersion in my work—which had so driven me in the past year especially—been more than she could balance on that fragile fulcrum of selfhood? Had my own existential anguish crept unheralded into her receptive psyche?

I don't know the cause. But night after night at bedtime, what she came to call her "feelings" would erupt anew. Tears would roll down her cheeks and well up in my own eyes. What *is* the reassurance of love, the affirmation of value that makes sense to a child? What can be balanced against the existential anguish of a child, eight years old, nearly nine?

Straining at the limits of my life, I taught my classes. I even delivered a second campuswide convocation lecture, again wrought from these materials, again distilled from the work on the book: "The Subversive 'I': Women's Voices, Women's Lives." But my own "I" was risking a destruction as fatal as Maggie Tulliver's conclusion; my dilemma felt as irresolvable as hers. In my journal, I wrote: "What if my conflicting needs prove to be as destructive, as fatal, as Maggie's? A fatal flood would be too easy—so then what?"

As if mirroring my own distress, Adriane's questions took a new turn. By her ninth birthday, she was asking aloud: "Mom, how can I want things for myself without being selfish? What about what other people want?" And still she persisted with the other refrain: "What is love? How do I know if I really love anyone?"

I HAVE SINCE READ that it is not uncommon for children at age eight or nine to face a new rupture in selfhood, as if they are growing up at uneven rates, leaving jagged edges of exposed vulnerability. For Adriane, as for these other children, the anguish was much more than childish self-indulgence; it was a new recognition of self, a new effort to make sense of life. In adult terms, she was depressed. Her depression may well have been a mirror of mine, but it refracted questions from the depth of her own emergent selfhood.

I have thought often of those anguished months, wondering whether I should have done something different: pursued therapy for her, sought out some pharmaceutical relief, simply told her that enough was enough. But I did none of those things. I held her and cried with her, listened to her, and tried to use words to bridge the chasm that had opened between us, the chasms within her.

And in the end, our family was not "ruined," nor was Adriane silenced. Slowly, cumbersomely, laboriously, each of the three of us began to form our fragile new understandings. Not least among our responses was our plan to move to London for the following year, when I had a one-year research leave—though this move would not be easy, especially given the necessity to earn more money to fund such a year.

Nor were we all in agreement about the plan. Adriane said, "I don't want to leave my house, my friends, my school, my cat." These were her touchstones, and she was still in the midst of her uneven growth in selfhood. I said, "It all seems too hard. I don't think I can get us all ready and across the ocean." But Kara said, "I'll help you, Mom. We need to go somewhere else for a while. I know we can do this."

Kara did help me to pack up the house, figure out plans, contact schools in London. Adriane reluctantly decided she could leave her house, her school, her friends, her cat. And in pursuit of financial resources, I agreed to teach summer school, found a place in an NEH summer seminar at Cornell while Kara and Adriane were with their father, rented the house for the summer and again for the academic year. By August, we were off, People's Express to London, a vagabond family of three. Still reeling from all that we had been through, we boarded the plane and left behind our house and our cat, left behind the place in which we had made our uncertain lives so far. Perhaps now we could learn to love each other better, even while we kept asking the ever more difficult questions, even while I did my work. Perhaps now we could continue to make our lives together, healing our rifted selves, resisting the categories that the culture around us continued to impose.

23

Finding the Blue Door

When you step into the Terraces, you enter a separate world, removed from the traffic of Cricklewood Broadway, from the pubs and clubs and greengrocers and retailers. Behind the larger trees that guard the entrance, a hush falls on the little parallel streets, the rows of attached houses facing each other across strips of green grass and surrounded by a brick and wrought-iron fence, with gates always standing open. These small homes, with dollhouse rooms on two levels, were built for railway workers late in the nineteenth century. That's what we were told by neighbors when we lived here for our year in London: 11 Johnston Terrace, NW2—the one with the bright blue door.

I have experienced that special hush each time I have again stepped into the Terraces, twice in the past two years, both times on a visit to Kara and Andrzej in their new life together in London. Most recently, this past June 2004, Kara and I took Andrzej and Ron with us to share this neighborhood that had so marked our validation as a single-parent family when we ventured forth from our roots in Wooster.

At the entrance, we paused and smiled at the new name for the street that leads into the Terraces: Kara Way, a private signal that the neighborhood acknowledges our residency there twenty years ago, even though all our friends have moved on. The name is official on my new map of London, though this same street has no name on my earlier map or in our memories. But that seems to be the only visible change.

The house itself looks unmarked by the passage of time. In back is the tiny "garden," as we were taught to call this patch of ground: flagstones and a clothesline surrounded by a fence, faced by the bare kitchen window, and lined along one edge by a short hall that leads to the bathroom, a twentieth-century addition and almost always cold. Upstairs, no doubt the three tiny bedrooms remain much the same. In front, the brick face still looks onto the strip of grass, lacy curtains hang unchanged in the window, and there is that distinctive blue door.

IN 1984, before we left Wooster, I had studied maps, made long-distance phone calls, and then blindly arranged this rental by good-faith agreement with a stranger. John and Rena, our good friends and family intimates from Wooster—in London for a few months that summer—had scouted out this Cricklewood address in advance, lest the neighborhood be too rough. And when we arrived, they escorted us across the sprawling city of London into the hush of the Terraces—which had won their somewhat skeptical stamp of approval—and toward the blue door awaiting us at 11 Johnston Terrace.

Rena, Kara, Adriane, and I took the train from Gatwick. John drove their small Austin 1300—temporary London car, soon to become ours—across London with our mounds of luggage nearly overflowing its limits. I had told Kara and Adriane that they could take whatever they felt they needed, and I had claimed for myself the need for many boxes of books as well as a special suitcase—which I had had to gate-check when boarding the plane—full of notes and papers for the writing I would be undertaking.

ACROSS THE ATLANTIC that August, family members looked at television maps in astonishment, hearing the word that they had first learned from us—"Cricklewood," unbeknownst to us making the news on the very day we arrived. We, new to this city and this neighborhood, watched the horizon in awe as we unloaded the luggage: flames shot into the sky and yielded a thick column of black smoke. We would later receive letters from the States asking us about this hugely expensive industrial fire, flashed across television screens around the world; still later I would answer the back doorbell to greet men in red suits examining our back garden for lingering pieces of asbestos. We were relieved to find out that no one was immediately hurt, though there was no telling about the apparent threat of possible lung damage. We could only shrug our shoulders and take this possibility in stride along with everything else that seemed so new.

EVERYTHING DID SEEM NEW AND STRANGE, despite the apparently shared language and customs and literature. I often fumbled with money at the grocery store, sorting through coins and bills in puzzlement as the groceries piled up, waiting for me to bag them myself. I paused at greengrocers, scrutinizing mounds of vegetables both familiar and unfamiliar but timid about making my selection when I was still uncertain about how to pronounce "aubergine" and "courgette" in the British way or what the customs were for making my own choices from the carefully wrought piles of green and red and orange and purple shapes. Kara and Adriane stood beside me, hanging back a bit as they, too, learned the ways of commerce in our new life.

At first, we went nearly everywhere together, bonded in our uncertainty as well as in our spirit of adventure. I welcomed their company and their help in carrying home bags of groceries and maneuvering through unfamiliar bus and tube schedules. We trekked together to different parts of the city, taking care of official business: registering as aliens, opening a checking account, locating shops and supplies, getting my pass to work in the reading room of the British Library—then still part of the British Museum right there in Virginia Woolf's own Bloomsbury neighborhood.

As long as John and Rena were still in London, even though across the city in Richmond, we felt a familiar aura of friendship as we made our way. We also had from them a strong provocation to soak in the cultural opportunities, trips to the Barbican Hall and the National Theatre and the Tate Gallery, bookings of plays and concerts. Early in our first month there, we took the train across to Richmond for the day, heading out on our own to Hampton Court Palace and then roaming with our good friends in Richmond Park and up and down little Richmond streets, seeking the plaque that bore Virginia Woolf's name and that of the Hogarth Press.

John and Rena had spent a number of leave years in London, beginning with their first when their own children were in primary school. They became for me a kind of model as to how one ventured into this new culture, though I would always be more hesitant, less sure of myself in new venues than they were. But from them I saw that it could be done, finding school placements for American children, learning the map of this great city, cultivating in one's children the taste for opportunities well beyond the scope of their small hometown in Ohio.

From them I learned as well the ways of British pub life, an occasional taste for LaPhroaig Scotch—which we were told on a "pub crawl" was the best Scotch there is—and a general sense that even I, as an adult responsible for my children and committed to my work, could indulge in the pleasures of the senses: food and drink and art and music and theater. We shared meals and walks and ice cream as extended family together, enough that we did feel a new possibility of belonging there before John and Rena returned to Ohio in September. We stayed—our single-parent family of three—grounded in Cricklewood, still finding our way in the larger London metropolis.

Early on, we had scouted out the school situation, relying on advance correspondence with the headmistress of Child's Hill School—a small borough school for children ages four to eleven—and with the more austere head of Hampstead comprehensive school, a much larger and more intimidating school for children ages eleven to seventeen. Not surprisingly, the adjustments were easier for Adriane in a class of twenty-five ethnically diverse children and a very supportive teacher who was thrilled to have her among her students: "What do they *do* in the States that she can read so well?!!"

At home with us, Adriane continued to grapple with questions about love and generosity, but at school she quickly made friends and settled in. Within a few days, she started bringing other children home to play, comfortably finding her way to and from school in her newly purchased uniform of gray pleated skirt, white blouse, gray cardigan; before long, she even began to sound British, adopting local rhythms and slang and clipped speech patterns.

Kara had more adjustments among the thousand students in her school, with classes that took her into unfamiliar sequences in the math curriculum and new subject matter, such as "design technology" and "games," and with peers already settled into cliques. At this level, the teachers were far less interested in accommodating an alien American student here just for the year. Still, Kara had been the driving force for this expedition to England, and she remained stalwart.

WHEN JOHN AND RENA DEPARTED, they left behind the white Austin 1300, which we had agreed to purchase from them at minimal cost: a car so that we could on occasion venture beyond the scope of public transport and pedestrian possibilities. But at first the car sat quiescent at the curb for days on end; I still lacked the necessary boldness of spirit to drive this manual-transmission vehicle, steering wheel on the right side, gearshift to my left, turning into traffic in what felt like the wrong lane, my clutch leg shaking and the engine threatening to die. Though Goldie, too, had a manual transmission, this car was no Goldie. We would rely, for the time being, on public transportation to get us to most of our destinations: walking to and from schools, taking the bus to the Brent Cross shopping center and the Tube into central London. And even later, after multiple timorous trips, the car never even took enough of a place in our lives to earn a name. It could only remain "the Austin" or simply "the car."

MOSTLY WE STAYED CLOISTERED in our Cricklewood home, which we still called a "flat," for that was how it had been advertised. It wasn't flat; it was two stories, but miniature, a dollhouse of a house. Here we clustered together, soaking up time with each other, leaning inward as we leaned on each other, a fragilely balanced tripod. At first, we were still disparate, strained by all of the transitions we were making, singly, collectively. But the rebalancing was essential to how we lived this year away from Wooster, sequestered with each other in Cricklewood, safe behind the blue door.

Upstairs in our dollhouse flat, inside Adriane's bedroom, was an actual dollhouse meant for play, on loan to her from our new friends Robin and Kirsten, slightly older girls who had outgrown doll play but empathized with the threat of displacement that a nine-year-old might feel—across the ocean from her house, her cat, her school, her friends. There Adriane could dramatize at will her fantasies, her angst, her terrors, for she had decidedly brought these emotions with her. When she ventured out, she lost items in shops and play areas—her red hooded jacket that her dad had bought for her the previous spring, her school bag, stocked with requisite equipment for school life: cardigan, umbrella, dictionary. When we ventured out together, she sometimes sulked in underground trains, sitting next to me, braiding the fringe on my scarf or moving up several rows of seats, her face red with tears. In the tube station one evening, she walked limply ahead of Kara and me, zombielike, mute, withdrawn into her private grief. Returned from such outings, she needed her private space, her own dollhouse life, a room of her own, safely tucked into the second floor of our flat.

Though Kara had no dollhouse fantasy outlet, she, too, needed her own room in which to muse, to read, to write letters, to turn inward onto herself. Downstairs, she would talk of her displacement, her alienation from school and culture. With the skies dripping bleakly outside, she would ask me, "Do you have any suggestions for getting rid of depression?" Upstairs in her small room, she sought her solitary answers—reading, writing, thinking.

In the third bedroom, especially once the girls had gone to bed in the evenings, I rehearsed our lives, retreating from the fears activated by Kara's question and Adriane's muteness on the Tube. I put away the excessive nightmare images that had leapt before me: of Adriane jumping down onto the tracks or dashing off wildly from me into some unknown danger, of her falling into a permanent silence, never again to speak to me. With my daughters safely sleeping in adjacent rooms, I sat in my own bed listening to Radio 3, while I studied maps of this huge city, tracing out the different colors of the London Underground lines and locating parks and neighborhoods, not just those familiar from Virginia Woolf and Doris Lessing and Margaret Drabble—"my" London writers—but also new ones in my immediate proximity. I became familiar with the many names that our own Cricklewood Broadway held as it angled its way up into NW2 from Marble Arch: Edgware Road, Maida Vale, Kilburn High Road, Shoot Up Hill, with other names to follow as it proceeded beyond Cricklewood.

Tired of mapping the city, I would sometimes lie naked on my bed, mapping instead the marks on my body. Beginning with my chin, I felt for the familiar scar, my first injury: a small child who fell from her tricycle into the cinders when a friend pushed too hard. At three years old, I had been either too adventurous or too trusting of a friend. On my neck, I found my smooth white necklace, residue of two thyroid surgeries. The first, at age twelve, had left a thick rope of angry pink tissue; the cortisone shots that followed shrank the rope into a flat band, half an inch wide. All that remained after a second thyroid surgery was my simple permanent necklace, lying over the top of my collar bone, dipping in the middle where the bone recedes, lined by dots on both sides, glistening relics left by surgical clamps.

As my hands mapped farther, I found the evidence of tree-climbing scrapes, surgical removal of warts and moles on my thumb and my left knee, an appendectomy scar angling down on the right side of my belly. On the lower rim of my navel—that first scar of selfhood—I could feel the tiny smile inscribed there by my tubal ligation three years earlier, when I had reached the limits of my ability to give to others. Tracing over my flesh, I honored the white rivulets that ran down the middle of my belly and fanned out on my breasts: inscriptions of motherhood.

SEQUESTERED IN A SLEEPING HOUSE, I also occasionally grabbed pen and paper or even turned on the typewriter, seeking words for thoughts that chased in my head. The typewriter was a special treasure, a testament, I thought, to my intrepidity and my commitment to writing. Early on, I had responded to a newspaper ad offering a used electric Olympia, office model, for sixty-nine pounds. It was an extravagant price for my budget, but my need was urgent. So I had set out to Hendon, an unknown neighborhood north of us, and when the Austin, sitting by the curb, failed to start, I simply took the city bus. With more boldness than I could usually muster, I had walked up to the door of a stranger's home and offered cash for this cumbersome machine. Pleased with myself, I had wrapped my arms around it, phoned a taxi and managed to lug it back to my own room in our flat.

Alone at night in my bedroom, I yearned for this typewriter to glow purple with the frenzy of new ideas. One night, late, I even drafted an opening scene of a possible novel: the female protagonist in an art gallery stood, vertiginous, before El Greco's *St. Sebastian*. But I could go no further, then; the Olympia could do only yeoperson's service, and that would be later, when I was ready to settle into scholarly projects. For now, I had to relinquish words and stories, merely trying to keep my balance.

But there in that same bedroom, I could not entirely constrain my own fantasy life, my own nightmare life—even if I could not yet activate words. I yearned for affirmation, yet to come from the University of Michigan Press, to which I had resubmitted my revised book manuscript. I yearned for the perennial fantasy lover, who might share in my joys and responsibilities. In terror, I recalled the chalkboard sign I had seen in front of a jewelry story out on the Broadway, a block down from the Terraces: "Metropolitan Police: Murder—between 10:15 and 11:00 a.m. on _____" (my journal records the message but not the actual date). The request to contact police with relevant information was reinforced by the small gathering of "bobbies"; the shop itself was closed for business. I had walked on by, heart thumping in alarm. In bed at night, I revived my own version of danger, dreaming that I was traveling with my daughters and yet another baby; in transit, I lost the baby and did not know where to look for her. In the morning, I wakened again to the convergence of responsibility: physical, financial, emotional.

DOWNSTAIRS IN OUR DOLLHOUSE FLAT, the rooms were at first also threatening. The radiators went mysteriously cold; the kitchen faucet—which I had not yet learned even to call a "tap," let alone to repair—dribbled ceaselessly; the bedsheets, laundered first thing in the morning in our miniature washer (no dryer), refused to dry before bedtime; excursions to the shopping center, where shops were organized on principles I failed to recognize, could not turn up the contact lens solution I needed or the right kind of fluorescent bulbs for the kitchen. Everything around us seemed alien, damp, and dreary, like the weather.

In the front sitting room, the three of us shared our angst over lost items, unfindable household supplies, troubling life griefs. We huddled together, tears in our eyes. Like life rafts in alien waters, we hugged each other, even as we ignored the pan of popcorn on the stove—our American comfort food— now burnt beyond salvagability. We couldn't have made real popcorn in any case; all we could find in the local shops was "maize," not even designated "popping maize," as it seems to be in more recent times. Small wonder that the pan had burned when the maize was so resistant to popping open.

AND THE WORK? With the girls off in school each day, I turned my attention to work, poking through the numerous boxes of books that I had brought or shipped, digging into my suitcase full of notes assembled before our departure. Much of this material was devoted to Virginia Woolf, to whom I had returned in my summer project for the NEH seminar at Cornell; much also supplied the grid of the book manuscript I had revised and sent back to the University of Michigan Press shortly before our departure. I did not know for certain whether I had brought this material out of genuine work necessity or simply as a touchstone, reassuring me of past thought.

As I sat in the front room, reading, I always kept one ear cocked for the twice-daily delivery of the Royal Mail. The post plopping through the slot into the cold hallway toward the bathroom would usually be preceded by the squeak of the gate into the back terrace. In my loneliness, I took comfort in the thought that twice a day these sounds might herald news from afar, connection to the life I had left on the other side of the Atlantic.

Even as my daughters and I settled into making our lives together, I still needed to figure out my relationship to my work. I made occasional excursions to the British Library, in awe of its scholarly history, smiling to think of my own position on the spoked wheel of library tables that I recognized from Woolf's *A Room of One's Own*. I purchased more books than I could afford on my visits to the Dillon's bookstore in Bloomsbury. But I could not find a systematic approach to the amorphous work on Woolf that I had initiated the previous summer or to the project on contemporary versions of omniscient narrative that I had proposed for this year of leave.

WHEN MY NOVEMBER BIRTHDAY coincided with the presidential election in the United States, I remained alone in front of the television long after the girls had gone to bed. Into the wee hours of the morning, I watched the map of my own country turn Reagan red one state at a time, grieving this political loss as I wearily acknowledged the passage of forty years of my own life. Alone in this flat in NW2, I also indulged in a glass of LaPhroaig to mark the date, lifting my glass in long-distance camaraderie when John and Rena phoned to wish me well.

Those birthday greetings were added to telephone wishes from my mother, my sister, my brother, cards from friends, and a private celebration with Kara and Adriane, my primary social allies. I had wakened that morning to apple muffins that Adriane had made and continued through the day in pleasant celebration: after school, a game of *Word Yahtzee*—a birthday gift—followed by a special birthday dinner that Kara cooked. Throughout it all, we took pleasure in each other's company: eating, laughing, admiring the flowers and gifts they gave me, blowing out all forty-one candles on their home-made cake. "One to grow on, Mom," my daughters chorused.

DEEP INTO THE NIGHT that began my forty-first year, I sat in our sitting room, trying to sort out my thoughts, swinging on the emotional pendulum of anxiety and excitement. The day before my birthday had been Guy Fawkes

Day. As I made my trip into the city for my weekly visit to Dillon's bookstore to do what I called my "research," I had regularly been greeted by the refrain "Penny for the Guy" from the costumed young people as I walked past. And instead of feeling accosted, I'd felt companionable, like I almost belonged. Inwardly I was also rejoicing, for in that day's post, plopped unceremoniously into the cold hallway in the late morning, I had received a letter from the University of Michigan Press with a new reader's report on my revised manuscript: "an astonishing transformation," the words said, "a superb job of revision." In short, the reader now recommended publication.

I was not yet done with revisions—further reader reports suggested more changes—and the official acceptance for publication in the Women and Culture series was another month in coming. It would be still longer before I would learn that the manuscript had won the University of Michigan's Alice and Edith Hamilton Prize for the best scholarly manuscript on women. But I was at last well on my way to realizing an actual book, no longer just a dream or a collection of ideas urging me into the unknown.

WE WERE SETTLING INTO this new life in the Terraces, making this space ours. Each time we came into our front sitting room, closing the blue door behind us, we turned toward each other, relieved at the sense that we were together. With the repaired radiators no longer cold, we gathered in the sitting room in the evening, indulging ourselves with Cadbury chocolate bars or not-quite popcorn and British telly, arguing that these shows were valuable cultural knowledge for us, especially the evening soaps such as *Coronation Street*. Somehow even *Dynasty*—pronounced in its alien way with the short *i*—was cultural knowledge for us: How else were we to participate in the dominant conversational topic among neighbors and school friends? On other evenings, each of us would pull out a deck of cards and lay them out on the sitting room floor for individual games of solitaire, a way to be together quietly, talking when we wished, otherwise occupied with our hands and private thoughts.

AS THE YEAR MOVED ON, Kara and Adriane and I began to reach out to other people, to make gathering places of our kitchen and sitting room. Having eaten dinner at neighbors' flats, we offered reciprocal hospitality in our own. At the home of Adriane's friend Priti, we learned to eat Indian food with chapattis and fingers instead of with knives and forks. At our own table with several friends, we engaged in political conversation, finding equal fault with the harsh policies of Margaret Thatcher and Ronald Reagan. We shared in games of *Trivial Pursuit* and *Monopoly* (British style) and sat around together in our own kitchen after our guests had gone home, collaborating on the clean up and sharing in the good feelings of a mutual social life. I was gratified by my daughters' companionship in this party debriefing, a new feature of our lives together after our relative isolation in our Wooster lives.

I took special pleasure in afternoons around the kitchen table when we were joined by Robin and K. J.—the neighbor friends approximately Kara's age who had lent the dollhouse to Adriane. The five of us often laughed in shared hilarity at the discrepancy in our language use; was it bangs or fringe that we had on our foreheads? A faucet or a tap through which our water came? Pudding or dessert with which we might end a meal? A bonnet or hood that covered a car's engine—a boot or trunk for luggage? And what on earth was Marmite? And when did one eat it—for tea? Lunch? Breakfast? We all found especially amusing Adriane's story from school of her request for an eraser being met by the acquisition of a "rubber." We enjoyed telling Robin and K. J. just what a rubber was likely to mean in the States; they equally enjoyed making fun of our inability to pronounce "Tube," instead coming out with something that sounded to them like "Toob."

As Christmas approached, we also learned together the lyrics of the two hit songs of the season, both released in December: Band-Aid's charity song "Do They Know It's Christmas?" and George Michael's "Last Christmas." We would all periodically break into song—poignantly aware of the famine in Ethiopia, which appeared in painful images on the television in our sitting room—and indulge in mock romantic suffering and self-protection: "Last Christmas, I gave you my heart, but the very next day, you gave it away." Oddly, the configuration of these two songs at the top of the charts spoke our own recurrent struggle with values: How do we reach out to others, even those on other continents, with a generous heart and genuine concern? Also, what are we to do with personal longings for love? And how avoid the ridiculous cultural clichés?

Adriane seemed to be coming to terms with her own griefs and judgments as we settled into our more fully shared mutual life in our Cricklewood flat. And though I continued to yearn after lost romantic possibilities—even now sometimes fantasizing that a letter from Michael might plop onto the floor in the cold hallway—I had finally given up on that as ever being a possibility, and I had made clear choices not to settle for other available relationships. I had turned instead to the powerful emotional satisfaction of life with my daughters. I remained lonely for intellectual peer conversations and for sexual intimacy, but I rejoiced in this new version of social life that we were constructing in Cricklewood.

When my mother came for a Christmas visit, we took special pleasure in sharing this city with her—Christmas decorations at Harrods and huge ravens at the Tower of London, plays at the National Theatre and music at the Barbican. We even found a scraggly Christmas tree, nailed into an X of two-by-fours, out on the Cricklewood Broadway near our favorite greengrocer. And Kara and Adriane and I quietly agreed to make a substantial contribution to Oxfam—admittedly enabled by a favorable exchange rate—acknowledging our gratitude for our material well-being and still wishing we knew how to ease the suffering in Ethiopia.

THE EARTH WAS TURNING; the winter solstice had come and gone. The sun still struggled to get off the horizon and reach over the roofs of the flats across the way from us on Midland Terrace. February continued to be dreary; laundry remained damp. But the kitchen table and the floor of the front sitting room had settled in as warm and friendly places to be. It's not that I had lost the cloud of depression or that Adriane had found a secure moral compass or that Kara had settled into a welcoming peer group. Though each of us had done much to shift away from these difficulties, we had not found some miraculous confidence to overcome alienation. Nonetheless, when February brought its own version of stresses, we were somehow better equipped to deal with them.

One evening in a hurry, I jammed my foot into the corner of a chair in our sitting room, breaking or severely damaging my fourth toe. I stared in shock as it jutted out to the side, emitting excruciating currents of pain. I heard the tiny cracking noises as I pushed it back into alignment and tied it up with the other three toes to act as splint. For several days, I watched in awe as it swelled up and a lurid, multicolored bruise spread over half of my foot. I could hardly walk but was grateful that Kara's feet were slightly larger than mine so that her boot made it possible for me to step out into the larger world, even if still hampered by currents of pain.

Another evening, when Kara phoned her father to discuss upcoming plans, his response was seventy-five minutes of righteous indignation, spouted hostilely into Kara's ear. He was angry at my failures: my inability to locate a place in London where he could repair one of his oriental rugs, my difficulty in figuring out how to accommodate him and his current woman friend for several nights during their anticipated visit to London, my apparent inflexibility in making plans for him to take his daughters for an extended trip to Ireland and then parts of Europe when he crossed the Atlantic in April. We had made this tentative agreement that he would travel with them at the end of their winter school term, but he had reached the conclusion that I was simply not accommodating enough, and so he spent his hour and a quarter abusing me—and indeed all Schultzes—and then threatening to withhold all support money as Kara sat stoic on the other end of the phone line. She and Adriane and I leaned into each other on the small love seat in our front sitting room, suppressing tears as she waited him out and then crying openly in the aftermath.

The pain of my daughters' split loyalties had crossed the Atlantic with us, but so had our pleasure in mutual interdependence. All of the struggles we had come through renewed our strength against this latest emotional assault. The pain of my broken toe receded into the shadows: we had each other.

At the kitchen table, we spent one afternoon drawing pictures of each other, seeking out our similarities and differences—noting family resemblances, Schultz or otherwise, with pride and pleasure. When I spent the semester in New York in 1998 all those years later when Adriane was a recent college graduate, she shared with me similar sketches that she had made of herself, her sister, her father, her mother. Then, too, she was groping for her place among her people. She and Kara have had to find their own way of being, distinct from both father and mother even while drawing resources from both. But, then, surely all children must do that?

SOMETIMES AT THE SAME TABLE, in that spirit of shared realities, our conversation opened onto more troubling concerns. I had recently been visited by a friend from the States who was wishing to continue a brief relationship that I had decided to end. He and I had spent several evenings together, visiting other parts of the city, attending plays and museums. We had walked together in Hyde Park, talking of Virginia Woolf's childhood at 22 Hyde Park Gate, imagining her on the Broad Walk, beside the Round Pond, perhaps even throwing a shilling into the Serpentine as her fictional Clarissa Dalloway does. One evening we had also walked through my Cricklewood neighborhood, over past the small library and into Gladstone Park as rain fell steadily, glistening in the street lights as we traversed nearby neighborhoods. He accused me of being "angry with men," unwilling to chance this relationship. And I *was* angry with men's easy and unthinking claim on privilege, just as I was angry that women have to do so much of the emotional educating. But I could not make him see that this anger was something altogether different from man hating. His eyes glistened with tears—Or was it raindrops gathered there?—as we stood in front of the little library in my simple neighborhood, far from the grand collections of the British Museum, far from the Stephens' family home in Kensington and from the Bloomsbury squares to which Virginia Stephen moved with her siblings after her father's death.

When Adriane and Kara wanted to know the significance of this visit, I told them as clearly as I could that this friend was not a romantic interest for me, but that I did still need a "lover" in my life. This response opened onto more questions, including the disappearance of Michael from our lives years ago. Because he was one of the very few men I had actually introduced them to—though that had happened only a few times when they were very young—Kara had retained a strong memory of these meetings. And as she had grown in age and awareness, I had become increasingly open about just what that relationship had meant to me. Now Adriane, too, was old enough for more open conversations about her mother's adult life.

Adriane's first reaction was anger at having been kept out of the secret until now: Why had Kara known about this secret relationship before she herself had been told? What did this mean about the bonds of trust between us? How would she ever know when to trust me now?

The wounds were raw, and her feeling was genuine that I had withheld something central from her. But now we were at last all on even ground: no more secrets, no more lies. Though these particular secrets had existed when she was a very small child, she could not understand that she would not have known everything about me, about what was going on in my life. Her commitment to speaking every thought sat in judgment on my silence. I told her that I had needed to keep certain things from her when she was too young in order to protect her, to protect the privacy of others—even to protect the emotional vulnerability of other children, Michael's sons.

I told her as well that I needed now for her to know that her mother had needs for adult intimacy, that this is an important part of adulthood, even if I had not been able to address these needs effectively. As central as my daughters were to my life, I did not want them to grow up thinking that motherhood is or should be the sole source of emotional satisfaction for them as women. Nor, in fact, did I want to burden them with the need to provide my primary emotional satisfaction—even if, at present, that was exactly what they were doing.

Adriane's concern in these current conversations brought her into a newly balanced three-way conversation with Kara and me. Now we could, at last, directly acknowledge her suppressed fear: that I might again have a secret relationship from which she would be excluded and by which she would feel denied in not knowing some central portion of me. And we could talk about her fear that in loving someone else, I might have less love—and less time—for her and her sister.

These fears were a child's concerns, and they were real. On the cusp of a new maturity, she could begin to comprehend that love was not finite, that it really was possible to love more than one person at a time—beyond that competition of "Who do I love more?" that had haunted her during her crises the previous year.

For me, this was among the most potent insights of parenthood: the wonder of my love for each of these two distinct human beings who were rooted in my heart, central to my life. I know that parents sometimes do sense a greater love for one child over another. But I could only be amazed that I truly did love each of them the most, each in her own way. Adriane by then had come to this knowledge for herself. Now she reached further up the ladder of insight to grasp that I might yet love someone else, too, without reducing the amount of love I had available for her and her sister.

NOW, IN THIS SUMMER OF WRITING, with my daughters so far away, I ache as I think back. Where was the time? How was I to balance the needs, the hurts, the yearnings? And yet that kitchen table, that flat behind the blue door, beckon to me. To be again at that table, sharing daily intimacy, cooking, laughing, talking. To be able, now, to reach out my arms and embrace each of my daughters in her unique physical presence. To enjoy now as I was only beginning to do then the distinctive pleasures of adult friendship with young women whose growth I have witnessed and shared.

Time, then, was in lovely surfeit even if I had my work to do. For once, I really could do most of it when they were busy with their own lives—school, friends, each other—and be there for them, with them, as we sat around the table, gathered in front of the telly, cuddled together on the love seat.

I RECENTLY HAD another minor surgical procedure, to remove a tiny heart-shaped mole of which I had been very fond. When the surgeon cut it out, he commented tersely, "Now that's gone."

"Yes," I responded. "I just keep having parts of me cut away."

The procedure had gone smoothly, seriously, routinely. But then, in unpredictable response to my wry comment, the surgeon had burst into hearty laughter. In that moment, I lay quietly upon the surgical table, calling to mind that old image of myself standing very still as multiple hands reached out and grabbed parts of me.

The small nevus of unusual shape was benign and could have remained in its comfortable familiar place on my left breast. But I didn't much mind. Instead, I lay very still and smiled at the remaining marks on my body, the striations of early mothering on my breasts and down my belly and the other scars: the map of my history, locating me over time, the bonds that have enriched rather than diminishing me.

Proprioception: the internal register of where one senses oneself to be physically in the world. There in Cricklewood, within the dollhouse flat behind the blue door, I struggled—alone and with my daughters—to register my location, to resist the locations that others had put upon me. No longer did I worry that others were grabbing the pieces of my flesh, taking my sustenance from me. I was learning step by step to relinquish the panicked self-protection, learning instead to lean inward as I also reached out into the world, learning that my primary location had to be internal: without that location, I could not sense where I was. Chief among my locators—internal and external—were my daughters, with whom I was finding my bearings.

24

Out from Cricklewood

The squirrels have become giddy with late summer: somersaulting on the knoll across the street, chasing after apple green walnuts. Crickets and cicadas hum and buzz with humidity. In the evenings, Ron and I sit on the porch, looking across at the walnut tree, graceful against the sky even in the heavy August air. Since he and I returned from our most recent trip to London, I have wandered through my summer days, thinking about the past, lost in inner reflection. In the mornings, I pick up the crystal and cradle it in the palm of my hand before returning it to the front window to split the morning sun. I know that this time of introspection will soon come to an end. The parking lot will fill with cars; the campus will fill with students.

Resisting thoughts of the college, I dawdle among summer memories: Ron's and my June visit to Kara and Andrzej, when we haunted London streets and went—the four of us—for a weekend in Paris, my initiation into the glamours of that city. Or I muse over my return to Bloomsbury to mingle with other impassioned scholars at the Virginia Woolf conference, the first to be held in her own neighborhood.

I return, too, to that deeper past nineteen years ago: May 1985, the arrival of spring after the earth had turned its way through the seasons of the London year with Kara and Adriane, the three of us leaning inward toward each other. As spring came on, the sun, which had lingered just at roofline over the flats in Midland Terrace through December, rose incrementally. The days lengthened; our Cricklewood adventure neared its end.

ON THE MORNING OF MAY 2, I waved good-bye to a taxi headed toward Euston station: Kara and Adriane departing for a four-week tour of Europe with Lawrence and his friend Kirstina, whom I had finally, nervously, agreed to host. Just as Lawrence had insisted when he phoned that winter, the five of us had managed to share a roof for four days in reasonable compatibility: no eruptions of anger from Lawrence, much good grace from Kirstina, excited anticipation for Kara and Adriane—and my own measured calm.

On that same afternoon—by a quirk of timing over which I must have had some control—I again sent off the manuscript of my book on which I had been working doggedly, revising, finalizing, lately without energy or interest. Through much of April, with Kara and Adriane off at school, I had sat alone at my desk, staring blankly at the wall. In front of me had sat the manuscript—final copy, retyped on the used Olympia—stacked neatly on top of the substratum of scattered note cards, draft pages, revised endnotes, xeroxed articles. From this detritus had surfaced the new version. But I had had to force myself to do the endnotes, the revised conclusion, the bibliography before I had finally been able to copy the entirety and post it off to Ann Arbor on the same day I sent my daughters off for their European vacation.

That was already nearly a week after I had stood in the doorway of our flat, smiling as I watched a simpler departure: Kara and Adriane setting off for their final day of school, hand in hand, a spring in their step, prepared to end their London adventure at the conclusion of winter term. So many departures, so much pull outward from the safe seclusion behind the blue door.

ALONE, I tried not to envy my daughters on their excursion to Ireland, Germany, Italy, Paris; I tried not to envy their father, sharing these new experiences with them. Alone, I sought ways to make this new aloneness my own. Now I would reclaim my solitude, return to my work, and await the return of my daughters, anxious that they not suffer undue stress in traveling with their father or unforeseen danger in taking on these new ventures. But I needed as well to venture out on my own, to expand beyond the cloistered life I had been living of late.

One Sunday—finally a sunny day—I set out modestly to Regent's Park, traipsing in and out and around and then up to the canal and along the bank. I sat for a moment to eat cheese and biscuits on a bench under a tree along the canal, a light rain falling on me, the London weather quixotic as always. Pleasantly lost, I meandered along the canal, aimless. At the end of the walkway, I ascended—eyes startled wide by a sudden return to human company—into a bustling market, populated by motley stalls and a fire-eater in the courtyard. I wandered among strangers, thinking of Lucy Snowe in *Villette,* erupting from her solitude into the frenetic activity of the carnival. But I resisted her agony and remained calm as I examined simple treasures and even made some purchases: a ring for Kara's approaching fourteenth birthday, a pair of earrings for me, a small leather bag. When the rain became serious, I set off to the cinema—*A Love in Germany*—from which I emerged to brilliant sunshine, a walk back through Regent's Park, a peaceful ride home on the tube.

But that evening, at home alone, I erupted into my own emotional turmoil after watching the late film on television: *The Effect of Gamma Rays on Man-in-the-Moon Marigolds,* with Joanne Woodward as a single mother of two daughters. During the last half-hour of the film, I could not stop crying: a great welling up of pain for the ways that people hurt each other, the terrible mechanisms of personal survival, the small possibility of hope, the yearning to give better comfort and hope to my own two daughters—and, still, to myself.

I kept thinking back on the months we had just come through, the stresses we had survived, the joys we had shared. I recalled in particular the period following the morning in mid-December when the post had come plopping through the mail slot on to the cold hallway floor, bringing with it exhilarating news: I had been awarded the Alice and Edith Hamilton Prize from the University of Michigan Press.

With the letter had also come an early impetus outward: the possibility of traveling to Ann Arbor in March to receive the prize in person. At first, this trip had seemed impossible—to recross the ocean for a mere few days, leaving my daughters behind in England as I made this uncanny reversal. But if the college would help to fund this trip? If the value would be actual exchange of ideas and time with interested colleagues? If I could somehow find my way out of the near agoraphobia I had developed during our early months in London?

Kara and Adriane had urged me to go, insisting on their pride in my accomplishments and their confidence in their own capacities. When I challenged Kara about how she would handle the hazards that might arise in my absence, she responded with eminent reasonableness that my examples of such hazards—fire, intruding strangers, unanticipated disasters—would be no easier for me to forestall than for her. And she assured me that our neighborhood network would provide ample support for her to be in charge during a brief four-day absence. Why would it matter, she wondered, that I would be thousands of miles away? I couldn't, in any case, always be watching over them, even when they were nearby.

Now alone, I wondered—as I continue to wonder all these years later—how I had convinced myself to make this difficult decision: to trust my daughters' approaching adulthood, Kara at nearly fourteen, Adriane at nearly ten. In some cultures, Kara *would* have been an adult, taking on a life of her own, though likely within a closely wrought network of kin. But not in my own culture; here—in England and in the United States—she was still a child. Indeed, I have since read of parents charged with child neglect when they have left children of similar ages on their own. And yet I *did* feel confident; I *did* recognize Kara's very real capacities to be in charge. I knew that both of my daughters would be responsible to each other, to our shared understandings. And, rightly or not, I trusted our mutual appraisal of what they could do.

EACH MORNING IN MICHIGAN, I had wakened abruptly at three o'clock— my body recognizing what would be time to arise in London. But I was not in our Cricklewood flat. Alone in an unfamiliar hotel room, I hadn't even been able to acquire the coffee that my body also called out for upon awakening. Prodded by jet lag, my mind had buzzed out of control. Pride in my daughters' strengths had chased after worry about the risks I had taken with their independence. Pleasure in meeting new people and being publicly feted had risen up in counterpoint with the fear of failure. Over all had fallen the shadow of an odd cultural dislocation: I was a foreigner in my own country.

My mother, proud of her daughter, had suppressed her concern about her granddaughters alone in England and driven to Ann Arbor to join in honoring my accomplishments. I felt her surge of support when I crossed the stage and again when we together joined English faculty in a celebratory dinner.

In a bizarre inversion, my return to Cricklewood had been a return home, the trip to Michigan an aberrant interruption in my sense of belonging. Kara and Adriane and I had gathered again around the kitchen table, talking, laughing, expressing mutual pride in the accomplishments of our four-day separation.

With them gone to Europe now, however, I returned to my earlier fear: What if something had happened to them in my absence? What if they were not now safe as they traveled in unknown places with their father?

I MISSED MY DAUGHTERS with a new fervor. After a year of being almost exclusively with them, I was bereft by this new absence, however much it fit the pattern of summers we had experienced throughout our years as a single-parent family. I had tasted some of this loneliness on the trip to Ann Arbor and indeed again on the return when we were visited by Kara's friend Sarah; that visit had inevitably shifted the balance of our triangulated family as Kara and even Adriane had turned from me toward this visiting "other daughter." The flat then buzzed with teenage vibrations, and I had felt anew my adult loneliness.

But that had been temporary, and despite Sarah's homesickness and all the additional stresses and distractions, the visit had been a delight for all of us, an expansion of our social horizon. Afterward, we happily returned to our own family of three.

NOW I WORKED ON, as during other summers balancing my freedom against my loss, though this time the loss held a new intensity. I tried to value my freedom through work, reviving other projects now that the book was out of my hands—taking notes, processing reading, feeling the time running through my fingers—but the work at present lacked urgency. I sought other freedoms as well: excursions to the theater and the Barbican and random tramps across Hampstead Heath, where sunlight slanted softly through the trees. I listened for the post to arrive each day, awaiting the occasional post-card from Kara and Adriane, awaiting word from the editor at the University of Michigan Press, telling me of the response to my revised manuscript. I phoned airlines daily, trying to determine the best arrangements for our imminent return to the United States, seeking arrangements that I could afford, that fit my time constraints. Anxious for the centripetal pull that would bring Kara and Adriane back to me, I was also becoming anxious for our shared return to Wooster.

ONE MORNING, my daily phone call to People's Express earned the desired result: three tickets booked for June 15 at a price I could afford. That same morning the post brought acknowledgment from the press, receipt of manuscript, but more than that a plan to publish the book in paperback as well: a triumph of my wish to reach a larger audience.

On that high note, with the sun shining brightly, I set out toward the Broadway and whimsically decided to try a greater adventure, despite the Austin's continued unpredictability. I had not taken the car beyond the city since my sister Eileen's visit early in March, when we had ventured out into the countryside—to Bath, to Oxford—reveling in her presence and taking courage from being in extended family. But now, buoyed by good news, I felt ready to hazard this solitary trip. I drove boldly right through the heart of London, straight south—miles and miles of city before I hit the countryside—hills, trees, the Downs: heading toward Sussex, Monk's House in Rodmell, Virginia Woolf territory.

Exhilarated by the time I reached Rodmell, I could not even be squelched by the news that Monk's House was only open from 2:00 to 6:00 PM on Wednesday and Saturday. On this Thursday midday, I would have to do my own investigation. I walked to the church behind Monk's House, climbed over a small stone wall and began to explore the back garden, replete with busts of Leonard and Virginia—famous images at which I paused honorifically (Were they really there, or have I inserted them mentally?), even as I was stopped by a groundskeeper cutting the grass.

"How did you get here?" he queried. But he was friendly, wanting to warn me that the Monk's House caretaker would be very "rude" if he saw me. Knowing that I was trespassing, I lingered anyway—overcoming my rule-abiding timidity, risking the rude encounter—and then inquired of the grass cutter just how I might get to the River Ouse: back out over the wall, through the churchyard and out to the road, a mile or so across the fields to the river bank.

The fields seemed flat and barren, and I had to face down the cows and climb over stiles, but I walked on, thinking of Woolf, taking in the surrounding fields, birds, cows, distant hills—looking back at the little church behind me. The river was ugly and harsh, bounded by uninviting steep banks, lined with rocks. I lay in the grass, feeling the hot sun, thinking of Woolf, of my own life. Words from *Mrs. Dalloway* echoed in my head: "He did not want to die. Life was good. The sun hot."

Already it was 4:00 PM, but I needed the ocean and so drove on to the coast, to walk on the beach in Newhaven, spotting the quay and the lighthouse—not Woolf's Cornwall lighthouse, but a beacon nonetheless—before heading back to the car and the drive north to the city.

But something was amiss. En route over hills, through the countryside, the Austin—about which I had become complacent—seemed rough, slow to accelerate, threatening to die. Even after I stopped and added three pints of oil and filled the tank with petrol, the engine kept dying out at crucial moments, on hills, at roundabouts. "If only I can get back to London"—I urged myself onward until, at the entrance to a huge roundabout connecting the A22 and M25, the engine gave a final death rattle and refused to restart.

Though I managed to get a lift to a service station and phoned the Automobile Association, I again found myself stranded when the AA driver simply took off, leaving me behind, once he discovered that the car started right up after sitting. As soon as I got on the roundabout, trying to follow the AA truck back to the station, I knew the car wouldn't make it and again pulled to the side. Now it was completely dark—10:00 PM—and I was out of options. When two police officers came by, finding me stranded along the road, their brusque command to move the car underlined my sense of desertion.

I stayed put, unable to move the dead car, helplessly awaiting the return of the AA driver, who managed against the odds to relocate me in the dark. With his "torch" pointed under the bonnet of the car, he set to work, aloof, disengaged, eventually discovering the distributor cap full of oil. Still taciturn, he wiped it clean and checked the oil level while I stood to the side, hovering desperately, posing as many questions as I could pull from my automotive ignorance and my panicked isolation. At last, he began to provide terse answers, and by the time the car started, he had become overtly helpful, suggesting that we reconnoiter at the station from which I had originally called him, though it would be closed by now.

Anxious not to lose this tenuous human contact, I backed onto the roundabout—a dangerous and unlawful act—so that I could follow him that five miles to the station, where we talked briefly, checked things out again.

Reassured, I thanked him repeatedly and set out on my own, now giddy with relief, gathering confidence as I drove through the dark and into the lights of the city: approaching home, safe, parking the car at the curb where it belonged alongside our back garden fence.

WHEN KARA AND ADRIANE RETURNED, I rejoiced, though I again needed to host Lawrence, this time without the buffering presence of Kirstina, who had already departed for the States. Even in her absence, I remained grateful for the care she had given my daughters during this extended travel time. But most of all, I delighted in my daughters themselves, grateful for their return to me, for the warmth of their presence, for the support they gave to me as I tried to do my best by them.

WHILE KARA AND ADRIANE WERE TRAVELING, I had made one last effort at undertaking some new work during this year that had been given over mostly to personal renewal and revisions of the old work: I wrote to Margaret Drabble, care of her publisher, asking whether I could meet with her. In shock, I welcomed her response—"6 June, teatime"—though when I telephoned to confirm, I had to inquire of her just when tea time was. I was still too American to know for certain that I should arrive at 4:00 PM.

With Kara and Adriane now gathered back to me, I prepared to set out for this meeting: nervous but supported. Kara said, "Don't worry, Mom. You'll get along fine. You're both Puritans." I was amused and impressed by the astuteness of this observation.

And, indeed, we did get along fine as we ranged informally over a series of topics that emerged in our conversation. I had not known what to expect—nor even what I myself wanted—but was at least comfortable as I sat conversing in the home of this writer whose work I admired so much, whose gracious welcome exceeded my hopes.

Balancing my cup of tea, regretting the lack of a tape recorder, I asked questions as they came to me, as they had struck me in my own musings. Knowing of her work on Arnold Bennett, I could not help leading with the question of writerly loyalties: Bennett or Woolf? And yet I knew it would not, could not be a question of choosing—nor was it. Both, of course, she responded, "I draw on *both* Bennett and Woolf, taking different things from each." Even as she disavowed Woolf as a "social personality," she spoke warmly and affirmatively of *To the Lighthouse* as "a very brave book."

I was amazed that she also spoke openly of her current work on the novel that would become *The Radiant Way,* describing the three main women characters and projecting the likelihood that this novel would be "depressing" because it takes on the Thatcher years and a number of feminist concerns. I welcomed her assertion that she develops a plot posing questions and then seeks the necessary answers. When I queried—"Do you see yourself as 'experimental'?"—I also appreciated her response that she wishes to solve certain kinds of narrative problems, but to do so in ways responsive to readers' wish that the novel seem "real." Her frank and open assertion that her characters are based on people she knows took me by surprise, as I had been so trained to the notion that one must avoid seeing any such life parallels.

But when she embraced the identity of "woman writer" and mother, too, I could hardly restrain my excitement. Her visible pleasure in her three children warmed me, as did her pleasure in their growing up, the perceptions that they gave back to her. And we shared our mutual honor for Doris Lessing as the first writer for both of us who actually treated her life as a woman in ways we could connect with our own lives.

I was exhilarated, reeling with ideas and observations, as I drove my way back to my daughters, who awaited me in our Cricklewood flat, where I could make notes, hoping to record the sense of this encounter. I thought especially about Drabble's comment that interview statements always need context—that they may even change in the course of the conversation itself. For I knew this also to be how genuine conversation works, each participant turning upon the words of the other, refracting insights and observations, shifting as thought itself is protean. And I anticipated just such a new turning together as I rehearsed this conversation with my daughters.

What was I to make of this actual encounter with a writer whom I taught, about whom I had written in my book? I was struck most palpably by her *realness,* her utter lack of pretension. And I reflected that she thinks of Woolf as a real person, not simply an icon, not simply the construer of magic upon the page.

When Kara asked how it had gone, I told her that I had quoted her comment about our shared "Puritanism" and that Margaret Drabble had comfortably acquiesced: this characterization suggested to her a belief in responsibility to other people. Her reply, too, seemed merely human—the person with whom I was having tea had responded to me as another person negotiating my own ways of being. I recalled as well her pause to answer the phone when her relatively new husband had called to check on dinner plans. "That was Michael," she said. "Some people live together without being married. We're married without living together." She had also noted that she did not think that she could have remarried while her children were still at home. Here, too, I enjoyed the bemused reflection on the ways in which we all make choices to structure our lives.

MY LAST IMAGE of our year in Cricklewood exists somewhere in a snapshot: the three of us gathered with endless piles of luggage next to the garden gate, the cab ready to transport us. The gate would no longer squeak for me; the laundry would no longer linger on the lukewarm radiators for us; the taps would run hot and cold for someone else. We had cleaned out all of our personal belongings—boxes of books and winter clothes to ship back to the States. And now we were gathered, the three of us and our mounds of luggage next to the cab that would carry us to Victoria Station. From there, the train to Gatwick and the People's Express to Newark and finally home to Ohio, where we would be met in Cleveland by Eileen and Jim: reunited with family, ready to make the drive home in reliable Goldie, which they had stored for us.

The entire extended Schultz family would soon gather briefly for a ceremonial burial of my father's ashes, delayed until all of us could be in the same place together. As usual, we would be squeezing this ceremony in among other commitments, with Kara and Adriane off to Bloomington to be with their father immediately after this gathering in Bluffton, where there would be a plaque and a tree remembering Harold B. Schultz, my children's grandfather.

After taking Kara and Adriane to Bloomington, I would return alone, as I had in summers for many years: to be again in Wooster. I was home, where my daughters and I made our ongoing lives. I was not home, for they were not here. None of us was home, for we had left a part of our sense of home in Cricklewood. Or perhaps we were finally assimilating the knowledge that had long been ours: home is not a place on the map, but a way of being in the world.

25

Bertha in the Attic

Already it is October, the current semester well under way, the college providing one continuity in this life I am telling. Alone during the day for the brief respite of fall break, I claim this time as my own. With my crystal, I chase the light, the rainbows. I chase memories, too, in frantic need to finish this story. But I know that narrative beginnings and endings are illusory, that in life there is no certainty.

Nineteen years later I wish I could tell you that magic happened upon our return from London, that fall when Kara and Adriane and I gathered once again in the house on Spink Street. Perhaps it was a kind of magic, the human kind that takes time and effort and conviction. It is true that we brought with us on our return the knowledge that we were a family, with resources of our own, both individually and collectively. And this knowledge was our magic. But it is also true that we returned to the buffeting of daily life, trying to hold steady the tripod family structure we had stabilized in Cricklewood.

WEATHER PERMITTING, Ron and I have continued through the early autumn to sit on our porch in the evenings. The oaks and maples glow red and gold even in the twilight, but the walnut tree is already nearly bare. Each day the sun angles lower in the sky, fading ever earlier; in the evenings, the crickets issue a subdued murmur. The squirrels make serious preparations for winter.

On the porch we talk, as always, of the details of our days, but also of larger changes in our lives. We note with pleasure Adriane's excitement about a recent decision in her own life: to resign her job in children's book editing and prepare for a different future, a return to the kind of work she did when she first moved to New York. Her plan now is to stay in the city she has grown to love, enrolling in a master's program in education, seeking dual certification in early childhood and special education. She will continue her commitment to her own writing and build upon her commitment to children, turning her attentions in a new direction. We celebrate the joy we hear in her voice as she tells us these plans.

AT THE TIME OF OUR RETURN from England, Adriane was still a child, but during our time away she had successfully bumped up the ladder of self upon which she had previously floundered in precocious questioning of love and morality. She returned to her house, her school, her friends, her cat with a new comfort in herself, a renewed trust in me and in our family. When she now reflects on that time, she recalls her home in Wooster as "warm, supportive, challenging"—a place where she learned to speak her mind with confidence, even as she often felt the need to quiet herself in public in the face of outward expectations. Though she continued to call on me as, in her phrase, a "moral compass" to whom she regularly confessed her anxieties and possible transgressions, she was increasingly growing into her peer world and seeking her own way beyond our household.

In those years, a crucial strategy for testing her understanding of the world lay in imaginative construction. She made up dramatic scenes with friends and acted them out in our living room, where Kara and I might serve as commandeered audience. Or she flopped out on her stomach on the kitchen floor while I was cooking and poured stories through her pencil onto the pad in front of her. She would remain still, lost in her fantasy, only once in a while looking up to confirm that I was still there.

These stories seemed to come effortlessly, the words rushing from her: imagined scenes of an Indian boy tracking and befriending a deer in the woods or of parentless children constructing their own survival in the wild. Later—but she was still very young, not yet in high school—she would imagine her way into the experience of a great white whale, isolated and hunted, *Moby Dick* from the whale's perspective. She regularly tried to fill in the gaps of the lives she thought remained untold.

Kara, too, was committed to stories as a way of knowing. Even before we had gone to England, she had been chosen to participate in "author day," where she had shared a book of her own making. She had fallen in love with reading early on—recall her hungry consumption of Austen and Brontë and Drabble on the brink of our departure for England—and she had identified her life goal: to be a writer. I remember telling this to Tillie Olsen when I met her during her first visit to the Wooster campus in 1980. Olsen had talked in my Virginia Woolf class of her own response to Woolf's luminous prose; she had read tearfully from "Tell Me a Riddle" to an audience packed with responsive students and faculty—participating in Woolf's affirmation that "we think back through our mothers if we are women."

Though I had felt that my daughters were yet too young to join in these public conversations, I vividly recall talking with Olsen about what she called the "college of motherhood" and about the creative capacities of her daughters and my own. By 1985, I could see that even young children can gain from such exposures, but in the earlier years I had been too apprehensive about my own professional life to risk including them in these public events. And yet the presence of women writers was a potent part of our lives together—through campus visits, through the books on our shelves.

When Kara recalls our return from London, she remembers not only that we selected new carpet and fresh paint to join the furniture we had purchased shortly before our departure, but also the central place held by new bookshelves in our living space and by writers in our lives. In the essay she wrote during her last semester of college—the same essay I quoted earlier—she tells it this way:

There were still lots of books. Now they were on two tall wood bookshelves. And everywhere else. They were brown, not dark, but definitely not light. The books had lots of colors. And lots of strange titles that made sense. Erica How to Save/Jong Your Own Life. *I used to read that book spine almost every day. It read like some sort of childhood to adolescent mantra. I said it really fast:* Erica-HowtoSaveJongYourOwnLife. *Then I read it slow:* Erica How to SaveJong Your Own Life. *It made sense both ways, even though I couldn't quite find the right sense every time. Then I learned that that wasn't the real title; I had missed part of the logic:* Erica Jong (comma) How to Save Your Own Life. *I think I still like the first way better, maybe there was more than one way to find logic.*

In college, Kara no longer said she wanted to be a writer, though she later returned to this goal. At the time she wrote this essay, she had scarcely taken any English courses and was instead committed to a major in international studies and to the work of learning multiple languages: a world of political action and global complexity compelled her energies.

But in this course in her senior year, she recalled the earlier draw of women writers as a presence in her Wooster home:

Actually, Erica Jong wasn't in the living room. She was in the dining room with Rita Mae Brown. And To the Lighthouse, *I think.* The Madwoman in the Attic *was in the living room; Gilbert and Gubar were there. I saw their names on the shelf; and then she* [Susan Gubar] *was actually there. A large presence in the room, but she did not impress me then. She looked normal enough. Did she have white hair? She looked older than my living room and I expected. She must have smiled. She was tall. She was tall, then. I wasn't so tall, but the madwoman in the attic seemed more important to me than this woman in my living room. She was more interesting. She was a part of my life.*

Maybe, after all, the women whose writing I taught in classrooms and whom I occasionally hosted on campus became a part of my daughters' lives. Kara understood this. Sometimes they were physical occupants of our living room—Susan Gubar and Gloria Steinem and Tillie Olsen—but more often they were simply a pervasive presence in our thinking. Either way, Kara had grasped the power of writing and of language and had pulled them into her world. Drawing on the metaphor that we—along with Gilbert and Gubar—had adopted from Charlotte Brontë, Kara went on to cite another new presence in our lives: the personal computer in which I had invested that same fall of our return from England. I had vowed never to write another book without this kind of technological assistance.

Jane Eyre lived in my room; and Bertha lived in my attic. Bertha was the new computer. She wasn't mine, but I got to help name her. I understood that she was creative genius, trapped. That she could be let out. My room had been in the attic before hers; before my blue, low pile carpet. I understood "the woman's quest for her own story." Jane Eyre's *madwoman sought it, our Bertha sought it,* EricaHowtoSaveJongYourOwnLife *sought it; I heard them telling. . . . They explained the scrawled papers on floors—past,—present, and—future.*

The scattered papers in that era represented the final urgings of my own first book, for that fall I was reading page proofs, constructing an index, concluding a process that had felt endless. The computer in the attic—Kara's former bedroom, now turned into my study—signified a commitment to future projects. I would not stop writing with this one book. We would all find ways to put words to our lives and thoughts.

IN A PERSONAL NOTE accompanying her college essay, Kara wrote to me:

Mom, you are a presence for me even when physically you are far away. I sense your mind, thoughts, and histories (and textual . . . angers?) when living my life; stemming from your own. You have embedded your strengths into my consciousness, even when they may feel faltering in yours (?). I frequently visualize you, not just you in the moment, but you through all the histories that exist in my memories. My memories of childhood, of adolescence, of your stories of life/lives prior to my own, of lives other than my own. I feel your presence almost everyday; and think about what it means, feel its significance and power. Powers that ebb and flow, but are always somewhere present; knowledges that push me through.

Kara's essay and her note, like my own narrative here, circle over the years, pulling in observations and fragments from disparate periods of our lives. But in that house in which the three of us, with Chang, made our home, she found insights that I now reecho, reverberations of my dialogue with both of my daughters over the subsequent years. Sometimes it is hard to know just who is echoing whom, just how all of these pieces fit together. A mother and her daughters. Must they be a coherent story?

THIS FALL, 2004, I am again teaching a course on Charlotte Brontë, a course that I first developed and taught twenty-two years ago. As a modernist, I was definitely stepping outside my expertise; indeed, I do not believe that I had ever formally studied any of the Brontë novels. But as a feminist, I was drawn to the spirit of resistance I saw at work. I remember that the first time I taught the course was in 1982 because I recall turning thirty-eight during that term—the age at which Charlotte had died.

The words and images are now almost as deeply woven into my thoughts as those of Virginia Woolf. These two writers join with many others as my literary ancestry. So it is no surprise that I recently wakened from sleep with a vivid image in mind: Bertha, flaming red and orange, grasping desperately at freedom as she falls to her death from the upper floor of Thornfield Hall. My dreams are also suffused with my own metaphors, drawing as they do on Brontë's: Bertha was our computer—as Kara says, our private metaphor for "creative genius, trapped"—but she was also our ongoing resistance to cultural norms, to finding ways to live lives of our own. Inside me—with my daughters—I was determined to free Bertha into life, not death, to join her with Jane Eyre and with Brontë, whose self was so complexly deployed in the creatures of her imagination.

In the year of our return from England, each of us in her own way still strained against the confines of our Wooster life. Like Charlotte Brontë— like Jane Eyre, pacing the corridor of Thornfield's third floor before she even knew of Bertha's existence—we yearned for a larger world, a world rich in possibility and vision.

KARA HAD RETURNED from our London year to a new social dynamic in her first year of high school: the rearrangement of her friends, who had formed different alliances in her absence, and now again as they tried to make sense of ninth grade and a new school for everyone. She chafed against the constraints of this small-town high school, and she grieved over a new distance in her friendship with Sarah. Struggling to define herself, she pushed herself still farther away from the norms of her peers. She did not even eat the way they did because she had that fall decided to become a vegetarian, having read much about nutrition and concluded that she wanted to eliminate meat from her diet. With this new expertise, she took on—with encouragement from me—the primary cooking in our home as one of her contributions to our family life. As she stretched toward unseen vistas, she also anchored herself more closely to us.

Adriane, in fifth grade, continued to test the limits of her environment. She, too, returned to shifts in her friendship circles, though her primary friends from third grade soon gathered together again: they were not, at least, entering a new school—those shifts would come later—and did not at this point feel challenged by her return to our neighborhood grade school. I rejoiced in living in a community that felt safe and allowed me to grant my children the freedom to roam. Yet I always knew that safety gives no guarantees, no matter where one lives: freedom to roam entails risks.

IN THE SPRING of that same fifth-grade year, Adriane and her friend Sherry set out on a bike ride one Friday afternoon. I had no trouble agreeing to the plan, though I could not have anticipated what actually did happen. They began their excursion with many hours of daylight left, and I was confident that they would be fine, but as dusk set in I became increasingly worried. Seven o'clock: At what point do I notify the police about missing children? Was I worrying too much or too little?

When the phone rang at 7:30—the night gathering quickly, for it was only midspring—I answered with apprehension.

"Mom, do you know where Overton Road is?"

I knew the voice and breathed a deep sigh of relief. I would find out where Overton Road was and drive there with a bike rack.

Was I angry or relieved when I learned that these two eleven-year-old girls had ridden their bikes out of town, onto the nearby highway—US 30— and on into unknown back-country roads? Was I angry or relieved when I learned that they had approached a house trailer and been welcomed inside for lemonade and the use of the telephone?

I quickly learned where Overton Road was and welcomed these two young adventurous girls to safety, not forgetting to thank the family who had offered lemonade and a telephone.

AT NIGHT, once Kara and Adriane were in bed, I would sometimes climb the stairs to the attic room, my new study. There I would hesitate before my recently acquired personal computer: Bertha was an early PC, much beyond my budget as well as outside my knowledge and experience. Because I didn't know how to begin with this foreign process, to learn an entirely new language system, I would at first simply pause, intimidated, and then turn away, leaving Bertha glowering but untouched.

One night I sat quietly before a dark screen, looking out across the street at the empty night sky, wondering how I could rise to this challenge. A sound at the side window drew my attention, and when I turned, I found myself eye to eye with a nocturnal raccoon, pausing on this third-floor windowsill before climbing on over the roof and toward an unknown destination. After its departure, I turned away from the window, from the empty night sky and from the threatening Bertha; defeated, I wound my way back down into the living room, where I took up my books, not yet ready to write by whatever mechanism.

Bertha remained confined and useless for months before I finally undertook tutorial lessons on word processing from a new friend that spring. For several afternoons, Roger and I hunched together over the keyboard, testing the ways of DOS and command lines. More knowledgeable than I, he was also extraordinarily patient as I contended obtusely with this new process. Grateful for his help, I invited him one evening to share in a simple vegetarian meal with Kara and Adriane and me.

Having followed Kara into her vegetarian diet, I had taken to shopping more frequently at the local food co-op, where I had met Roger. And so began one of my own new pathways, for I was still seeking for someone to share in my life with my daughters, someone with values similar to my own. Roger did share a number of my interests: not just vegetarian eating, but also a resistance to consumer culture, a curiosity about the world, a love of learning, a respect for the minds of children. Indeed, he had earlier spent time teaching in a local nursery school, though he was reserved in reaching out to my daughters; he would later tell me that he knew he was moving on and didn't want to make bonds that would be wrenching to break.

"Hiya," he would greet me in genuine friendliness when I walked into the co-op or pushed open the door to his house. "Hiya," he would say, too, when he arrived unheralded on my front porch. His own pursuit of simplicity included not having a telephone, so we relied on impromptu arrivals and casually shared meals. We would often work together, side by side, on projects at one house or the other or on individual studying efforts. We were comfortable, side by side, learning and talking. But there was that plan to leave. And what's more, his approach to relationships was something he called "nonattachment," premised on a preference for living exclusively in the present. As for me, I tried, again, to balance the yearning for constancy and caring with the outward pull toward renewal and adventure.

As I recall that summer, I feel the turning of the earth, the changes that life brings. Again I knew loss: my valued friend and colleague, Jim Turner, was snatched away unexpectedly by early death. When I attended his memorial service and shared public grief with friends and colleagues, with his children and his widow, I forced myself to recognize another grief, for Jim's untimely death reminded me that we were no longer so close to Sarah as we had been during the childhood years: in the ways of adolescent shifts, Sarah, my "other daughter," had drifted on, inexplicably. Roger, who was away that summer, wrote to me of his own sense of Sarah's distinctive presence, for he had known her as a preschooler when he had worked in the local nursery school years earlier. And though I knew that children do need to move on in the mysterious ways of growing up, I missed this other special child who had been a part of our Wooster lives.

I continued to rely on John and Rena but felt again the rifts of time and change as I acknowledged that other friends had drifted away. Elizabeth was no longer a regular part of my life; Michael was long since gone, and other colleagues had moved away or wandered on with their own lives. Roger, new friend and intimate, awkwardly woven into my daily life, was continuing with his plans to leave as well, though not for another year.

But when I shake the kaleidoscope differently, I recall other changes that nourished the present. I recall that this was the year when my book actually came out: an object to hold in my hands, evidence that my thoughts had wound their way out into the world beyond Wooster. This, too, was the year when my mother moved into northeast Ohio on her seventieth birthday— making the effort to be near both of her daughters while she was still able to make a new life in a new place: a model for me in her ability to move on, even after having lived forty years in the same town. Her presence an hour away enabled not only weekend visits for all of us, but also individual time with her granddaughters.

THE FOLLOWING SPRING, April 1987, I thought about all of these changes en route home from a conference in Ann Arbor, Michigan. Finally adjusted to word processing, I had managed to draw on Bertha's capacities to help me construct a paper on narrative strategies in Virginia Woolf. The presentation of the paper had gone well; I had enjoyed the exchanges with colleagues from other parts of the country. I would return to a full professional life on campus and likely to the usual impromptu time with Roger. I would return as well to a celebration of Adriane's twelfth birthday. I did not have the relationship I thought I wanted, but I could see that my life was rich in rewards. And it was a life still centrally balanced with the lives of my daughters.

I began the drive on bare roads, gray skies above, mind free to wander, to reflect on the complexities of my life. But when I was about fifty miles from home, the weather changed suddenly, and I was startled back into full attention to the road before me. I turned off the freeway onto a two-lane highway, and the light rain turned to freezing rain and then snow, gathering in ridges beneath my tires. Driving in the snow—as I would so many years later en route to New York—I watched it gather around me, shocked that this could happen in April. Still moving with traffic, which was light, I felt the ridges build beneath my tires, deepening with startling speed as dusk gathered. I followed the tail lights of the car ahead of me until it turned off the road, and then I drove on, peering into the dark, guided by my own headlights that poked through the blur of white falling all around.

In Ashland, still twenty miles from home, I had to stop and ask which road to take, for all of the signs were covered in snow. *This is death,* I thought. My mind now was chillingly focused; I did not see how I could survive this drive on icy roads into the unknown night.

When the last vehicle ahead of me turned off—an eighteen-wheeler that had led the way for me out of Ashland—I tried to carry forward. But the ruts in the snow were by now too deep for my subcompact car. Goldie could go no farther. I was alone on the highway, no cars in sight, no markers on the road.

At least I saw the lights of a house just up the hill and hoped to find people and perhaps some help. But when I had trudged through the snow and stood shivering on the porch, the woman at the door told me she could not help, nor would she let me use her phone since she didn't see that there was anyone I could call. Through the storm door, I saw them there around the table, playing cards. But I had no claim on their companionship or their assistance. And I had no energy to insist on my need.

Wearily, I returned to Goldie, still stranded in snowdrifts now rising above the bumper. Again I thought, *this is death.*

I would not have known what to do had help not come along unsolicited. But I knew to welcome a four-wheel-drive pickup with a towrope when it stopped to check on me. And I knew that it was my good fortune to be towed through the snow and to find a resting place on an unknown couple's couch, surrounded by dogs, until the roads could be cleared enough for travel.

When I tried to phone home from this helpful stranger's house, the operator said, "It's a snow emergency. Only emergency calls are allowed."

And I said, "This is an emergency. My children are home alone and I need to speak to them."

The next day was Adriane's twelfth birthday. I had long since become accustomed to leaving Kara and Adriane home alone while I attended short conferences. I had seen no particular reason to expect difficulties on this three-day trip with plans to be home by Saturday night so that I could host a birthday party on Sunday. Kara, a very grown-up fifteen, was perfectly capable of being in charge. But I had certainly not expected a freak blizzard in April: this *was* a state of emergency. My daughters needed to know where I was; I needed to know that they were okay.

The next morning I drove into Wooster on streets emptied of cars and glistening with snow. I went past Roger's house but did not stop; I was aiming straight for home. We postponed the birthday celebration with Adriane's friends that had been scheduled for that afternoon. The three of us spent the rest of the day in the quiet relief of each other's presence.

THE FOLLOWING ACADEMIC YEAR, 1987–88, I knew for certain that changes were in the air. As chair of the Women's Studies Program, I was in the midst of planning a tenth-anniversary celebration in the spring; I had successfully acquired the funding to invite a number of prominent feminist scholars to campus. My success was sealed one night that fall when I sat alone on my bed and answered a ringing phone: Adrienne Rich agreeing to keynote our celebration. I had also signed on to write a book about Tillie Olsen. And I was applying for jobs elsewhere, knowing that a change in my life was imperative.

That fall Roger had left for the West Coast, pursuing his own independent plans. I had good-naturedly helped him to do much work on his house and pack up all of his belongings. As he put it, "We've put up with too much from each other not to be friends." And I agreed. I waved good-bye to him and returned to my full life in Wooster. Increasingly, I understood that the coasts, with their ocean beat, were not where I would be making my life.

Much else was in motion. That summer my mother and Adriane helped me to move from one office to another—still in Kauke, this time in proximity to my English department colleagues. Regretfully, I left behind my interdisciplinary hallway and the proximity to such colleagues as John Hondros and Jim Turner's now-empty office. I planned as well a move of household, for the college had bought all of the houses around me and now offered to buy my house too, generously giving me ample time to seek a new home by the following spring.

That summer and fall Kara worked on her driving skills, following the requisite driver's education class. We would take Goldie to an empty parking lot on campus where Kara could practice the jerky transitions from gear to gear. Motion was the purpose, and she was persistent. Adriane, too, moved on: beginning junior high school, she experienced that next bump up toward adulthood. When she returned home from her first day at the new school, I saw immediately that she was somehow more grown up.

As if cleansing myself of past griefs, I fell mysteriously ill that same fall. I could retain no food. Though I persisted in my teaching commitments, I gripped the edge of the desk for balance as I swayed light-headedly, while tiny arcs of light flashed in my eyes. Between classes, I retreated to my bed, trying to find some food I could manage. In eleven days, I lost twelve pounds; my white blood cell count rose dramatically. But even with the help of a specialist in gastroenterology, we could never determine the problem. My body gradually returned to some kind of stability, enough at least that I could visit the West Coast over fall break, confirming the ongoing if distant friendship with Roger. And I made plans to attend the Modern Language Association convention in San Francisco in December. Planning for change, knowing it was urgent, I asked myself repeatedly: "Have I ever been happy? Do I even know how to be happy?"

AT THE CONVENTION, I interviewed for new jobs—actively seeking the change I felt to be coming in my life. But on the way there—on the plane to San Francisco just after Christmas—I met change, unplanned. I looked up from the work I held on my lap, settled in the window seat, straight into eyes both familiar and unknown: here was Ron, though I did not know I was looking for him.

Two days later we walked and talked on Ocean Beach, swept away by each other's presence. When he returned me to the conference hotel afterward, he said, "Let's stay friends."

I responded, "I need more than a friend. I have friends all over the world."

I got out of the car with his other words echoing in my ears: "What's twenty-seven hundred miles compared to the moon and the stars?"

READER, you already know what happened next. Within two years, Ron and I were married. Two days after the wedding, Kara set off, alone in Goldie, for her first year of college in the East. Ron and I—with Adriane and Chang and Bertha loaded into Goldie's successor along with books and papers and clothes and camping gear—headed west for a year's leave in California. Camping in the Medicine Bow Mountains en route, Ron and I stayed up late around a campfire, looking up into the night sky and listening to the raccoons, whose eyes barely pierced the dark around us and whose voices scolded us toward sleep.

We returned together to our third home in Wooster, successor to the one we had left behind on Spink Street: a newly constituted family of four, coming and going in different arrangements. We had to leave Chang's body behind in California, where we had honored his inexplicable death by walking on the beach together with daisies in our hands. Bertha returned with us, facilitating the next book—on Tillie Olsen—and finally retiring to a box in the attic, replaced by a ThinkPad, which still roams the house with me, resisting the confinement of any single room.

ON THE EVENING OF OCTOBER 27, 2004, Ron and I again sit on our porch. It is a Wednesday, a full teaching day, and I have work yet to do. But these pauses are essential, the time we spend sharing our respective days, interpreting the events of our lives. On this night, we have as well a further purpose: to await the eclipse of the moon.

The evening is unseasonably warm, the skies clear, with dusk closing into darkness. We look out across the street at the nearly empty parking lot. The bare branches of the walnut tree are etched against the sky over Kauke Hall as the moon comes up full and bright. We ate earlier than usual in order to keep this date with the lunar eclipse.

In awe we sit together, watching the distant white sphere transform eerily before our eyes. We watch the dusty orange shadow move almost imperceptibly over the moon, like a giant mouth biting most of it away and leaving visible a slim white crescent. Then we watch as it shape-shifts again, glowing red in total eclipse, spherical but obscured: a blood moon. All of the sunsets and sunrises, refracted by the earth's atmosphere, have momentarily converged as the earth moves across the path of the sun's light. The earth has taken its bite, but the light persists.

At the peak of the eclipse, we watch, too, when our new neighbors, still strangers to us—a young couple, she visibly pregnant—walk out across the street seeking a better view. Compelled by these transformations, Ron and I sit together on the porch, awaiting the conclusion of the drama. After midnight, the moon shape-shifts above the trees one more time: full and bright, it casts its white light on us and on the earth around us.

Epilogue
December 24, 2005

J ulian's face changes in fleeting moments, like clouds passing over the sun in the London sky. For a brief quiet time, I sit alone with my grandson, watching these changes: it is the morning of his first Christmas Eve. He, in turn, watches my face intently as I talk with him. He periodically breaks into open-mouthed smiles, paced by smaller ones, glimmering in his lips and eyes. These are the most ready responses I have yet seen in him. He is, after all, only five and a half weeks old, and no one expects much from him. Yet he *is* responding, and this is pure joy to me.

I do not know exactly what Yeats meant by "honey of generation," but holding my grandchild now, I am rinsed in sweetness. I place my hand on his nearly naked head and examine him closely: his little bow mouth, probing tongue, and quivering chin; his faint eyebrows and round cheeks, a single dimple on his right cheek echoed by multiple dimples on his knuckles; the pointed tip of his ear and his button nose; his uneven breath and periodic deep sighs. As I talk with him, the wraiths of my two daughters' infancies rise before me. I see simultaneously the protean selves my grandson will become: shape-shifting through his growing years, still shape-shifting in adulthood even after I will no longer be here to note his many ways of being. But now he is fully present. Tears prickle in my eyes.

I see, too, my own protean selves: the child sitting high up in the crook of the tree reading books, the sister trailing after siblings, the daughter proud of similarities to both parents, the student eager to achieve, the professor, writer, scholar, wife, mother to my daughters, walking my own path.

EARLIER THIS MORNING I walked alone across Hyde Park. The sun had barely risen when I left the apartment in Notting Hill, where Ron and I are staying during this holiday visit to Kara and Andrzej and Julian. I listened to the clock at Kensington Palace ring the nine o'clock hour as I followed the Broad Walk past the Round Pond. I watched the morning mist rise from the pond and listened to a flock of geese come noisily in, joining seagulls on the pond's shore. I could feel droplets of water in the air, barely discernible—the sensation of mist on my skin. The sun rose in front of me as I walked straight south.

On the other side of the park, I stopped at 22 Hyde Park Gate, Virginia Woolf's childhood home, where I noted the plaques on the front of the house. Then I walked down Queen's Gate Road with the sun shining directly into my eyes, a lightness in my step. Ahead of me my people were beginning to gather: Ron would follow me from Notting Hill by Tube; Adriane would arrive soon, having flown in from New York on the 6:50 flight into Gatwick; Julian's other grandparents would arrive shortly into Heathrow; Kara and Andrzej and Julian were stirring awake in the apartment in South Kensington. We were coming together for Julian's first Christmas, but also, more significant, for his first family celebration. Alone, I walked toward the sun, toward the gathering family, my heart full.

Acknowledgments

I am grateful to the College of Wooster and to the Henry Luce III Fund for Scholarship at the college for invaluable support and release time to work on earlier versions of this book. I owe much to colleagues in the English Department and the Women's Studies Program (now the Women's, Gender, and Sexuality Studies Program) for conversation and shared insights into narrative, feminism, and the urgencies of gender transformation. My thinking about memoir and gender also owes much to students at the college over my thirty-three years of teaching, especially in these courses: "Virginia Woolf," "Charlotte Brontë," "Women's Studies Seminar," "Feminist Perspectives on Motherhood," and, most recently, "Memoir as Literary Genre." I am grateful to them and to independent-study students for helping me to understand the power of story and language and the ways in which gender is part of our everyday lives.

I am grateful to Paulette Bates Alden and William Kloefkorn for careful reading and response to earlier versions of the manuscript, as well as to Vivian Gornick for encouragement and comments in workshops as I worked through several early sections of the book. Byrdcliffe Arts Colony provided time for reflection and focused work on portions of the manuscript. Intellectual support for this project and powerful exemplary writing on motherhood came from Jane Lazarre and Tillie Olsen.

I owe special thanks to Kathie Clyde and Jennifer Hayward for reading sections of the manuscript and for ongoing support, as well as to Mary Lou Cummings and Mary Knocke for reading and talking about the entire manuscript in progress. My parents, Harold and Bunny Schultz, gave me foundations for all of my thinking about family; my father never had a chance to know of this project, but I received loving support from both of my parents.

From my mother I received much encouragement in the actual writing right up until her death in January 2007. I am grateful, too, for ongoing encouragement from my brother, Don Schultz, and my brother-in-law, Jim Burry.

My sister, Eileen Burry, was there for me and for the project in its many stages and through its arduous birth. So, too, were my daughters, Kara Frye Krauze and Adriane Frye, and my husband, Ronald Tebbe. I am deeply grateful to all of them for careful reading, much support, and many ongoing conversations. I could not have written the book without their loving encouragement.

A slightly different version of chapter 7, "Professor-Mother," was previously published as "Making a Living, Making a Life," *Journal of the Association for Research on Mothering* 5, no. 2 (Fall–Winter 2003): 21–28, reprinted by permission of the Motherhood Initiative for Research and Community Involvement, successor to the Association for Research on Mothering. Grateful acknowledgment is made for permission to reprint it.

Permission to quote or reprint from the following sources is also gratefully acknowledged: an excerpt from Adrienne Rich, "Origins and History of Consciousness," in *The Dream of a Common Language: Poems 1974–1977*, copyright © 1978 by W. W. Norton & Company, Inc., used by permission of the author and W. W. Norton & Company, Inc.; an unpublished letter from Harry Frye, dated May 17, 1976, used by permission of Caroline Kratz, Richard Frye, and Patricia A. Frye-McLaud; unpublished notes written by Lawrence O. Frye, July 3–4, 1994, used by permission of Adriane E. Frye and Kara Frye Krauze; unpublished essay by Kara Frye, dated March 1, 1993, and unpublished personal note from Kara Frye, dated March 2, 1993, used by permission of Kara Frye Krauze.